A GUIDE TO
ASIAN STOCK MARKETS

ROBERT LLOYD GEORGE

Longman Financial Services Publishing
a division of Longman Financial Services Institute, Inc.

PREFACE

This book is intended to provide the general reader with everything he or she will need to know in order to invest in Asian stock markets. Where appropriate, each chapter covers the following topics:

1. An introduction to, and history of, the stock exchange.

2. The performance of the stock market over the last five years, according to the most commonly used index.

3. Practical information about each stock exchange, namely:
   - the address and telephone number of every major national or regional exchange;
   - the trading days and hours of each exchange;
   - details of settlement procedures in each market;
   - rules concerning disclosure; and
   - custody services (and charges) offered by banks and brokers.

4. The largest quoted stocks, in terms of both market capitalisation and turnover.

5. Major types of investors, including institutions, retail investors, and brokerage houses, as well as major government or quasi-government organisations that may significantly influence the market.

6. Costs for investors in each market, such as brokerage commissions and stamp duty.

7. A list of major securities houses, including international brokers.

8. Listing requirements on each stock exchange.

9. Mutual funds or unit trusts available to international investors for each Asian market.

10. Rules for foreign investors, including:
    - foreign investment restrictions;
    - foreign exchange controls;
    - taxation, including capital gains taxes, income taxes, and withholding taxes; and
    - shareholder liability and protection.

The author welcomes readers' suggestions and any additional information that may improve this book in future editions.

ROBERT LLOYD GEORGE
Hong Kong
October 1989

CONTENTS

ACKNOWLEDGEMENTS

The compilation of material for this book was a team effort by fund managers and analysts at Indosuez Asia Investment Services Limited. I would particularly like to thank Ray Jovanovich and Alice Leung, who compiled the statistics and the general information on the various stock markets.

For their contributions to the material on individual markets, I would also like to thank the following: Colin Abraham and Yoriko Tada of Indosuez Asset Management (Japan) Ltd (Japan); the staff of W.I. Carr, Taipei, especially Sunny Chen (Taiwan); Ray Jovanovich (Malaysia, Bangladesh, and Pakistan); Lisa Stewart (Thailand); Emil Nguy (Indonesia); Michael Lee (Singapore); Nerissa Lee (Hong Kong); and Robert Ho (the Philippines). For information.on Nepal, which proved the most difficult country in which to gather statistics, I am grateful to Banque Indosuez Kathmandu.

Also a special word of thanks to Beth Rosenthal, Daisy Lee, Jamie Chan, and Peggy Wong who worked for long hours to help prepare the typescript on time.

I am grateful to Sally Rodwell of Longman Law, Tax and Finance for commissioning this book, and to my editor, Robyn Flemming, for her patience and perseverance in helping me to get the book into shape.

FIGURES

Introduction

Japan

Taiwan

South Korea

Hong Kong

Singapore

Malaysia

Thailand

The Philippines

Indonesia

India

Pakistan

TABLES

1

ASIA'S EMERGING EQUITY MARKETS: A GENERAL INTRODUCTION

Imagine an Asian country where the stock exchange has just reopened after ten years of destructive warfare or Communist dictatorship. Much of the nation's industry has been entirely wiped out. There are few exports, and the economic prospects for the nation seem to be purely those of an agricultural country. Rice is the principal staple diet, and much of the population is undernourished. Military occupation continues. The original programme of the military government has included land and shareholding distribution to the people at large, and many of the major industrial groups have been broken up. The stock exchange is moribund. Market capitalisation stands at less than US$1 billion. On some days, daily turnover drops below US$100,000. Only a handful of security houses retain experienced staff with knowledge of the market and their profession.

The country described could well be one of a number of Asian countries analysed in this book in 1989; the description would also have applied to Taiwan, Korea, or Thailand 10 to 15 years ago, such has been the rapid pace of economic and market development. However, the answer to the riddle is, in fact, Tokyo, in 1949. The parallel is drawn simply to emphasise the real need for vision when investing in Asia's emerging equity markets today. Prospects for recovery in some countries may presently appear as unlikely as they did in post-war Japan, or Korea, or Taiwan in the 1960s.

In Asia, generally, it has been the human, rather than the natural, resources which have resulted in phenomenal long-term returns for the patient investor. The key to selecting the most rewarding investment opportunities is generally to find the most hard-working and resourceful people.

Asian Outperformance

No observer of the international investment scene during the past 20 years can fail to be struck by the consistent outperformance of the Asian securities markets, when compared over the same period (1969–1989) with those of the United States, or the European markets. The index figures are indeed remarkable (Table 1.1).

The most consistent long-term performance of any large capital market has of course been that of the Tokyo stock market which, starting at the same level in 1968 as the Dow Jones Index in New York (both were then at the 1,000 level on the Index, with the Nikkei Dow Jones modelled on the American original), stood in mid-1989 at nearly 35,000, as compared with 2,600 in New York.

Table 1.1 Performances to 31 December 1988*

Market	%
Hong Kong	+ 1,900
Japan	+ 1,320
Singapore	+ 500
United Kingdom	+ 450
France	+ 340
Germany	+ 110
United States	+ 150
World	+ 400

Source: Capital International.
Note: Index = 100 at 1 January 1970.

Coupled with the strength of the yen in 1985–1988, this has meant that the capitalisation of the Japanese equity market overtook that of the American market in 1987 and has become by the end of the 1980s easily the largest market in the world, accounting for 40% of world capitalisation, compared to 32% for the United States.

An Economic Assessment

We may begin our analysis of this phenomenon by taking a general look at the region. The Asian country statistics table (Table 1.2) includes the relevant data on population, Gross National Product (GNP), and exports, as well as information about the different stock markets, to give an idea of the relative size of each country and each market.

It is immediately apparent that Japan dominates the Asian region economically, both in terms of its economic size, which is 70% of the Asian total GNP, and its market capitalisation, which is 89% of the Asian index as at 31 March 1989.

As Figure 1.1 demonstrates, beside the three major elements of the world stock market — Japan (40%), the United States (28.5%), and Europe (21%) — the rest of Asia (at 5.5%) looks small. However, it is, in fact, the most dynamic and fastest-growing region of the world, with a large population, natural resources, and growing export volumes. One need only look back ten years to realise that it would have been right to have overweighted this region in a global portfolio when it was merely 1% of the index. We may now possibly look forward to the year 2000, when it may reach 15–25% of the world market.

But should these growing Asian markets be overemphasised at the expense of Japan? Here the evidence of the past is not so clear. Japan has outperformed all other major markets to reach its

Figure 1.1 World Equity Market Index

Source: Capital International.

Figure 1.2 Asian Equity Market Index

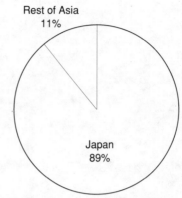

Source: Indosuez Asia Investment Services research.

Figure 1.3 Asian GNP

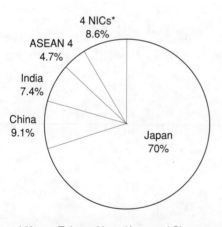

* Korea, Taiwan, Hong Kong and Singapore

Source: Indosuez Asia Investment Services research.
Note: * Korea, Taiwan, Hong Kong, and Singapore.

Figure 1.4 Asia's Exporters

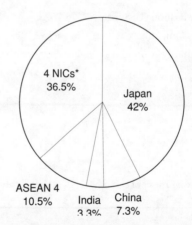

Source: Indosuez Asia Investment Services research.

present size — 40% of the world, and a full 89% of the Asian total stock market capitalisation (Figure 1.2). Can it remain so large in relation to its neighbours? Other measures of relative economic size need to be examined.

If one looks at economic, rather than capital market, size (Figure 1.3), the share of Japan in Asian markets falls to 70%; this is due not only to the powerful rise of the Asian NICs (Newly Industrialised Countries: South Korea, Taiwan, Hong Kong, and Singapore), but also to the rise of China, India, and the ASEAN members (the Association of South East Asian Nations: Indonesia, Thailand, Malaysia,

Table 1.2 Asian Country Statistics, as at 31 March 1989

Indicator	Japan	Taiwan	S. Korea	Hong Kong	Singapore	Malaysia	Thailand
Population (mn)	122.5	20.5	42.0	5.7	2.6	16.9	54.0
GNP (US$bn)	2,946.2	124.0	156.1	54.6	21.2	31.0	54.5
Real GNP Growth (%)							
1987	4.2	11.9	12.0	13.5	8.8	5.2	7.0
1988	5.5	7.0	12.1	8.5	10.9	8.1	10.3
1989F	4.5	6.5	8.0	6.5	7.0	8.0	8.5
Per Capita Income (US$)	24,051	6,045	3,750	9,650	8,154	1,881	1,009
Trade as % of GNP	34.4	102.3	70.0	224.9	297.0	106.0	56.7
Domestic Exports (US$bn)	458.4	61.6	59.0	27.8	20.1	17.0	15.1
US (% share)	33.8	39.1	35.5	33.2	31.3	16.6	19.2
Japan (% share)	–	14.4	19.9	5.1	10.6	19.5	15.5
Exports Manufactured (%)	100.0	98.1	84.4	99.5	75.2	41.7	66.5
Market Capitalisation (US$bn)	3,757.0	179.5	107.2	82.9	27.2	26.2	10.0
No. of Listed Companies	1,132	150	496	292	129	232	139
Index Performance in 1988 (%)	39.9	228.4	72.8	16.7	26.1	36.8	35.7
P/E Ratios							
1988	73.5	67.5	31.4	11.5	20.9	20.4	12.4
1989	63.0	40.6	24.8	10.5	14.5	19.0	11.0
EPS Growth							
1988	23.0	50.0	1.9	18.0	34.2	36.4	50.0
1989	20.0	15.0	8.5	16.5	10.3	15.1	20.0
Average Daily Turnover (US$mn)	8100	848	275	66	16	10	26

Sources: W.I. Carr; International Monetary Fund – International Financial Statistics; Indosuez Asia Investment Services
          research.

Notes

1. GNP/GDP and export figures for 1988 are estimates; all other figures are the most recent.
2. All growth rates are on an annual basis.

Philippines	China	Indonesia	India	Pakistan	Sri Lanka	Nepal	Bangladesh
58.4	1,100.0	178.0	816.8	103.8	16.6	18.3	110
34.0	377.0	75.0	243.0	40.0	7.0	3.4	15.0
5.0	9.3	4.2	4.1	6.5	1.5	7.1	3.0
6.6	8.5	4.9	2.5	5.8	3.5	4.5	5.7
6.2	7.8	5.8	9.0	7.5	3.0	7.1	3.5
582	343	419	297	385	422	164	145
40.0	28.0	33.7	12.6	28.1	55.5	26.5	28.93
4.9	49.0	19.7	11.07	4.3	1.5	0.23	1.41
28.5	3.1	20.9	13.2	11.1	6.5	5.0	N/A
16.9	6.6	42.7	11.9	11.4	17.4	10.5	N/A
45.1	66.3	36.3	51.5	52.5	48.6	66.0	77.3
4.0	0.5	1.0	31.6	2.5	0.5	0.032	0.45
143	25	24	5,250	422	176	31	111
4.2	N/A	269.5	48.9	15.0	-20.9	N/A	4.2
6.7	N/A	20.0	16.8	18.0	18.9	N/A	7.8
5.8	3.3	18.0	14.0	15.0	15.5	25.0	6.0
66.7	N/A	19.7	20.0	17.0	5.0	N/A	N/A
14.8	80.0	25.0	22.0	20.0	13.0	N/A	N/A
3.9	N/A	0.3	35	0.72	0.05	0.001	0.02

Brunei, and Singapore). The region thus appears somewhat more balanced, although it is still highly dependent on the Japanese consumer buying goods from South-East Asia, for instance, and on the Japanese tourist spending in Asian cities and resorts.

The real picture emerges when one measures the relative share of Asian exports. Japan accounts for only 42%, and the four NICs for over 35%, of this total volume, representing a growth in world export market share that is not yet reflected in their capital markets. The ASEAN four are also becoming more and more dynamic as exporters (although commodities are still very important), as are China and the socialist bloc (Figure 1.4). Many observers even predict that Vietnam will be the surprise winner of the early 1990s: their forecast is that as soon as its military withdrawal from Cambodia is completed foreign investment will pour in, and the large numbers of discharged soldiers will be put to work on textile and electronics production assembly lines. Tourism and offshore oil exploration are other promising areas.

Two Key Questions

With the Asian economy broadly assessed and the data set out, two questions of relevance to the equity investor present themselves and accordingly merit an explanation. First, why has the Japanese stock market outperformed — that is, what are the main elements behind its successful long-term record? Second, will other Asian markets demonstrate the same trends as Japan?

Briefly enumerated, the answers to the first question are:
1. Hard work.
2. A high savings rate.
3. An undervalued currency.
4. Consistent export success, leading to an unsurpassed corporate earnings record over a 30-year period.
5. Government intervention in the capital markets, particularly during periods of weakness, structural change (during the oil shocks), or international crisis.
6. Powerful business groups with holdings which underpin the share prices of their member companies.
7. Asset backing in the phenomenal real estate prices prevalent in urban Japan today.
8. A large and growing population of shareholders who are both conservative and (as was demonstrated during the week of 20–25 October 1987) less liable to spates of panic selling than their Western counterparts.
9. Powerful securities houses — the 'Big Four' — who are also prepared to support the market.

As to the second question, many of the characteristics highlighted as underlying the strength of the Japanese market — close business/political connections, strong securities houses, high savings rates, and export success — are also true, to one degree or another, of Korea, Taiwan, Hong Kong, and Singapore. The first two countries in particular (which have had, coincidentally, a Japanese educational system) show some of the same discipline and organisation which tend to impress the international investor analysing their industrial success and capital markets performance.

The Markets Themselves

Turning to the more specific part of our analysis, which examines the size of, and activity in, each national stock market, Table 1.2 above shows the total capitalisation, the number of listed companies, and the average daily turnover. However, foreign investors should be aware that the number of active stocks in an Asian market is usually far less than the number of listed companies. Even in Japan, where there are three sections to the market — first, second, and 'over the counter' — there are many stocks which are very thinly traded. This is even more true of the smaller Asian markets where a relatively large capitalisation does not guarantee good marketability of the shares.

It is very common practice in Asia for the founding family or a large business group to hold up to 70% of the available shares. Sometimes the 'float' (the shares publicly available) might not exceed 10–15% of the total. This may not pose an obstacle for individual investors, but for large international investors the ability to buy and sell shares in a given market in blocks of up to US$5 million a day is an important guarantee of liquidity, which may not always be available in Asian markets.

· Professional fund managers based in Asia can advise on each individual market. The best advice, of course, may simply be patience and careful selection. For a longer-term investor, it is always possible to accumulate quality shares in these small markets, but selling can be a problem.

The price/earnings (P/E) ratios for 1989 (prospective) (Figure 1.5) are as accurate as can be ascertained. They are intended to be helpful indicators of the relative multiples between the different markets. Coupled with the estimates for growth and corporate earnings for each country, they give a good standard of measurement for comparison with Western stock markets.

Figure 1.5 Asian Stock Markets' Price/Earnings Ratios, as at 31 March 1989

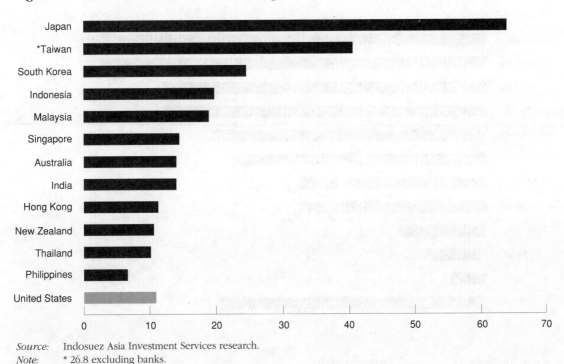

Source: Indosuez Asia Investment Services research.
Note: * 26.8 excluding banks.

Japan is indeed famous for its high P/E multiples, and although the present level is high even by historic standards, the Japanese market has never been especially cheap, and it has always paid to take a longer-term view.

As will be seen for the smaller markets such as Bangkok, Manila, Hong Kong, and Bombay, multiples are still low because of perceived political risk or the immature state of these capital markets. First-hand research, and visits to each stock exchange and to individual companies, are essential for a serious fund manager or international investor. The true quality of management and the financial prospects for individual businesses are notoriously difficult to judge from a distance.

It should be further noted that P/E ratios throughout Asia can prove baffling by international comparison. More detail will follow in the individual chapters on countries' different accounting practices, which helps to explain the relative differences in multiples. Japanese P/E ratios at 67 times are, generally speaking, not consolidated and can understate the true earning power of companies, whereas in Hong Kong, for example, P/E multiples are usually low not only because of the perceived political risk of 1997 but also because, with the low tax rate of 15%, there is no great incentive for companies to hide their profits. Hong Kong businesses therefore tend to report in full and to pay out generous dividends to their shareholders.

As to dividends, Figure 1.6 shows that Japanese shareholders scarcely benefit at all in dividends paid from the growth of the company. They have been more than compensated, however, by the capital growth in share prices. Japanese companies tend to reinvest a very large part of their profits into new plant and equipment, and as this is well understood by stockholders, the foreign investor should bear such a relationship and performance in mind when considering the Tokyo market.

Figure 1.6   Dividend Yield of Asian Stock Markets, as at 31 December 1988

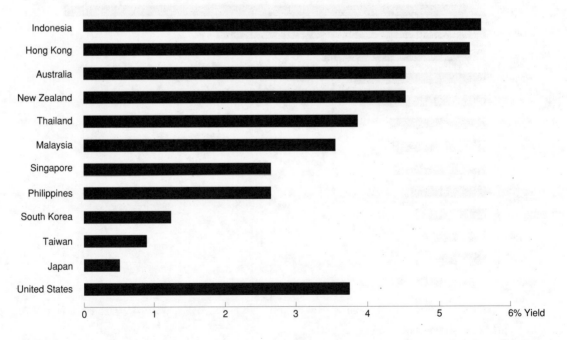

Source: Indosuez Asia Investment Services research.

Accordingly, while this book provides and analyses a comprehensive set of statistics for the investor approaching the Asian securities markets for the first time, it is important to stress the need

other factors prevalent in Asian countries, which can

veloped economies in Asia, it is obvious that few
narkets for the time being (and, indeed, many of these
to international investors). However, given the rapid
consequent rise in the value of their capital markets,
clude statistics on these large Asian nations with very
he rapid changes which have taken place in countries
asonable to imagine that, at the same speed of change,
g capital markets in the 1990s. The swift development
)78 has now reached the point where smaller securities
(adjacent to Hong Kong), Guangzhou, Shanghai, and
en to foreign investors, there is clearly the possibility
vill need to raise capital and may tap its large pool of

lle class of nearly 150 million people, with 10 million
in all these Asian capital markets is considerable.
, this is not something which is culturally acceptable
tings are rather tame affairs and do not involve very
ception may be made for Japan, where directors
stockholders by 'sokaiwa', or bouncers.)

Japanese Influence

Since the beginning of the 1980s, Japan has replaced the United States as the world's major creditor. Tokyo is rapidly surpassing New York (as New York surpassed London a generation ago) as a global banking centre. Japan's overseas financial assets are climbing rapidly and will probably reach US$1,500 billion by the end of the 1990s. The bulk of Japan's large trade and current account surplus is being recycled into US government bonds. In addition, the growth in direct investment into real estate by both Japanese institutional and individual investors is clearly apparent in Hawaii, California, and other US states (see Figures 1.7 and 1.8).

In South-East Asia, there is a profound economic impact from an increase not only in bank loans but also in direct investment by Japan, as indicated in Table 1.3. Additionally, one cannot neglect the growing impact of Japanese tourism on the region. Hong Kong, for example, has benefited enormously in its hotel and retail trade from the more than 1 million Japanese tourists who visit the territory annually.

When the Japanese yen started to move up against the dollar in 1985, it produced a knock-on effect not only in Japan itself but in all the other Asian economies as well. This is illustrated in Figure 1.9. The cost of producing textiles in Japan became prohibitive. The business moved first to Taiwan and Korea; then, in 1986, the new Taiwan dollar also started to move up against the US dollar, and the Taiwanese textile producers moved en masse to Thailand as well as to Malaysia. This was one of the reasons for Thailand becoming a major focus of investment in 1987 and 1988. A practical investment philosophy in Asia is to concentrate on niche businesses in each country. For example, in Japan today it is the service industries— including tourism, leisure, and retailing— and the high-

Figure 1.7   Capital Flows from Japan, 1987 (US$ billion)

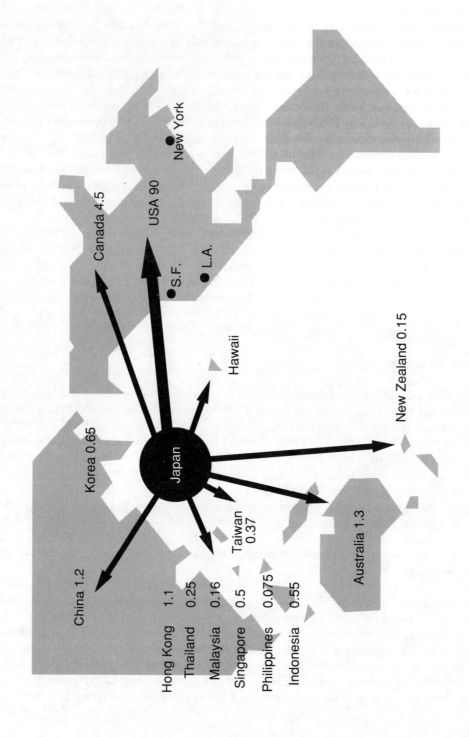

Canada 4.5

USA 90

New York

S.F.

L.A.

Hawaii

China 1.2

Korea 0.65

Japan

New Zealand 0.15

Taiwan 0.37

Australia 1.3

Hong Kong   1.1
Thailand   0.25
Malaysia   0.16
Singapore   0.5
Philippines   0.075
Indonesia   0.55

Source: Japanese Ministry of International Trade and Industry.

Figure 1.8 Japan's Direct Foreign Investment, 1976—2000E

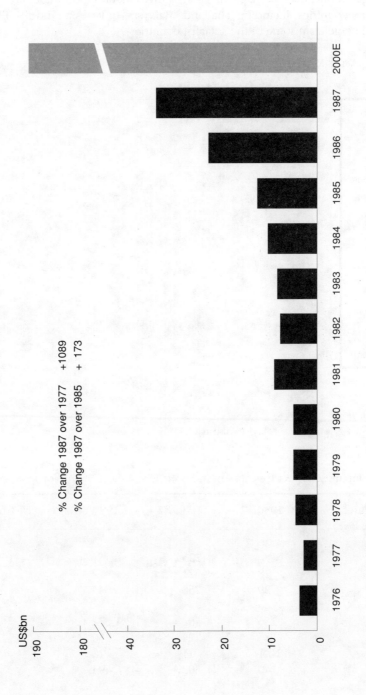

% Change 1987 over 1977   +1089
% Change 1987 over 1985   + 173

Source: Tokyo Economic Planning Agency; Japanese Ministry of International Trade and Industry; Indosuez Asia
Investment Services research.

technology industries which are attractive. Korea is the most efficient producer of a number of middle-range products, but perhaps the greatest investment opportunities are now emerging in the lower-income countries, including Thailand, Malaysia, Indonesia, and the Philippines, and will eventually emerge from some of the socialist countries.

Figure 1.9 Asia's Move Upmarket into the 1990s

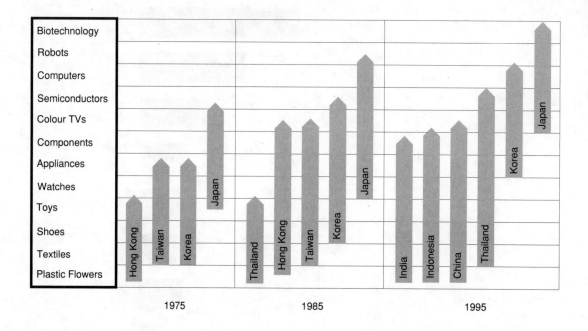

Source: Indosuez Asia Investment Services research.

Table 1.3 Japanese Direct Investment in South-East Asia (US$ million)

Year End March	1980/81	1986/87	1987/88	% Change 1986–1987
China	N/A	226	1,226	+ 442
Philippines	78	21	72	+ 243
Indonesia	529	250	545	+ 118
Hong Kong	156	502	1,072	+ 114
Thailand	33	124	250	+ 102
India	N/A	11	21	+ 91
Singapore	140	302	494	+ 64

Year End March	% Change 1986–1987
South Korea	+ 48
Taiwan	+ 26
Malaysia	+ 17
Other Asia	+ 83
South-East Asia Tot	+ 109
Australia	+ 39
New Zealand	+ 30
Other Pacific Islan	+ 289
Pacific Total	+ 42
World Total	+ 49

Sources: Japanese Ministry of Finance; indo.....   ..... research.

Note: The surge in Japanese direct investment overseas is the single most important structural change affecting the Asia-Pacific region. In the year to March 1988, Japanese direct investment in South-East Asia rose 109%, to US$4.9 billion — 15% of the total.

Japanese Finance

A further explanation of the strong performance of Asian economies and markets may be found in the relatively low cost of borrowing which has prevailed in these countries since 1945. Japanese companies, for example, can borrow at an average cost of about 5%, compared to prime rates in the United States of around 12%, bestowing a very important competitive advantage (see Figure 1.10). Japanese companies have of course also raised an enormous amount of capital in the stock market over the past 20 years. The consumer electrical companies such as Matsushita, Sharp, Sony, and Pioneer were able to finance their aggressive global expansion in the 1970s with proceeds from such capital issues. In the 1980s, it has been the turn of the semiconductor, or 'chip', manufacturers such as Fujitsu, NEC, and Oki. Here again, they were able to raise finance much more cheaply than their American competitors such as Texas Instruments and Motorola.

But it is in the financial sector that the greatest international impact may be felt in the future. When, in 1988, the internationally accepted Cooke Committee published its new rules for capital ratios for banks, it was widely expected that the Japanese banks would suffer the most and lose their competitive edge since they had, on average, only 2% of equity capital relative to the large size of their loan portfolios — compared with a 5% average among Western banks.

The 'Cooke Ratio' was set at 8% (equity as % of total assets) by the end of 1992, so to meet this challenge all international banks must raise a great deal of capital. However, Western observers had not reckoned with the strength and breadth of the Tokyo stock market, backed by the enormous

Figure 1.10   Prime Interest Rates Throughout Asia, as at 31 December 1988

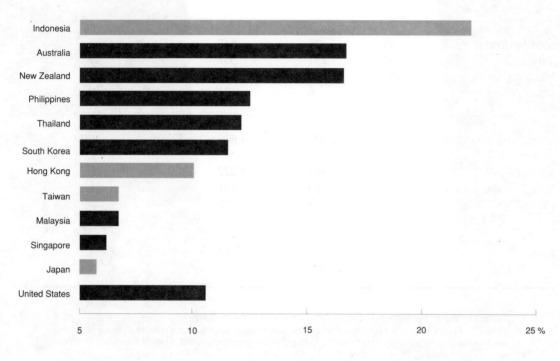

Source: Indosuez Asia Investment Services research.

power of Japanese savings. Already, major banks such as Sumitomo, Fuji, Mitsubishi, Sanwa, and the Bank of Tokyo have been able to raise very large amounts of capital from the market without difficulty.

   Another strange phenomenon in some Asian markets is that, after a large rights or bonus issue of new shares, the share price does not adjust downwards, as one would logically expect, but usually rises so that the nominal price does not change.

   To give an idea of the ease with which even second-line Japanese companies, with their excellent credit ratings, can raise finance in international markets, the average convertible bond warrant issue made to Swiss investors by Japanese companies carries a coupon of 2.5%.

Liquidity and Confidence

Taking a broad view, then, what could be the major reasons for the outperformance of the Asian securities markets over the past 20 years, and what are the major trends in the region today?

   Two of the main reasons for the superior performance of Asian capital markets over the past 20 years can be identified as *liquidity* and *confidence*. Liquidity is almost entirely attributable to the high rate of savings which is prevalent throughout the 'Confucian' world (China, Japan, and Korea, and the overseas Chinese communities).

Figure 1.11 shows the average savings rates in the Asian countries, compared to Australasia and the United States. It is estimated, for example, that the Japanese population as a whole saves US$1 billion per day. When this is compared with the low savings rate in the United States (around 5% average in the past five years), one can readily appreciate why the Japanese market has outperformed New York.

Figure 1.11   Savings Rates in Asia, as at 31 March 1989

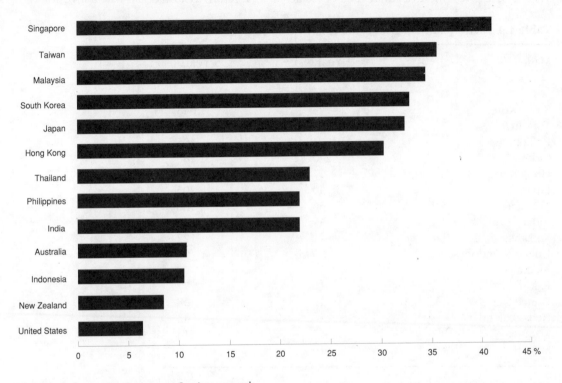

Source: Indosuez Asia Investment Services research.

In any attempt to understand the motivation for such high savings rates, however, one must distinguish within Asia itself between the voluntary savings in countries such as Hong Kong and Taiwan, and the government-directed schemes in Singapore and Malaysia (called the Central Provident Fund).

As to investor confidence, it is worthwhile remembering the events of the week of 19–23 October 1987. The day after the New York market had fallen 508 points, retail investors in Seoul and Tokyo were aggressively buying the shares of their leading national companies — not simply for patriotic motives, but from a genuine belief in their own future growth potential. This might have seemed absurd to a Western observer at that time, since Korea, for example, is highly dependent on the United States as an export market. If the US economy had followed the New York market into a deep recession, Korea would clearly have been badly affected. However, the remarkable fact about that week was that it was Tokyo, among all the other major markets, which led the recovery of confidence, and it was Japanese individual investors who provided the necessary cash and buying power to spur that recovery and restore the confidence that would avert collapse.

Evaluating Performance

In commenting on the performance of the different Asian markets, it is useful to take the five-year performance figures in Table 1.4, together with the currency appreciation or depreciation figures in Table 1.5, to give a more accurate idea of the actual total return to a US dollar-based investor.

Table 1.4   Performance of Asian Stock Markets, to 31 December 1988

Market	1 Year (%)	5 Years (%)
South Korea	73	648
Taiwan	228	572
Philippines	4	495
Indonesia	270	280
Hong Kong	17	207
Japan	40	205
Thailand	36	188
India	49	138
Sri Lanka	-21	122
United Kingdom	6	97
Australia	13	92
Pakistan	15	77
United States	12	68
New Zealand	-6	43
Malaysia	37	14
Singapore	26	4

Source: Country stock exchanges.

Table 1.5   Performance of Asian Currencies vs US Dollar, to 31 December 1988

Country	Currency	1 Year % Change	5 Years % Change
Japan	Yen	- 1.9	+45.8
Taiwan	Dollar	+ 1.3	+30.0
South Korea	Won	+13.7	+14.0
Singapore	Dollar	+13.7	+ 8.5
Hong Kong	Dollar	0	0
New Zealand	Dollar	- 4.4	- 4.0

Country	Currency	1 Year % Change	5 Years % Change
Australia	Dollar	+ 18.4	- 5.2
Thailand	Baht	- 0.7	- 9.7
Malaysia	Ringgit	- 8.9	- 16.1
Bangladesh	Taka	- 3.4	- 29.1
Sri Lanka	Rupee	- 7.4	- 32.1
Pakistan	Rupee	- 6.9	- 38.1
India	Rupee	- 16.1	- 42.5
Philippines	Peso	- 2.6	- 52.4
Nepal	Rupee	- 16.7	- 65.8
Indonesia	Rupiah	- 5.0	- 74.1

Source: IMF/ International Financial Statistics; Indosuez Asia Investment Services research.

Clearly, there has been a great advantage in being invested in those currencies (the Japanese yen, Korean won, New Taiwan dollar, and Singapore dollar) which have appreciated in the past three years against the US dollar. The major underlying reason for this appreciation has been the trade surplus which each East Asian exporter achieved in its bilateral trade with the United States, as well as, of course, US diplomatic pressure to revalue — from the 1985 'Group of Seven' accord, which began the yen's revaluation, to the 1987–1988 pressure on Taiwan and Korea. Hong Kong, for political reasons, in October 1983 pegged its dollar at a fixed exchange rate of HK$7.8 to US$1.00 and thus escaped US pressure. However, Hong Kong has, in contrast with its competitors, suffered from a much higher inflation rate as a result of this undervalued exchange rate.

Stock market performance, therefore, has been partly (but by no means wholly) linked to currency movements. The most important factors have been underlying economic growth, corporate earnings, and dividend growth. Korea and Taiwan have topped the league here, and currency revaluation has also helped to maintain substantial liquidity within the country, supporting share prices.

The Philippines and Indonesia have both been special cases. All of the movements in the Manila index occurred during the two to three months following Mrs Aquino's coming to power in February 1986. In Indonesia's case, the Jakarta market actually doubled *in one week*, in December 1988, bounding out of the doldrums it had endured for the previous three years. Hong Kong and Thailand recorded more consistent performances, since investors receive, on average, an annual dividend yield of around 5%.

The Tokyo market continues to perform consistently better than any other large world market, recording an average 40% annual growth over the last five years including 1987. Taken with the appreciation of the yen, this compares very favourably with the performance of the US (+68% in five years) and the UK (+97%) markets.

Many investors have therefore concluded that Japan is permanently the safest and best market for their pension funds or individual savings. However, past performance, as any unit trust prospectus will warn, is no guide to future growth. It is unlikely, for example, that world markets will see a US dollar devaluation in the next five years of anything like the extent since 1985.

Volatility has been a characteristic of Asian markets over the years. Hong Kong is a prime example of this. The Hang Seng Index rose from 100 to 1,800 in 1970–1973, then fell to 150 in 1973–1974. From a low of 750 during the 1983 crisis of confidence, it rose to 4,000 in the week preceding the October 1987 crash, then fell 33% in a day.

Nonetheless, the long-term trend over 20 years has shown a very powerful upward momentum, in large part based on the phenomenal growth of corporate and personal wealth in Asia during this period.

Potential Growth and Returns

What is the longer-term potential for each Asian stock market? In addition to the underlying growth rate of the economy, exports, and domestic savings, it may be useful to compare the size of the capital market with that of the economy (Figure 1.12).

Figure 1.12   Asian Stock Market Capitalisation as a Percentage of GNP, as at 31 December 1988

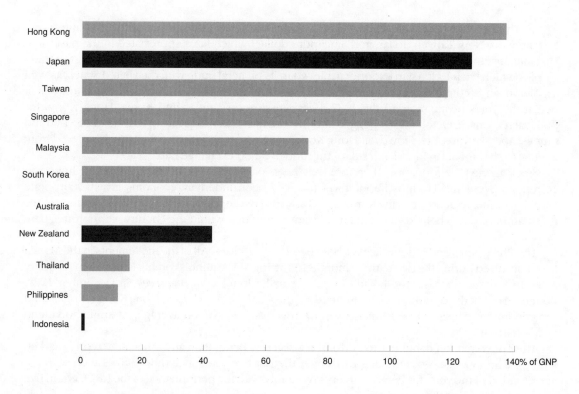

Source: Indosuez Asia Investment Services research.

Two comments should be made. In the case of small entrepôt 'city-states' such as Hong Kong and Singapore, it is quite normal for foreign trade to exceed GNP by 200%; therefore, the stock market does not necessarily look overvalued in this perspective. However, for larger economies such as Taiwan and, especially, Japan, it is surprising that the capitalisation of the nation's quoted corporations would exceed the size of the GNP (which includes all the private, unquoted corporations and the government share of the economy). One of Japan's leading economists, Professor Hisao Kanamori, Chairman of the Nikkei Research Centre, has said that once the Tokyo stock market reached 140% of Japan's GNP, it was fundamentally overvalued. For the time being, however, the large pool of liquidity from Japan's recurrent export surplus and high savings rate seems quite sufficient to maintain the index at high levels.

Emerging Markets

Turning to look at the emerging equity markets in Asia, however, one can easily spot the laggards with the greatest potential for growth: South Korea, Thailand, India, and the Philippines, all the way down to Indonesia, whose market is barely 1% of GNP. Korea's case is both encouraging and instructive: ten years ago, the capital market was less than 10% of GNP; however, with official encouragement, a small intake of foreign capital, and — most importantly — a rapid growth in the number of Korean investors (both individuals and institutions), the Seoul market has taken off in the 1980s and now equals about 65% of GNP.

Thailand is about five years behind Korea, having risen recently to 25% of GNP, and still appears relatively undervalued. Of all the other markets, India is perhaps the most promising, with Bombay and the other 15 stock exchanges still having a capitalisation equal to about 9% of GNP. However, one leading Indian analyst commented that the stock market cannot reflect the entire US$275 billion Indian economy because 'the government owns so much in India', including the whole of the banking sector and most of the heavy industry (except for special cases such as Tata Iron and Steel).

One striking indicator (see Table 1.2 above) is the rise in personal incomes in the four NICs, with Hong Kong almost touching US$10,000 annually per capita and South Korea, with a much larger population of 42 million, advancing towards US$5,000. These are important statistics in that they tell a great deal both about the growth in domestic consumption in each country and the number of potential shareholders in each stock market.

The degree to which each economy is geared to the world trade cycle is also reflected in its trade as a percentage of GNP, as is also shown in Table 1.2. To a large extent, this will reflect the potential growth rate of the economy as a whole. Figures included (showing the percentage distribution of each country's exports among the United States, Japan, and Western Europe) are important, since an investor should be aware of the degree to which each country is dependent on developments in the US economy or in the EEC.

Also included are figures showing the percentage of exports accounted for by manufactured goods. In the case of Japan, it is 100%, indicating that virtually none of Japan's exports are agricultural or basic commodities. Taiwan and Hong Kong are also very close to this 100% figure.

For the other Asian nations, the high percentage of exports which are in fact manufactured is remarkable. Given the tendency of stock markets to be biased in their reflection of the economy, mainly towards listed manufacturing companies and service companies, this figure is an important indicator of each country's stage of evolution. Only recently (in 1980), for example, Thailand was dependent on rice exports for nearly 50% of its overseas trade. Now, manufactured exports make up over 60% and agriculture less than 20% of total exports.

Of course, such analysis only highlights the potential in these markets and does not have in itself any predictive value. The West German economy, for example, continues to be much larger than the

British economy, but for historical and cultural reasons the London stock market (capitalisation US$763 billion) is disproportionately broader and more liquid than Frankfurt (US$230 billion) or Paris (US$226 billion).

Investment Opportunities in Funds

Despite the evident attractions of high-growth South-East Asian markets, it is often difficult or physically impossible for investors to find an entry point into them. Accordingly, a growing number of closed-end 'country funds' have been launched (Table 1.6) by investment management companies to meet the needs of investors wishing to gain access to restricted Asian markets. Given the limitations of marketability within the small Asian markets themselves, the ideal solution has been to list the shares of the funds in London or New York. The creation of these funds for Korea, Taiwan, and Thailand in the 1980s may be compared to the early Japan funds created in the 1960s, which were also closed-end funds with a fixed life of from five to seven years.

Table 1.6   Investment Vehicles in Restricted Asian Markets

Country	Fund	Manager	Inception Date	Listing (if applic.)	Size (US$mn)	R/C*
South Korea	Korea Int'l Trust	Korea Inv. Trust	Nov 1981	N/A	251	R
	Korea Trust	Daehan Inv. Trust	Nov 1981	N/A	198	R
	Korea Fund	Scudder Stevens & Clark	June 1984	NYSE	576	C
	Seoul Trust	Daehan Inv. Trust	Apr 1985	N/A	204	R
	Seoul Int'l Trust	Korea Inv. Trust	Apr 1985	N/A	216	R
	Korea Growth Trust	Citizens Inv. Trust	Mar 1985	Hong Kong	207	R
	Korea Europe Fund	Korea Schroder Fund Management	June 1987	London	190	C
	Plus convertible bonds issued by Daewoo, Goldstar, Saehan Media, Samsung, and Yukong					
Taiwan	Taiwan (ROC) Fund	Int'l Inv. Trust	Oct 1983	NYSE	369	R
	Formosa Fund	Kwang Hwa Securities	Mar 1986	London	225	R
	Taipei Fund	National Inv. Trust	May 1986	London	190	R
	Taiwan Fund	China Securities Investment Trust Corp.	Dec 1986	NYSE	88	C
Philippines	JF Philippine Trust	Jardine Fleming	July 1974	Hong Kong	5.2	R
	Thornton Philippines Redevelopment Fund	Thornton	May 1986	Hong Kong	4.0	R
	The Manila Fund	Indosuez Asia	Oct 1989	London	50	C

Country	Fund	Manager	Inception Date	Listing (if applic.)	Size (US$mn)	R/C*
Thailand	Bangkok Fund	Bangkok First Inv. Trust	1985	London	58	C
	Thailand Fund	Mutual Fund Co.	Dec 1986	London	65	R
	Siam Fund	Indosuez Asia Inv.	Jan 1988	London	100	C
	The Thai Fund	Mutual Fund Co.	Dec 1988	NYSE	146	C
	Thai Euro Fund	Mutual Fund Co.	1988	London	80	C
	Thai Inv. Fund	Yamaichi/Asia Secs.	1988	London	34	C
	Thai Prime Fund .	Mutual Fund Co.	Dec 1988	Singapore/ London	155	C
	Thailand Int'l Fund	Fidelity	Dec 1988	London	80	C
Malaysia	Malaysia Fund	Merrill Lynch	Mar 1987	NYSE		C
	Malaysia Fund	Morgan Stanley	Dec 1987	NYSE	84	C
Indonesia	Malacca Fund	Indosuez Asia Inv.	Jan 1989	London	35	C
	Indonesia Fund	Jardine Fleming	Mar 1989	N/A	25	C
India	India Fund	Merrill Lynch/U.T.I.	June 1986	London	102	C
	India Growth Fund	Unit Trust of India	Dec 1988	NYSE	60	C

Plus convertible bonds expected 1989/90 by leading Indian corporations

Source: Indosuez Asia Investment Services research.
Note: * R = Redeemable; C = Closed-end.

One can only hope that within the next ten years, many of these markets will be larger in both size and turnover as well as much more open to international investors. At present, however, in addition to the funds, a number of convertible bonds have been directly issued by leading Korean corporations. Leading Indian corporations may follow this example, since the promising Indian capital market has hitherto only been open through two funds.

Individual investors should study carefully the performance of these funds, particularly how their Net Asset Value (NAV) compares with the daily market price in London or New York. It is very common to see a new country fund launched at, say, a price of US$10.40, and trade with a 10–15% premium at US$11.50–12.00 for the first two months. Six months later, the NAV market price may be selling at a discount of 5% (US$12).

Such a pattern can happen for a number of reasons. At the time of launch, there is great enthusiasm and interest in the exotic market for which the country fund is destined. The shares go to a premium because it is a closed-end fund, and so the issue is oversubscribed. The underlying asset value of the shares may take some time to begin to perform, and when it does, the premium is likely to diminish.

If the underlying market, and thus the NAV, should fall, then it is quite possible to see the discount widen to 20–30%. This was, for example, the case with the *India Fund* in 1987–1988. An additional factor was the devaluation of the rupee. If the market goes out of fashion and many investors wish to get out at any price, the discount widens further. If this occurs, there may well be a bargain to be had.

Some closed-end funds, or investment trusts as they are known in the United Kingdom, have been purchased outright by outside investors who will then liquidate the underlying shares so as to realise a hefty profit. By contrast, international investors' continuous demand for Korean paper and Korean funds has meant that there has been a 100% premium, on average, prevailing on the Korean issues listed in Hong Kong during the past few years. However, during the October 1987 crash, although the underlying price of the Korean shares hardly changed, the premiums fell overnight from 100 to 50%.

Pension Funds and Savings

One aspect of these developing markets which investors should consider in the coming decade is the potential demand for shares that may come from the increasing mobilisation of the Western world's personal and corporate savings — not only through mutual funds, but also, and more significantly, through pension funds.

The magnitude of the potential inflow is considerable. At present, not more than 2% of the estimated US$1,400 billion of tax-exempt institutions in the United States (including pension funds, retirement plans, savings plans, endowments, and foundations) is estimated to be invested in foreign securities. However, by the mid-1990s, this proportion is likely to grow to 5% of the total, while the size of the total pension fund pool is expected to continue to increase at around 10% per annum.

In Japan, also, with the generally high savings rate of the Japanese population (accumulating US$1 billion per day), pension funds are becoming more and more established. Nevertheless, it is the 12 large life insurance companies — Nippon Life, Dai Ichi, Meiji Life, Sumitomo, Chiyoda, and so on — who are leading the slow but massive flow of Japanese capital overseas. In 1988–1989, more than half of these major insurance companies established investment offices in London, New York, and Hong Kong. Dai Ichi, one of the largest players, with US$110 billion of assets, purchased 1% (the maximum allowed) of Hongkong and Shanghai Bank shares, 2% of Cie Financière de Suez, and several other strategic stakes around the globe. Observers in Japan comment that this trend has barely begun and will start to have a significant influence in share markets, especially in South-East Asia, in the 1990s.

In the Asian countries themselves, surplus capital and savings are beginning to be felt in share markets, as institutional players become more influential than retail investors and tend to stabilise markets with their continuous cashflow. In Hong Kong, for example, the government passed legislation to establish provident and pension funds for all smaller Chinese manufacturing companies, a measure which is likely to have a significant medium-term effect on demand for equities, as well as for fixed-income instruments.

Other countries are also active in this respect. In Singapore, the government already exerts a great influence on the capital markets and interest rates through the medium of the *Central Provident Fund*, which absorbs over 20% of national income. In Thailand, domestic savings are mainly channelled into the Mutual Fund Company, a monopoly fund management corporation belonging to the Ministry of Finance.

In a very similar way, the government-owned Unit Trust of India, with US$7 billion under management and a remarkably successful series of funds, owns over 10% of traded shares on the Bombay Stock Exchange and effectively acts as a cushion for the market with its buying power (supported by over three million customers all over the subcontinent). In Indonesia, such a stabilising role is played by the government agency Danareksa which, together with the Capital Markets Executive Agency (BAPEPAM), is attempting to develop the local securities market by attracting retail investors.

Many Asian governments have taken steps to encourage savings, and offer fiscal incentives to shareholders through means such as the famous 'Loi Monory' issued in France in 1976, enabling small investors to offset about 5,000 francs (US$1,000) of dividend income against income taxes. The privatisation of large state corporations throughout Asia during the 1980s has also dramatically increased the number of shareholders. For example, the large share issue of NTT in Japan, which took place in three tranches in 1987–1988, raised in total over US$180 billion — 5% of the total capitalisation of the Tokyo stock market.

One of the most discussed international dilemmas of the 1980s was the problem of 'Third World debt', which appeared to threaten the international banking system, as had occurred twice before in the 1890s and the 1930s. Approaching 1990, the dilemma seems less threatening, and there is an abundance of surplus capital in the developed world (especially in Japan). Furthermore, it should not require any great imagination to devise attractive and performing investment vehicles to channel these surplus savings into the markets of the developing world.

Converging Elements

Another interesting component of Asian equities markets to consider is the role that the International Finance Corporation (IFC), the private sector affiliate of the World Bank in Washington, is now playing in promoting the further development of emerging markets in the developing world, especially in Asia. Clearly, many of these countries have very small, illiquid markets which place severe constraints on foreign investors, so it is natural that the public and private sectors form a partnership to invest in such developing countries. Fund management companies and international banks need the political and moral support of an international agency such as the IFC, and the IFC in turn requires the on-the-spot expertise and technical know-how that small, flexible management groups specialising in a particular region can provide. By the spring of 1989, the IFC had co-sponsored investment funds for six countries: South Korea, Thailand, and Malaysia, all quoted in New York; a private fund for Brazil; and debt-conversion funds for the Philippines and Chile. The debt-conversion funds buy discounted foreign debt for hard currency and then invest in local shares, being 'locked in' for five years. In addition to these, the IFC has two proprietary funds: the *Emerging Markets Growth Fund* and the *Emerging Markets Investment Fund*.

Tables 1.4 and 1.6 clearly demonstrate that these 'emerging' markets are not merely of interest to international agencies but also to profit-oriented and competitive companies, such as fund management organisations. Many respected international groups have seen the long-term attraction of such 'developing country' investment at an early stage and started to accumulate equities in such places as Chile, Nigeria, and Pakistan.

As can be seen, there is today a convergence of interest occurring among agencies, such as the IFC (a World Bank affiliate), private and institutional investors such as pension funds, and the host countries and populations of the Third World themselves.

Political Change

In any discussion of the development of equity markets in Asia, one must also consider social and political changes. There has been a clear failure of socialism in the region, as elsewhere in the world, which is recognised by many governments desperate to raise capital for development. Even China concedes that the centrally planned economy idea does not work. On the other hand, China does not want to borrow heavily and run up a large foreign debt, so it may in time turn more to capital markets in Shanghai, Shenzhen, Guangzhou, and other cities.

The shift in Asia, as in Europe, to free market ideas in the 1980s has been remarkable, though it has not been without political repercussions. The return to democracy of Korea and Taiwan, for example, has coincided with a rapid growth of their stock markets.

Ready for a Change in Attitude?

The question then presents itself as to whether a country such as India or Brazil is ready to allow foreign investors to come into its equity markets. Will they not lose 'control' or 'ownership' of their national companies, or even precious mineral resources? There is an emotional issue here which does not affect the more straightforward business of lending. Many countries, especially those who have lived under the rule of colonial powers until as recently as 40 years ago, cannot countenance the prospect of abandoning any share ownership to foreign investors. There are varying degrees of this attitude: complete prohibition as in Pakistan; limited entry (to offshore funds, managed locally) as in Korea; a specific percentage of ownership permitted as in Thailand; or an apparently unrestricted (but culturally difficult) 'open door' policy to foreign investors as in Japan.

Of the markets discussed in this book, probably only Hong Kong has a completely *laissez-faire* attitude to international investors to the extent of allowing takeover bids, for example. (But then, in Asia, things are seldom as they appear on the surface, in this as in many other aspects of life.)

There has nevertheless been an important shift of attitudes on the part of central banks and political leaders who do not wish to, or cannot, increase the burden of foreign debt and must look to new sources of financing. The equity market can tap both domestic savings and international capital sources; it can be carefully regulated; and ownership and control need not be sacrificed. The Asian attitude to the institution of the stock exchange itself has evolved rapidly in the past five years.

A stock market is not merely a casino for speculators: it is a vital part of a nation's economy. It is, further, the most accurate barometer of national economic well-being, of corporate health, and of confidence in the government and in the currency. It may indeed become a source of national pride.

'The cult of the equity is taking over India', a senior official in Delhi told the author in March 1989. If this is true, it is a remarkable commentary on the global *'Zeitgeist'*, or spirit of the Age, that this Western concept has attained the socialist corners of Asia, including China (as Chapter 16 describes). Some would even argue that there is a more profound political and philosophical meaning to this change. Owning a share in a company is very much akin to having a vote in a democracy. The gradual spread of 'a share-owning and property-owning democracy' in East Asia, as in Margaret Thatcher's England, could have broad political repercussions.

Deregulation of barriers to trade and capital flows; privatisation of state-owned entities, such as airlines — in a word, liberalisation: all this will be beneficial to the development of Asian securities markets.

Some Initial Advice

The chapters that follow offer specific market information and advice. However, in summary, the best advice to investors based in Europe or North America would be: Have the courage of your convictions — hold on to Asian investments for the best long-term gains. And to a short-term trader who is closer to the Asian scene: Buy on corrections to achieve the most outstanding capital gains.

The foregoing general data and analysis should give some clues as to growth prospects and therefore to where one should invest for the best risk/return ratio in a diversified Asian portfolio. The potential investor is advised to ignore the overwhelming weight of the Tokyo market capitalisation today—to 'look beyond Japan', in other words—and to place a bet on the growth of the smaller Asian exporters. Even if one of these markets stumbles, the loss is cushioned by diversification, as graphically displayed in Figure 1.13. The greater likelihood is that among these Asian 'tigers' will be the world's investment winners in the 1990s, as they have been in the 1980s. Indexing will certainly not produce the best results.

Figure 1.13   An Asian Model Portfolio, 1989

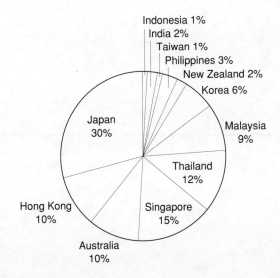

Source: Indosuez Asia Investment Services research.

Asia is an exciting region with a dynamic future. While the cautious investor can reduce volatility by spreading his investments broadly across the region, he must also have fortitude to ride out the cyclical and political dips.

2

JAPAN

Introduction

When the Tokyo Stock Exchange reopened for trading in April 1949 after almost a decade of closure, Japan's industry lay shattered after its defeat in the Pacific War, and the population subsisted on rice. International observers gave the economy little chance of recovery, and it was widely announced that Japan would henceforth only be an agricultural producer. Under the radical programme of the US occupation to destroy the tenacious hold of the *'zaibatsu'* (large industrial groups), large holdings of land and industrial shares were redistributed to the people. In brief, the outlook for an investor appeared bleak. Yet somewhere in the suburbs, Akio Morita, with two friends, was preparing to start manufacturing radios. His company would later become Sony. Elsewhere, Konosuke Matsushita and Kenichiro Honda were founding the businesses which now bear their names. A visionary investor with US$1,000 to spare who purchased a handful of these companies' shares would have seen his stake multiplied hundreds of times over the next four decades.

In fact, Tokyo in 1949 was not very different from the situation in many Asian capitals in recent years, and even today in the 'emerging markets'. Yet the Tokyo Stock Exchange Index was to rise no less than 113 times during the next 40 years (see Figure 2.1). No market in world history has shown such a comparable and consistent appreciation over such a long period of time.

Historical Background

The first Japanese stock exchanges were established in Tokyo and Osaka in 1878. The majority of transactions on these exchanges were in government bonds, but due to the remarkable economic growth of Japan after the Meiji restoration, the stock market was already contributing to the financing of long-term capital for industry by the 1920s. Defeat in the Pacific War meant that trading was suspended for a time, but a new stock exchange was established in 1949 based on a securities exchange law modelled on American practice. Margin trading was introduced in 1951, and in June 1961 a Second Section was opened on three exchanges — Tokyo, Osaka, and Nagoya. Japan's post-war economic growth has meant that the stock market has become a central pillar of the financial markets, and in early 1987 (in terms of market capitalisation) the Tokyo Stock Exchange became the largest stock market in the world (Table 2.1).

Note: US$1.00 = ¥146.3.

Figure 2.1 Tokyo Stock Exchange (TOPIX) Performance, 1949–1989

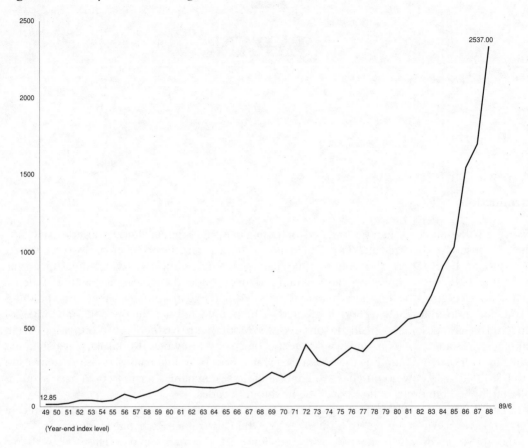

(Year-end index level)

Figure 2.2 Japanese Yen vs US Dollar, Weekly, 1983–1989

Source: Datastream.

Table 2.1 Stock Market Performance, 1985–1989

Market Indicator	1985	1986	1987	1988	1989E
Nikkei-Dow Index	13,083.18	18,701.30	21,564.0	30,159.0	37,000
Market Index (TOPIX)	997.72	1,323.26	1,963.29	2,134.24	2,600
Annual Growth Rate (%)	(22.3)	(32.7)	(48.3)	(8.7)	(21.8)
Listed Companies	1.487	1,504	1,533	1,576	1,640
Listed Stocks (mn shares)	258,635	267,680	280,745	295,406	310,000
Total Market Value (US$bn)	937.7	1,694.0	2,625.4	3,721.0	4,055
Daily Trading Volume (US$mn)	1,362.2	3,400.0	7,135.3	8,161.3	9,000
PER (times, TSE 1st section)	35.2	47.3	58.3	58.4	60*
Market Cap/GNP (%)	59.9	86.2	97.6	129.9	132
No. of Investors (% of pop.)	18.2	15.2	17.2	19	21
Ownership of Institutional Investors (%)	76.6	77.4	79.0	79.1	79.3
Corporate Earnings Growth	(2.4)	(.9)	15.8	28.0	15.0
Funds Raised through Equity (US$mn)	3,763.8	4,762.3	22,600.0	35,375.5	70,000
Dividend Yield Ratio (%)	0.92	0.74	0.59	0.51	0.45

Sources: Tokyo Stock Exchange; Tokyo SEC.
Note: * The PER for 1989 is prospective.

Stock Exchange Details

Figure 2.3 shows the location of stock exchanges in Japan.

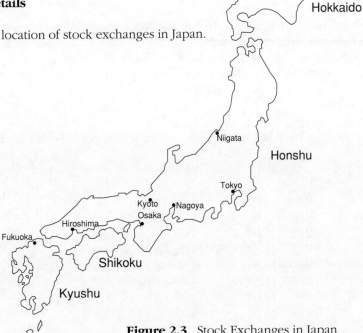

Figure 2.3 Stock Exchanges in Japan

Addresses

Tokyo Stock Exchange
2-1-1, Nishombashi-Kayaba-cho
Chuo-ku
Tokyo 103
Tel: 666 0141
Tlx: 02522759 TKOSE J

Osaka Securities Exchange
2-1, Kitahama
Higashi-ku
Osaka 541
Tel: 203 1151
Tlx: 05225118 OSASE J

Nagoya Stock Exchange
3-3-17, Sakae
Naka-ku
Nagoya 460
Tel: 241 1521

Kyoto Stock Exchange
66 Higashinotoin-Higashiiru-Tachiuri-Nishimachi
Shijo-dori Shimokyo-ku
Tel: 221 1171

Hiroshima Stock Exchange
14-18, Kanayama-cho
Naka-ku
Hiroshima 730
Tel: 41 0094

Fukuoka Stock Exchange
2-14-2, Tenjin
Chuo-ku
Fukuoka 810
Tel: 741 8231

Niigata Stock Exchange
1245, Hachiban-cho
Kamiohkawamae-dori
Niigata 951
Tel: 22 4181

Sapporo Stock Exchange
5-14-1, Minamiichijo-Nishi
Chuo-ku
Sapporo 060
Tel: 241 6171

The Tokyo, Osaka, and Nagoya exchanges have two trading sections each, while the Kyoto, Hiroshima, Fukuoka, Niigata, and Sapporo exchanges have only one section. The Tokyo Stock Exchange, situated in the city's famous 'Kabutocho' business district, is the most significant exchange, accounting for 86.1% of the total national turnover of stocks in the year to December 1988.

Trading Days/Hours

Dealing hours on the eight stock exchanges are from Monday to Friday, as follows:

	AM Session	*PM Session*
Tokyo	9.00 – 11.00	1.00 – 3.00
Osaka	8.50 – 11.00	1.00 – 3.00
Nagoya	9.00 – 11.00	1.00 – 3.00
Fukuoka	9.00 – 11.30	1.00 – 3.30
Hiroshima	9.00 – 11.30	1.00 – 3.30
Sapporo	9.00 – 11.30	1.00 – 3.30
Kyoto	9.00 – 11.00	1.00 – 3.00
Niigata	9.00 – 11.30	1.00 – 3.30

Main Indices

The two main indices commonly used to assess the 1st section of the TSE are the Nikkei Stock Average (NSA 225) and the Tokyo Stock Price Index (TOPIX). It is necessary to keep in mind the different representations of the indices in order to accurately monitor the TSE. The NSA 225 is a simple arithmetic means of the stock prices of the 225 selected stocks and does not fully represent the real average price of the stock market. TOPIX, on the other hand, is a more accurate index, as the influence of each share is weighted proportionately. TOPIX can be further subdivided into three categories: large company index (stocks of companies with 200 million plus listed shares), medium company index (over 60 million, and under 200 million shares), and small company index (under 60 million shares). TOPIX tends to be more influenced by price movements in the more heavily capitalised companies. The very large sectors — the financials and utilities — account for about one–third of the total market capitalisation. Underperformance of these sectors could drag the TOPIX, while having less impact on the NSA 225, as these two sectors have less than 12% weighting in the Nikkei. Table 2.2 shows the difference in weightings between the two indices as at March 1989.

Table 2.2   Index Weightings, as at March 1989

% Weighting	NSA	TOPIX
Mining	0.9	0.2
Fisheries	0.7	0.3
Construction	5.8	4.8
Foods	7.0	2.5
Textile	5.4	1.9
Pulp/Paper	2.4	1.0
Chemical	10.8	7.1
Oil/Coal	1.8	1.0
Rubber	0.8	0.5
Glass	4.7	1.7
Iron/Steel	3.8	5.0
Non-ferrous	6.2	1.6
Machinery	4.0	3.0
Electronics	8.0	9.1
Transport	4.6	6.1
Precisions	1.4	0.9
Other Manufacturing	1.7 ·	1.3
Commerce	6.2	6.4
Financials	10.7	29.5
Real Estate	2.1	1.7
Land Transport	3.6	3.6
Marine Transport	1.2	0.8
Air Transport	0.5	1.1
Warehouse	0.9	0.2
Communication	0.5	2.1
Elec. Power/Gas	0.9	5.8
Services	3.4	0.8

Source.   Tokyo Stock Exchange.

TOPIX is now the official index of the Tokyo Stock Exchange due to its better representation of the overall price movements of the market. It has a tendency to avoid overstatement and distortion of price movements, to which the NSA 225 is more frequently prone.

Japanese Stock Exchange Review

Japan's capital markets are undergoing a period of radical change and development. The main forces for change are:
- the internationalisation of Japan's stock markets;
- the liberalisation of the domestic financial structure; and
- the development of derivative instruments such as Index Futures.

It is interesting to speculate whether these trends will make Japan's stock markets more similar to stock markets in other developed countries. Our conclusion is that the Japanese stock market will retain many of its unique characteristics. These include the influence of stable shareholders, the stabilising influence of the Ministry of Finance (MOF) and the Tokyo Stock Exchange (TSE), and the trading orientation of many institutional investors. Thus, despite these trends, Japan will continue to be a market which foreign investors will have to work hard to understand. The Japanese market offers many opportunities to the active investor who understands its special nature and dynamics of change.

One of the distinctly Japanese features of the corporate structure is the crossholding of shares. Japanese companies believe in the importance of stable stock ownership. As shown in Figure 2.4, 25% of total shares are held by corporations. (This stems from the tight business relationships, mostly through the *'zaibatsu'* corporate alliances.) In recent years, this practice has been challenged by Japanese speculative groups as well as overseas corporate raiders, exemplified in conflicts such as the present ongoing battle between Koito Manufacturing and T. Boone Pickens. To avoid hostile takeovers or buyouts, companies also seek financial institutions such as banks and life insurance companies as core shareholders. This accounts for the highest ownership of 45%. Of the banks, trust banks account for more than 90%. This is mainly comprised of tokkin and fund trusts, which are money trusts for securities portfolio investments. It is estimated that about 50% of all shares quoted on the TSE are held by other quoted companies. This unique structure of crossholdings, by taking into account the double counting of the value of the company's holdings of other companies' shares and earnings, has frequently been used as one of the main arguments for the Japanese high PER compared with other major stock markets.

Liberalisation of the Japanese Financial Structure

The institutional structure of Japan's financial system is determined by Article 65 of the Constitution. The Japanese equivalent of the *Glass Steagall Act*, it was introduced by the US occupation forces after the Pacific War with the aim of preventing the development of the excessively powerful financial groups. Article 65 was therefore seen as part of the same process which broke up the *'zaibatsu'* industrial groups.

At present in Japan there is a clear distinction between city banks, long-term credit banks, trust banks, non-insurance, life insurance, security brokers, and investment trusts. Article 65 restricted competition in the financial system; each industry lobbied the authorities to defend its protected

Figure 2.4   Share Ownership by Market Value, 1988 (%)

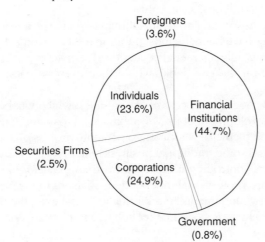

Source: Tokyo Stock Exchange.

market. In many cases, price rates (such as brokers' commissions) were fixed so as to prevent price competition. Competition was in terms of financial muscle and sales power, not price or perform-ance. There is now pressure for the removal of many of these barriers to facilitate 'Universal Banking'.

The development of the investment advisory business is an interesting 'test case' of these trends. Until the *Asset Management Act 1986*, the advisory business barely existed in Japan. The 1986 Act defined the industry and effectively created it. There are now over 400 investment advisory companies, of whom 145 have a full discretionary asset management licence. It is of interest that very few of these companies are truly independent, most being controlled by security companies and banks. In many cases, this is the first time they have emerged from their protected environment to compete directly with each other. This is likely to set a precedent for other financial areas.

The development of the investment advisory industry created competitive pressure for further market liberalisation, particularly of the pension industry and the investment trust industry. At the time of writing, pension fund management is a monopoly of the life insurance and trust bank companies. Again, this was something which was established in the immediate post-war period. It is expected that legislation will be passed in the autumn of 1989 to allow investment advisory companies to manage pension funds. Although it is only a partial liberalisation, it is an important first step. Total pension assets are about ¥17 trillion (US$130 billion). This is small compared to Japan's total financial assets of ¥650 trillion (US$5,000 billion). The relatively low level of present pension benefits suggests that pension assets are likely to grow substantially in coming decades. Institution-ally managed pension funds could come to have a dominant influence on stock market activity as they do in the United States and the United Kingdom.

Following their breakthrough in pension funds, the investment advisers immediately turned their attention to another, and much larger prize: the investment trust industry. This shows that in a complex, interrelated world, it is difficult to have partial liberalisation. The investment trust industry was set up in 1951. Initially, 14 licences were granted to brokers to manage trusts. This was reduced to nine after the stock market crash of 1964 and the industry remained stable until the 1980s. Recently, however, many people have begun to invest in unit trusts. At present, there are 14 investment trust management companies, all of whom are controlled by major stockbrokers. Their total assets are in the region of ¥55 trillion (US$380 billion), as at April 1989.

It is this rich prize that the advisory companies are lobbying to manage, and it is interesting to note that foreign advisory companies have been the most public in their demands. In principle, the MOF may wish to grant investment trust management licences to advisory companies. However, to do so would open a Pandora's box, for the city banks would then exercise enormous pressure to be allowed to participate.

Japan's financial system has begun a process of liberalisation which will be difficult to reverse. It will be associated with the development of universal banks in Japan and ultimately the abolition of Article 65. The end result will be the development of a highly professional investment advisory industry, breaking in the process some traditional business relationships. In addition, some of the conflicts of interest (eg brokers controlling investment trust companies) may be corrected. One implication of this is that a more professional independent advisory industry will be less trading-oriented and more influenced by fundamental stock valuation. However, the process will be likely to take over a decade before it changes stock market behaviour in Japan.

Development of Derivative Instruments

In the stock market crash of October 1987, the Japanese market fell less, but then recovered more quickly, than most other markets. Though it is still unproven, the conventional wisdom is that one important reason for the crash on Wall Street was the activities of index arbitrageurs and portfolio insurance policies. At the time, no such instruments existed in Japan. However, since then, the type and volume of derivative instrument, such as futures and warrants, have expanded, removing in the process part of the safety factor hitherto present in the Japanese stock market.

Index futures had been available since September 1986 on the Nikkei Index in Singapore (SIMEX), although the contract was relatively illiquid, making it not very useful for arbitrage purposes. However, in September 1988, two stock index futures began to trade onshore. These were the Tokyo First Section (TOPIX Index), which trades on the Tokyo Stock Exchange, and the Nikkei Stock Index, which trades in Osaka. In July 1989, this was taken an important step further when options on the Nikkei Index began to trade on the TSE. As in 1985 when bond futures began to trade, the significance of this development was first appreciated by American investment banks. In a well-publicised coup, several American investment brokers realised large profits by holding the Nikkei Index long until the expiry date and then ramping up the underlying issues to create an artificial move in the Index futures. This was rather a shock to the system, since it was the first occasion on which the cash market had been driven by the futures market. The emotional impact was heightened further by the Nikkei Index clearing the 30,000 level. However, the 'system' responded quickly: the MOF promptly imposed regulations to prevent brokers dealing for their own accounts in the last half-hour of a trading session on any day. This response by the authorities sent out a clear message: the Japanese stock market will not tolerate excessive arbitrage trading and index speculation.

It is likely in the future that traded options for shares will be created and actively traded. At present, only synthetic options exist which are created by a very small number of American investment houses. These are not liquid or tradable instruments, but tend to be held for a long time (between one and three years). They are therefore of limited use in the financial strategies of normal investors.

Table 2.3 shows that there has been a significant expansion in the last three years in two derivative instruments: onshore convertible bonds, and Eurobonds with warrant issues. Many of these issues are for '*zaiteku*'— that is, money borrowed at a low nominal rate of interest is then deployed in the financial markets at a higher rate of interest, thereby earning a substantial margin. It seems clear that many Japanese corporations do not understand the concept of future dilution of earnings which such a strategy implies.

Table 2.3 Warrants and Convertible Bonds, 1982–1988 (¥ billion)

Year	Domestic Bonds			Overseas Bonds		
	Straight Bonds	Convertible Bonds[1]	Warrants	Straight Bonds	Convertible Bonds	Warrants[2]
1982	1,140.5	4,475	44	406.8	672	99
	(70%)	(27.3%)	(2.7%)	(34.5%)	(57.1%)	(8.4%)
1983	648.0	827.0	10	632.3	1,080.1	128.6
	(43.6)	(55.7)	(2.9)	(34.3)	(58.7)	(7.0)
1984	812.0	1,208.5	13	614.8	1,331.9	448.8
	(39.9)	(59.4)	(0.6)	(25.7)	(55.6)	(18.7)
1985	789.5	1,904.0	10	1,672.4	1,187.9	684.6
	(29.2)	(70.4)	(0.4)	(47.2)	(33.5)	(19.3)
1986	976.0	2,743.5	116	1,632.0	429.8	2,025.6
	(25.4)	(71.5)	(3.0)	(39.9)	(10.5)	(49.6)
1987	943.0	5,256.0	33	1,396.8	994	3,202,4
	(15.1)	(84.3)	(0.5)	(25.0)	(17.8)	(57.3)
1988	910.0	6,640.0	0	1,429.5	922.4	3,722.5
	(12.1)	(86.9)	—	(23.5)	(15.2)	(61.3)

Sources: The Bond Underwriters' Association of Japan; Nomura Securities.
Notes
1. CBs now account for 87.9% of total domestic issues.
2. Growth in overseas warrants financing, while no domestic warrants issues took place in 1988. Overseas warrants now account for 61% of total overseas financing.

The Euro-dollar convertible bond market has been in a secular decline for some years. The reason for this is that it is normally possible to finance at a lower rate of interest using bonds and warrant issues. The only exceptions to this rule are the city banks and trust banks, who are prohibited by law from issuing warrants. They therefore continue to utilise convertible bonds.

Although several onshore yen bond and warrant issues were developed some years ago, this market is now moribund due to the decision of the MOF to prohibit the splitting of bond and warrant issues into separate traded instruments. This, of course, removed the essential attraction of bond and warrant issues. However, there are now indications that the MOF wishes to exert greater control over such an important source of finance for Japanese companies. This has been mirrored by the move of trading activities and warrants from London to Tokyo. At present, the main market-making activity remains in London, but it is clear that the strongest final demand is in Tokyo.

The size and complexity of the warrant market looks set to increase gradually, offering investors the opportunity to pursue various investment strategies beyond simple gearing. It is likely that Japanese investors will take a large share of trading activities in warrants, which may have dramatic implications for warrant pricing which is as yet relatively inefficient. As improvements are made to publicise warrant pricings, individuals are expected to become increasingly active in the warrant market.

The growth of derivative instruments has had only marginal effect as yet on the total Japanese market. This may be of some comfort to foreign investors, since it means that, at least for the foreseeable future, Japan will retain its attractive quality of index stability. At the same time, the proliferation of these instruments offers the sophisticated foreign investor the possibility of developing financial strategies to match his or her risk profile.

Over the next year, additional financial derivative products are expected to be introduced in Japan. The Tokyo Financial Futures Market is scheduled to open in June 1989, where futures on US Treasury bonds, Euro-yen and Euro-dollar interest rates and foreign exchange will commence trading. Following the Nikkei Index options in the OSE, the TSE will also begin TOPIX Index options in the fall. The Nagoya Exchange is also starting the 'Option 25' Index option, targetting individuals and smaller corporate investors.

Major Market Players

The major market players in Japan are individual investors, foreign investors, and domestic institutions.

Individual Investors

In the past few years, individual investors have become a dramatic force in changing the direction of the Japanese market. While the memory of October 1987's Black Monday is still vivid, the aggressive return of the individual to the Japanese market (while institutional and foreign investors continued to be net sellers) is also noteworthy. The confidence of retail investors was one of the major reasons why the Nikkei became the first market to recover from the crash. According to a Bank of Japan study (Table 2.4), the total size of personal financial assets grew from ¥347 trillion (US$1,500 billion) in 1980 to ¥703 trillion (US$5,300 billion) in 1987. As shown in Table 2.5, the proportion of savings deposits declined from 51% to 46% in the same period, and cash from 13% to less than 10%. On the other hand, individuals' securities holdings rose from 16% to 20%.

The abolition of the *'maruyu'* system in April 1988 the low interest rate environment, and rising land asset values from the exceptionally strong real estate market in 1986–1988 have led investors to seek products with high risk and high returns. Individuals are expected to continue to play a more significant role in the Japanese market, and securities firms are therefore strengthening their retail operations.

Table 2.4 Total Size of Personal Financial Assets, 1980–1987

Year	¥ trillion	US$ billion
1980	347.43	1,500
1985	574.23	2,800
1986	643.20	4,000
1987	703.14	5,300

Source: Bank of Japan.

Table 2.5 Breakdown of Personal Financial Assets, 1980–1987 (%)

	Securities	Equity	Bond	Cash	Savings	Insurance
1980	16.3	7.3	7.5	12.5	51.3	13.0
1985	19.0	8.5	7.6	9.8	48.4	15.4
1986	211	10.9	6.6	9.6	46.2	16.3
1987	20.1	9.9	5.5	9.7	45.5	17.5

Source: Bank of Japan.

Foreign Investors

Foreigners have been net sellers of about ¥13.7 trillion since 1983. In 1987 alone, net selling by foreign investors amounted to ¥7 trillion, though this was exaggerated by the market crash. However, foreign investors have begun to re-evaluate the Japanese market. The fact that the Tokyo market has shown the fastest recovery since Black Monday and that it will continue to be supported by sound economic fundamentals, strong currency, and low inflation has resulted in foreign investors becoming net buyers as of September 1988 — the first time this has occurred in five years.

Domestic Institutions

Total assets of domestic financial institutions (including city banks, trust banks, and life and non-life insurances) have expanded from ¥3,064 trillion (US$23 trillion) in 1985 to ¥8,057 trillion (US$60 trillion) in 1988. Sales of single-premium deferred annuities have been brisk, supported by the fact that it is the highest-yielding instrument to be introduced in the 'post-*maruyu*' period. This pressure to produce higher yields in a low interest-rate environment has gradually eroded the practice of paying out dividends to policy holders from interest and dividend income and turning to the domestic market for equity investment.

Net assets of investment trusts have surged from ¥20 trillion (US$150 billion) in 1985 to ¥55 trillion (US$400 billion), as at April 1989 (see Table 2.6). The proportion of stock trusts has grown to account for 75% of the total. This has been triggered mainly by the preference of both corporations and individuals for new types of products, such as index funds.

Table 2.6 Net Assets of Investment Trusts, 1980–1988 (¥ trillion)

Year	Total	Of which Equity Investment Trusts	%
1980	6.05	4.03	66.6
1985	19.97	10.38	52.0
1986	32.08	19.12	59.6
1987	42.91	30.61	71.3
1988	52.90	39.25	74.2

Source: The Investment Trust Association.

It is expected that liquidity will be supported from the inflow of new money coming from the public sector. Over the next three years, redemptions of government bonds with coupon rates between 6% and 8% are estimated to be ¥23 trillion, while the current market coupon of 4.7–5.2% could shift more funds into equities. Also, under the current financial deregulation, the government is in the process of further relaxing the equity investment for postal life insurance, Ministry of Health and Welfare pension funds, postal savings, and agricultural co-operatives. It is estimated that this will provide more than ¥2 trillion (US$15 billion) for equity investment for fiscal year 1989. Moreover, corporate pension funds totalling ¥30 trillion (US$200 billion) in fiscal year 1989 may increase their equity investment proportion from 30% to 50%, according to some Japanese brokerage houses.

The market has been supported by the low interest-rate environment and the strength of the Japanese economy. The last three years of the strong yen have shifted corporations' efforts to rationalisation of their costs. This has led to greater production efficiency, such as closing down factories in order to redevelop land assets. The effect of these rationalisation plans has come at a time when the economy has started to recover. As a result, basic industries have benefited the most from this structural change, as was reflected in the performance of the stock market. Between January 1987 and December 1988, the steel sector advanced by +308%, followed by the marine transport sector at +164% and the paper and pulp sector at +129%.

Tokkin and Fund Trusts

As at March 1989, tokkin and investment trusts accounts amounted to ¥39 trillion, a tremendous increase compared with ¥8.8 trillion in December 1985. Up until mid-1987, tokkin funds grew at a faster pace than fund trusts, driven by corporations' efforts to take advantage of the active TSE to increase their non-operating income to offset the negative impact of the *endaka* on the corporate earnings and the overall economy. However, with the recovery in the economy from late 1987, companies began shifting their efforts away from '*zaitech*' as their mainline business began to pick up. After the experience of Black Monday, firms have become more sensitive to risk management. Several companies, such as Renown, Orix, and Nippon Yusen, have announced plans to reduce their '*zaitech*' activities. Tokkin and fund trusts were one of the major forces in the 'triple-merit', liquidity-driven bull market of 1986–1987. However, leadership in the market force will likely shift to individuals and investment trusts.

Stock Trading Volume and Value

There are four stock trading methods on the Stock Exchange: (a) 'regular way' transaction settled on the third business day following the day of the contract; (b) 'cash' transaction settled on the day of the contract or on the next business day; (c) 'special agreement' transaction settled within 14 days of the day of the contract (this trading method, established for executing orders from overseas investors, is not used at present); and (d) 'when issued' transaction settled in new shares after their issuance. In reality, however, 'regular way' transaction accounts for 99.9% of total trading volume.

In 1988, combined annual share volume, as well as the value of the first and second sections of the TSE, increased to 282.6 billion shares and ¥285.5 trillion respectively (see Table 2.7). The daily average volume and value also increased to 1,035 million shares and ¥1,045.9 billion respectively.

Table 2.7 Stock Trading Volume on all Stock Exchanges, 1949–1988

Year	Tokyo (%)	Osaka (%)	Nagoya (%)	Other Exchanges (%)	(mn shares) All Exchanges
1949	256 (60.2)	119 (28.1)	25 (5.9)	25 (5.9)	425
1950	512 (56.2)	256 (28.2)	53 (5.8)	90 (9.8)	911
1951	812 (56.9)	398 (27.6)	84 (5.8)	139 (9.6)	1,443
1952	2,003 (57.3)	867 (24.8)	230 (6.6)	397 (11.4)	3,497
1953	2,092 (54.5)	1,061 (27.6)	264 (6.9)	423 (11.0)	3,839
1954	1,238 (56.4)	613 (28.0)	132 (6.0)	210 (9.6)	2,195
1955	2,505 (66.3)	826 (21.9)	189 (5.0)	256 (6.8)	3,777
1956	6,692 (63.2)	2,683 (25.4)	531 (5.0)	679 (6.4)	10,586
1957	7,692 (63.9)	3,072 (25.5)	688 (5.7)	595 (4.9)	12,046
1958	11,684 (65.8)	4,421 (24.9)	876 (4.9)	776 (4.4)	17,758
1959	21,201 (66.7)	7,898 (24.9)	1,286 (4.0)	1,397 (4.4)	31,782
1960	27,230 (62.8)	12,486 (28.8)	1,803 (4.2)	1,811 (4.2)	43,331
1961	31,457 (65.1)	13,109 (27.1)	1,882 (3.9)	1,876 (3.9)	48,324
1962	35,971 (67.9)	13,142 (24.8)	2,128 (4.0)	1,731 (3.3)	52,972
1963	40,779 (69.0)	13,982 (23.7)	2,308 (3.9)	2,047 (3.5)	59,117
1964	29,345 (70.2)	9,734 (23.3)	1,476 (3.5)	1,233 (3.0)	41,789
1965	34,838 (69.0)	12,407 (24.6)	1,603 (3.2)	1,637 (3.2)	50,483
1966	35,938 (69.1)	12,860 (24.7)	1,665 (3.2)	1,578 (3.0)	52,041
1967	28,805 (68.3)	10,669 (25.3)	1,636 (3.9)	1,049 (2.5)	42,159
1968	46,886 (71.4)	15,529 (23.7)	2,145 (3.3)	1,081 (1.6)	65,541
1969	50,986 (74.1)	14,719 (21.4)	2,247 (3.3)	902 (1.3)	68,853
1970	42,753 (74.9)	11,778 (20.6)	1,794 (3.1)	773 (1.4)	57,099

Year	Tokyo (%)	Osaka (%)	Nagoya (%)	Other Exchanges (%)	(mn shares) All Exchanges
1971	60,819 (74.7)	17,746 (21.8)	1,988 (2.4)	883 (1.1)	81,436
1972	100,358 (74.1)	30,021 (22.2)	3,473 (2.6)	1,622 (1.2)	135,475
1973	59,248 (74.7)	16,799 (21.2)	2,169 (2.7)	1,145 (1.4)	79,361
1974	51,001 (78.4)	11,325 (17.4)	1,963 (3.0)	793 (1.2)	65,082
1975	51,906 (82.6)	8,549 (13.6)	1,710 (2.7)	689 (1.1)	62,855
1976	69,941 (84.7)	9,553 (11.6)	2,299 (2.8)	806 (1.0)	82,597
1977	71,195 (83.7)	10,723 (12.6)	2,362 (2.8)	830 (1.0)	85,111
1978	98,555 (83.2)	15,579 (13.2)	3,546 (3.0)	814 (0.7)	118,494
1979	98,246 (85.0)	12,828 (11.1)	3,497 (3.0)	1,022 (0.9)	115,594
1980	102,245 (86.0)	12,454 (10.5)	3,317 (2.8)	917 (0.8)	118,931
1981	107,549 (83.8)	14,863 (11.6)	4,817 (3.8)	1,089 (0.8)	128,318
1982	78,474 (86.0)	9,179 (10.1)	2,546 (2.8)	1,026 (1.1)	91,241
1983	104,308 (85.3)	13,469 (11.0)	3,375 (2.8)	1,168 (0.9)	122,320
1984	103,737 (83.4)	16,247 (13.1)	3,331 (2.7)	1,030 (0.8)	124,346
1985	121,863 (83.3)	18,295 (12.5)	5,151 (3.5)	990 (0.7)	146,302
1986	197,699 (82.9)	29,028 (12.2)	10,394 (4.4)	1,231 (0.5)	238,354
1987	263,611 (83.6)	37,133 (11.8)	13,199 (4.2)	1,495 (0.4)	315,441
1988	282,637 (86.1)	31,690 (9.7)	12,485 (3.8)	1,496 (0.4)	328,311

Source: Tokyo Stock Exchange.
Note: 'Other exchanges' are composed of Kyoto, Hiroshima, Fukuoka, Niigata, Sapporo and Kobe, but Kobe Exchange was dissolved on 31 October 1967.

The turnover ratio was 98.1% on the volume basis and 70.2% on the value basis (see Table 2.8).

Table 2.8   Stock Trading Volume and Value, 1984–1988

	No. of Trading Days	Total Volume (mn shares)	Daily Average	Turnover Ratio (%) (based on volume)	Total Value (Yen mn)	Value (¥bn) Daily Average	Turnover Ratio (%) (based on value)	No. of Trades (mn)
1984	287	103,737	361	42.5	67,974	236.8	47.1	23.08
1985	258	121,863	428	48.0	78,711	276.2	44.7	26.05
1986	279	197,699	709	75.1	159,836	572.9	67.2	34.48
1987	274	263,611	962	96.1	250,737	915.1	80.6	41.59
1988	273	282,637	1,035	98.1	285,521	1,045.9	70.2	41.30

	No. of Trading Days	Total Volume (mn shares)	Daily Average	Turnover Ratio (%) (based on volume)	Total Value (Yen mn)	Value (¥bn) Daily Average	Turnover Ratio (%) (based on value)	No. of Trades (mn)
Jan.	21	12,903	614	4.6	13,318	634.2	3.7	2.58
Feb.	22	16,623	756	5.9	17,749	806.8	4.5	3.24
Mar.	24	31,333	1,306	11.1	28,256	1,177.3	6.8	3.89
Apr.	23	21,812	948	7.7	21,928	953.4	5.1	3.81
May	21	22,202	1,057	7.8	20,078	956.1	4.7	4.06
June	24	42,469	1,770	14.8	34,828	1,451.2	8.2	4.94
July	24	35,306	1,471	12.2	36,176	1,507.3	8.2	3.84
Aug.	25	15,548	622	5.4	19,604	784.2	4.5	2.54
Sept.	22	19,588	890	6.8	20,447	929.4	4.8	2.47
Oct.	23	22,216	966	7.6	23,101	1,004.4	5.4	2.90
Nov.	22	24,878	1,131	8.5	29,401	1,336.4	6.6	3.61
Dec.	22	17,760	807	6.0	20,636	938.0	4.4	3.38

Source: Tokyo Stock Exchange.

The number of trades in 1988 was 41.3 million, which was about the same as the 41.6 million recorded in 1987.

The Thirty Largest Stocks

If we compare the 30 largest companies in Japan measured by various criteria (see Tables 2.9, 2.10, and 2.11), it is clear that Nippon Telegraph & Telephone (NTT) has by far the largest number of shareholders following its widely publicised listing in 1986–1988. However, it is the Japanese banks, led by IBJ (Industrial Bank of Japan) whose market capitalisation is the largest, with the financial sector accounting for over 40% of the total market. By contrast, the most popularly traded stocks in terms of daily turnover are the steel stocks, led by Nippon Steel.

Table 2.9 The 30 Largest Quoted Stocks by Number of Shareholders, as at 31 March 1988

Company	No. of Shareholders ('000)
Nippon Telegraph & Telephone	1,210
Tokyo Electric Power	491
Nippon Steel	353
Kansai Electric Power	327

Company	No. of Shareholders ('000)
Toshiba	280
Chubu Electric Power	240
Hitachi	234
Mitsubishi Heavy Industries	233
Tohoku Electric Power	171
Mitsubishi Electric	170
Osaka Gas	165
Sumitomo Metal Industries	163
NKK	158
Japan Air Lines	143
Toray Industries	140
Sanyo Electric	138
Fujitsu	136
Kobe Steel	125
Tokyo Gas	125
Kawasaki Steel	121
Sumitomo Chemical	116
Fanuc	114
Matsushita Electric Industrial	113
Asahi Chemical Industry	111
Shikoku Electric Power	108
Kyushu Electric Power	106
Taisei	100
NEC	97
All Nippon Airways	97
Nippon Express	95

Source: Tokyo Stock Exchange.

Table 2.10   The 30 Largest Quoted Stocks by Market Capitalisation, as at 31 December 1988

Company	Market Value (¥bn)
Industrial Bank of Japan	10,229
Sumitomo Bank	9,989
Nippon Telegraph & Telephone	9774
Fuji Bank	9,397
Tokyo Electric Power	9,257
Dai-chi Kangyo Bank	9,090
Mitsubishi Bank	8,924
Sanwa Bank	7,536

Company	Market Value (¥bn)
Toyota Motor	7,185
Nomura Securities	7,147
Nippon Steel	5,774
Matsushita Electric Industrial	4,949
Hitachi	4,711
Long-Term Credit Bank of Japan	4,612
Kansai Electric Power	4,556
Mitsui Bank	4,237
Tokai Bank	4,217
Mitsubishi Trust & Banking	4,197
Sumitomo Trust & Banking	3,681
Tokyo Gas	3,653
Mitsubishi Estate	3,361
Chubu Electric Power	3,319
Tokyo Marine & Fire Insurance	3,308
Mitsubishi Heavy Industries	3,292
Bank of Tokyo	3,253
Daiwa Securities	3,103
Toshiba	3,089
NKK	2,997
Nissan Motor	2,923
NEC	2,915

Source: Tokyo Stock Exchange.

Table 2.11 The 30 Most Active Stocks by Volume, 1988

Company	Volume of Shares (mn)
Nippon Steel	20,670
Kawasaki Steel	14,528
NKK	13,269
Sumitomo Metal Industries	9,287
Mitsubishi Heavy Industries	9,179
Kobe Steel	8,236
Toshiba	6,726
Kawasaki Heavy Industries	6,241
Ishikawajima-Harima Heavy Industries	5,101
Mitsui Engineering & Shipbuilding	4,767
Mitsubishi Electric	4,591
Nisshin Steel	3,187
Sumitomo Heavy Industries	3,169

Company	Volume of Shares (mn)
Tokyo Gas	2,785
Hitachi	2,782
Japan Line	2,497
Hitachi Zosen	2,354
Nippon Yusen	2,241
Nissan Motors	2,235
Mitsui Mining and Smelting	2,214
Mitsui O.S.K. Lines	2,128
Fujitsu	2,074
Nippon Mining	1,958
Sumitomo Chemical	1,899
Toray Industries	1,859
Keisei Electric Railway	1,654
Fuji Electric	1,574
Sanyo Electric	1,571
Japan Steel Works	1,552
Marubeni	1,452

Source: Tokyo Stock Exchange.

The number of listed companies (Table 2.12) shows the dominance of the Tokyo Exchange. There are in fact 32 local stocks listed only in Osaka, and 14 in Nagoya. However, the strength of Japan's financial and securities exchange system also depends on its strong regional character. Slightly more than 50% of all trading volume is accounted for by the 30 largest stocks.

Table 2.12 Number of Companies Listed on all Stock Exchanges, as at 31 December 1988

	Tokyo		Osaka		Nagoya		Kyoto	Fukuoka		Sapporo
	1st Sec.	2nd Sec.	1st Sec.	2nd Sec.	1st Sec.	2nd Sec.	Hiroshima	Niigata		
No. of Listed Companies	1,130	441	812	279	417	101	233	191	242	197	189
Listed on Single Exchange	296	349	32	164	14	70	1	7	17	9	13
Listed on 2 or more Exchanges	834	92	780	115	403	31	232	184	225	188	176
Listed on 8 SEs	95	—	95	—	95	—	95	95	95	95	95
7 SEs	24	—	24	—	23	—	18	19	23	20	17
6 SEs	31	—	31	—	28	—	18	19	26	17	16
5 SEs	32	—	32	—	29	—	13	8	18	14	14
4 SEs	55	1	54	1	42	—	18	7	17	17	12
3 SEs	231	13	232	14	138	9	41	21	27	10	8
2 SEs	366	78	312	100	48	22	29	15	19	15	14

Source: Tokyo Stock Exchange.

Brokerage Commission Rates

The various brokerage commission rates as applied to stocks and convertible bonds with or without warrants are shown in Tables 2.13 and 2.14 respectively.

Table 2.13 Stocks, Warrants, and Subscription Rights, as at March 1989

Trading Value		Commission in % of Trading Value
Up to	¥1 million	1.20%
Over	¥1 million and up to ¥3 million	1.00%+¥2,000
Over	¥3 million and up to ¥5 million	0.90%+¥5,000
Over	¥5 million and up to ¥10 million	0.75%+¥12,500
Over	¥10 million and up to ¥30 million	0.60%+¥27,500
Over	¥30 million and up to ¥50 million	0.40%+¥87,500
Over	¥50 million and up to ¥100 million	0.25%+¥212,500
Over	¥1 billion	0.15%+¥712,500

Source: Tokyo Stock Exchange.
Note: Commission on trading value less than ¥200,000 is fixed at ¥2,500.

Table 2.14 Convertible Bonds and Bonds with Warrants, as at March 1989

Trading Value		Commission in % of Trading Value
Up to	¥1 million	1.00%
Over	¥1 million and up to ¥5 million	0.90%+¥1,000
Over	¥5 million and up to ¥10 million	0.70%+¥11,000
Over	¥10 million and up to ¥30 million	0.55%+¥26,000
Over	¥30 million and up to ¥50 million	0.40%+¥71,000
Over	¥50 million and up to ¥100 million	0.25%+¥146,000
Over	¥100 million	0.20%+¥196,000
Over	¥1 billion	0.15%+¥696,000

Source: Tokyo Stock Exchange.

Table 2.15 lists only the 15 largest Japanese brokerage houses, although there are a very large number of smaller firms.

In the past three years, a growing number of international securities firms have been established in Tokyo, although only those firms listed in Table 2.16 are full trading members of the TSE.

Table 2.15 Major Japanese Brokerage Firms

Member Securities Companies	Address	Tel.
Nomura	9-1, Nihombashi 1-chome, Chuo-ku, Tokyo 103	211-1811, 3811
Nikko	3-1, Marunouchi 3-chome, Chiyoda-ku, Tokyo 100	283-2211
Daiwa	6-4, Ohtemachi 2-chome, Chiyoda-ku, Tokyo 100	243-2111
Yamaichi	4-1, Yaesu 2-chome, Chuo-ku, Tokyo 103	276-3181
Nippon Kangyo Kakumaru	6-1, Marunouchi 1-chome, Chiyoda-ku, Tokyo 100	286-7111
Wako	6-1, Nihombashi-Koami-cho, Chuo-ku, Tokyo 103	667-8111
New Japan	6-20, Kyobashi 1-chome, Chuo-ku, Tokyo 103	561-1111
Sanyo	8-1, Nihombashi-Kayaba-cho 1-chome, Chuo-ku, Tokyo 103	666-1233
Okasan	17-6, Nihombashi 1-chome, Chuo-ku, Tokyo 103	272-2211
Yamatane	7-12, Nihombashi-Kabuto-cho, Chuo-ku, Tokyo 103	669-3211
Marusan	5-2, Nihombashi 2-chome, Chuo-ku, Tokyo 103	272-5211
Kokusai	26-2, Nishi-Shinjuku 1-chome, Shinjuku-ku, Tokyo 163	348-7211
Tachibana	13-14, Nihombashi-Kayaba-cho 1-chome, Chuo-ku, Tokyo 103	669-3111
Dainana	10-9, Ginza 3-chome, Chuo-ku, Tokyo 104	545-9111
Toyo	20-5, Nihombashi 1-chome, Chuo-ku, Tokyo 103	274-0211

Table 2.16 Major Foreign Securities Companies in Tokyo (with TSE Membership), by Country

United States

Citicorp Scrimgeour Vickers Int. Ltd	ARK Mori Bldg, 24th Floor, 12-32, Akasaka 1-chome, Minato-ku, Tokyo 107
First Boston (Japan) Ltd	Asahi Seimei Hibiya Bldg, 5-1, Yurakucho 1-chome, Chiyoda-ku, Tokyo 100
Goldman Sachs (Japan) Corp.	ARK Mori Bldg, 10th Floor, 12-32, Akasaka 1-chome, Minato-ku, Tokyo 107
Kidder, Peabody Int. Corp.	Shin-Tokio Kaijo Bldg, 13th Floor, 1-2-1 Marunouchi, Chiyoda-ku, Tokyo 100
Merrill Lynch Japan Inc.	Ote Center Bldg, 1-1-2, Otemachi, Chiyoda-ku, Tokyo 100
Morgan Stanley Japan Ltd	8th Floor, Ote Center Bldg, 1-3 Otemachi 1-chome, Chiyoda-ku, Tokyo 100
Prudential-Bache Securities (Japan)	Sumitomo Shiba-Daimon Bldg, 2-5-5, Shiba Daimon, Minato-ku, Tokyo 105
Salomon Brothers Asia Ltd	ARK Mori Bldg, 9th Floor, 12-32, Akasaka 1-chome, Minato-ku, Tokyo 107
Shearson Lehman Hutton Asia Inc.	12-32, Akasaka 1-chome, ARK Mori Bldg, 36th Floor Minato-ku, Tokyo 107
Smith Barney, Harris Upham Int. Inc.	Mitsubishi Bldg, 5-2 Marunouchi 2-chome, Chiyoda-ku, Tokyo 100

United Kingdom

Baring Securities (Japan) Ltd	10th Floor, Shin-Kasumigaseki Bldg, 3-2 Kasumigaseki 3-chome, Chiyoda-ku, Tokyo 100
County Natwest Securities (Japan)	AIU Bldg, 2nd/3rd Floors, 1-3 Marunouchi 1-chome, Chiyoda-ku, Tokyo 100
Kleinwort Benson Int. Inc.	810-Kokusai Bldg, 1-1 Marunouchi 3-chome, Chiyoda-ku, Tokyo 100
S.G. Warburg Securities (Japan)	New Edobashi Bldg, 1-7-2 Nihonbashi-Honcho, Chuo-ku, Tokyo 103
Schroder Securities (Japan) Ltd	ARK Mori Bldg, 17th Floor, 12-32, Akasaka 1-chome, Minato-ku, Tokyo 107
W.I. Carr (Overseas) Ltd	Yaesu Osaka Bldg, 4th Floor, 1-1 Kyobashi 1-chome, Chuo-ku, Tokyo 104

Switzerland

Swiss Bank Corp.	Shin Kasumigaseki Bldg, 20th Floor, 3-2 Kasumigaseki 3-chome, Chiyoda-ku, Tokyo 100
Union Bank of Switzerland	Yamato Seimei Bldg, 7th Floor, 1-7 Uchisaiwaicho 1-chome, Chiyoda-ku, Tokyo 100

France

Sogen Securities (North Pacific)	Sumitomo Shiba Daimon Bldg, 12th Floor, 2-5-5 Shiba, Minato-ku, Tokyo 105

West Germany

Dresdner-ABD Securities Ltd	Shionogi Honcho Kyodo Bldg, 7-2 Nihonbashi-Honcho 3-chome, Chuo-ku, Tokyo 103
DB Capital Markets Asia Ltd	ARK Mori Bldg, 22nd Floor, 12-3 Akasaka 1-chome, Minato-ku, Tokyo 107

Hong Kong

Jardine Fleming Securities Ltd	Yamato Seimei Bldg, 1-7 Uchisaiwaicho 1-chome, Chiyoda-ku, Tokyo 100

Taxation

Tax Reform in Japan

The tax reform law of 1988, which has been effective since 1 April 1989, represents the most dramatic overhaul of the tax system since the early 1950s. Introduction of the consumption tax — the centrepiece of the reform — is a historic event because it shifts the burden of revenue away from income taxes and towards indirect levies on goods and services. Under the new tax system, a 3% tax shall be levied on consumption of most goods and services.

As to securities taxation, the principle of capital gains tax, which had not been taxable, was changed. A new tax is imposed on income generated from sales of equities, subscription rights, warrants, convertible bonds, and bonds with stock subscription warrants. Investors can choose to pay either an effective 1% withholding tax on the value of the sale or 20% of the profits from the sale. On the other hand, the securities transfer tax was lowered to 0.30% of the value of shares sold, from the previous 0.55%, and to 0.16% on the sale of convertible bonds and bonds with warrants, from the previous 0.26%.

Securities Transfer Tax

The securities transfer tax, payable by a seller, is described in Table 2.17.

Table 2.17 Securities Transfer Tax (Payable by a Seller), as at April 1989

Securities/Seller	(% of Trading Value)	Other than Securities Company
Shares and Stock Investment Trust Certificates	0.03	0.12
Convertible Bonds and Bonds with Warrants	0.16	0.06

Dividend Tax

Individual
As of April 1989, an individual's tax liability on dividend is as follows:
1. If annual dividend per issue of stock is ¥100,000 or less, choice from the following:
    (1) Aggregate taxation (20% tax withheld at source); or
    (2) No statement of dividend in tax return — hence separate taxation (20% tax withheld at source).
2. If annual dividend per issue of stock is more than ¥100,000 but less than ¥500,000, and further, if individual owns less than 5% of shares of the company, choice from the following:
    (1) Aggregate taxation (20% tax withheld at source); or
    (2) Separate taxation (35% tax withheld at source).
3. If annual dividend per issue of stock is ¥500,000 or more, or the number of shares held is 5% or more of the total outstanding shares, aggregate taxation is applicable (20% tax withheld at source).

Corporations
For a corporation, the dividend income on stock investment trusts and bond investment trusts is taxed as follows: Separate taxation (20% tax withheld at source). The amount of dividend received is not taxable up to 90% of the amount of dividend paid.

For a corporation's dividend income on shares, where the amount of dividend received is in excess of the amount of dividend paid, 87.5% of the excess is not taxable.

Capital Gains Tax

Individuals
The taxpayer may elect to pay a 1% withholding tax on the value of the sale of shares, or alternatively, 20% of the realised profits.

Corporations
Capital gains taxes are the same as for an individual, with the additional option of deducting capital losses from taxable income.

Withholding Tax for Foreign Investors

Withholding tax on dividends or interest paid is deducted at source. The standard rate for non-residents is 20% on both dividends and coupons. However, in the case of residents of the countries listed below (Table 2.18), the effective withholding tax rate is lower because of special double taxation agreements between these countries and Japan. Dividends are freely repatriable for overseas investors depending on the tax treaties in the investor's country.

Table 2.18 Non-resident Withholding Tax Rate

Country	Dividends on Stocks and Stock Investment Trusts (%)	Interest on Debentures, Bonds, and Bond Investment Trusts (%)
Australia	15	10
Austria	20	10
Belgium	15	15
Brazil	12.5	12.5
Canada	15	15
Denmark	15	10
Egypt	15	(domestic law applies)
Eire	15	10
Finland	15	10
France	15	10
Italy	15	10
Korea	12	12
Malaysia	15	20
The Netherlands	15	10
New Zealand	15	—
Norway	15	10
Pakistan	—	30
Philippines	25	15
Singapore	15	15
Spain	15	10
Sri Lanka	20	—

Country	Dividends on Stocks and Stock Investment Trusts (%)	Interest on Debentures, Bonds, and Bond Investment Trusts (%)
Sweden	15	10
Switzerland	15	10
Thailand	25	10
United Kingdom	15	10
United States	15	10
West Germany	15	10

Disclosure and Reporting Requirements

The most important documents regarding disclosure in Japan are the securities registration statement and prospectus, the securities report, and the semi-annual and current (annual) report. The securities registration statement must be filed with the MOF by a company intending to carry out a capital increase, with certain minor exceptions. The contents of this statement are prescribed by ministerial regulations and include details of the company's business operations and financial structure for two consecutive accounting periods. The statement must also contain the report of a certified public accountant. Copies of the statement are made available for public inspection at the MOF and must also be made available at the head office and principal offices of the company.

The same general regulations also apply to the securities report and the semi-annual and annual reports. The annual report must be filed with the MOF within three months of the end of the relevant financial period. Regulations are passed from time to time in order to protect further the interests of the investing public. The most important revision in recent years required the financial statements contained in the semi-annual report of companies to be audited by certified public accountants (applicable to financial years commencing on or after 1 April 1977) in the same manner as the annual accounts.

Apart from these main methods of disclosure, the *Tokyo Stock Exchange Regulations for the Supervision of Listed Securities* provide for the prompt, accurate, and wide dissemination to investors of information about companies which may influence stock prices, in an attempt to maintain a fair and orderly market. The *Securities Exchange Law* also makes provisions against insider trading, although it should be noted that since 1953, directors and major shareholders of a listed company are not required to report on their respective shareholdings. The Recruit Cosmos scandal, which brought down Prime Minister Noboru Takeshita's regime in 1989, however, could lead to a review and overhaul of these shareholder protection regulations in future.

Listing Requirements

The TSE has certain minimum criteria which must be fulfilled before a company is accepted for listing. These requirements apply, for example, to the amount of paid-in capital, the number of 'floating shareholders' (shareholders with between 500 and 50,000 shares) and 'floating shares', period of time since incorporation, total net assets, net profits, and dividends per share. The company must produce share certificates in conformity with exchange requirements. No company will be accepted for listing if the audit report accompanying the company accounts states that false information has been recorded.

New companies are normally listed on the Second Section of an exchange which has two — Tokyo, Osaka, and Nagoya — while in other cases it will be listed on the First Section. On the fulfilment of certain additional requirements, a company may be later transferred to the First Section.

Share Ownership in Listed Companies

The National Conference of Stock Exchanges, consisting of all eight stock exchanges in Japan, has been conducting an annual share ownership survey of all domestic companies listed on any one of the stock exchanges. The annual survey is carried out by sending each company a questionnaire on various data of its shareholders available from the shareholders' record, as at the close of the business year ending between 1 April of the previous year and 31 March of the present year. The 1988 statistics thus reflect the total of an individual company's figures at business year-end ranging from April 1987 to March 1988. Since 1986, the survey covers only such shareholders who own one or more 'unit of shares'. One unit consists generally of 1,000 shares.

The 1988 survey disclosed the following highlights: (a) the individual ownership decreased by 0.3% to 23.6%; (b) the ownership of trust banks rose to 8.4%, up 1.3% from the year earlier; and (c) the foreign ownership declined by 1.1% to 3.6% from 1987. It is interesting to note in Table 2.19 that foreign ownership of Japanese shares reached a peak of 6.3% in 1984.

Table 2.19 Share Ownership by Type of Investors — all Listed Companies, 1951–1988 (%)

	Govt and Local Govt	Financial Institutions	Investment Trusts	Securities Companies	Business Corporations	Individuals and Others	Foreigners
1951	3.1	12.6	—	11.9	11.0	61.3	—
1952	1.8	13.0	5.2	9.2	13.8	57.0	—
1953	1.0	15.8	6.0	8.4	11.8	55.8	1.2
1954	0.7	16.3	6.7	7.3	13.5	53.9	1.7
1955	0.5	16.7	7.0	7.1	13.0	54.0	1.7
1956	0.4	19.5	4.1	7.9	13.2	53.1	1.8
1957	0.3	21.7	3.9	7.1	15.7	49.9	1.5
1958	0.2	21.4	4.7	5.7	16.3	50.1	1.5
1959	0.3	22.4	6.6	4.4	15.8	49.1	1.5
1960	0.2	21.7	7.6	3.7	17.5	47.8	1.5
1961	0.2	23.1	7.5	3.7	17.8	46.3	1.4
1962	0.2	21.4	8.6	2.8	18.7	46.7	1.7
1963	0.2	21.5	9.2	2.5	17.7	47.1	1.8
1964	0.2	21.4	9.5	2.2	17.9	46.7	2.1
1965	0.2	21.6	7.9	4.4	18.4	45.6	1.9

	Govt and Local Govt	Financial Institutions	Investment Trusts	Securities Companies	Business Corporations	Individuals and Others	Foreigners
1966	0.2	23.4	5.6	5.8	18.4	44.8	1.8
1967	0.2	26.1	3.7	5.4	18.6	44.1	1.9
1968	0.3	28.2	2.4	4.4	20.5	42.3	1.9
1969	0.3	30.3	1.7	2.1	21.4	41.9	2.3
1970	0.3	30.7	1.2	1.4	22.0	41.1	3.3
1971	0.3	30.9	1.4	1.2	23.1	39.9	3.2
1972	0.2	32.6	1.3	1.5	23.6	37.2	3.6
1973	0.2	33.8	1.3	1.8	26.6	32.7	3.5
1974	0.2	33.9	1.2	1.5	27.5	32.7	2.9
1975	0.2	33.9	1.6	1.3	27.1	33.4	2.5
1976	0.2	34.5	1.6	1.4	26.3	33.5	2.6
1977	0.2	35.1	1.4	1.4	26.5	32.9	2.6
1978	0.2	35.9	2.0	1.5	26.2	32.0	2.3
1979	0.2	36.6	2.2	1.8	26.3	30.8	2.1
1980	0.2	36.9	1.9	2.0	26.1	30.4	2.5
1981	0.2	37.3	1.5	1.7	26.0	29.2	4.0
1982	0.2	37.3	1.3	1.7	26.3	28.4	4.6
1983	0.2	37.7	1.2	1.8	26.0	28.0	5.1
1984	0.2	38.0	1.0	1.9	25.9	26.8	6.3
1985	0.2	38.5	1.1	1.9	26.9	26.3	6.1
1986	0.8	42.2	1.3	2.0	24.1	25.2	5.7
1987	0.9	43.5	1.8	2.5	24.5	23.9	4.7
1988	0.8	44.6	2.4	2.5	24.9	23.6	3.6

Sources: Ministry of Finance; The National Conference of Stock Exchanges.
Note: Figures are based on the number of 'unit' shareholders since 1986.

Foreign Investment in Japanese Stocks

While purchases by foreigners (notably large UK and US pension funds) continued to grow in 1986 and 1987 (see Table 2.20), net sales were far higher, and most Western money managers regarded the Japanese market as far too expensive. Japanese investors, by contrast, continued to be large net buyers of their own markets.

The total volume of foreign investment in Japanese stocks (purchases plus sales) in 1988 declined by ¥7,523 billion (or 15.4%) to ¥41,236 billion from the previous year. Foreign purchases of Japanese stocks decreased slightly to ¥20,674 billion, while foreign sales declined to ¥20,562 billion. As a result, foreign investors became net buyers of Japanese stocks for the first time since 1983.

By regions, European investors were the largest net sellers, with ¥411 billion (see Table 2.21). The amount of net purchases by US investors was ¥46 billion. The amount of net sales by Asian investors

Table 2.20 Foreign Investment in Japanese Securities, 1979–1988 (¥ billion)

| | Stocks | | | Bonds | | |
	Purchases	Sales	Net Balance	Purchases	Sales	Net Balance
1979	1,104	1,235	−132	2,071	1,720	351
1980	2,873	1,688	1,185	3,601	2,352	1,249
1981	5,340	4,577	763	5,179	3,953	1,226
1982	4,000	3,620	380	6,971	5,846	1,125
1983	7,684	6,641	1,043	9,747	9,214	533
1984	8,441	10,158	−1,717	14,777	13,961	816
1985	9,381	10,161	−780	25,194	24,045	1,149
1986	17,027	20,617	−3,590	41,143	41,529	−386
1987	23,371	30,823	−7,451	43,909	42,916	993
1988	21,995	21,745	250	36,088	38,894	−2,806
Jan.	1,226	1,026	201	2,501	2,420	81
Feb.	1,977	1,705	272	3,012	3,175	−163
Mar.	2,419	2,153	266	2,664	2,753	−89
Apr.	1,896	1,836	59	2,741	2,835	−94
May	1,629	1,881	−252	2,660	2,940	−280
June	2,110	2,518	−408	3,212	3,165	47
July	2,228	2,681	−453	3,922	4,052	−130
Aug.	1,658	1,866	−208	2,968	3,270	−302
Sept.	1,061	1,147	−86	3,388	3,932	−544
Oct.	1,865	1,506	360	3,203	4,072	−869
Nov.	2,368	2,027	341	3,207	3,473	−257
Dec.	1,558	1,400	158	2,611	2,807	−196

Source: Ministry of Finance.
Note: Calculated on the basis of 'Indirect Investment', which means acquisition of shares less than 10% of the outstanding shares of a company by a foreign investor. Figures collected at the time of trade settlement.

decreased largely to ¥16 billion from the preceding year. Other regions' investors were the largest net buyers, with ¥493 billion.

Foreign Investment Restrictions

In the past, there have been limitations and restrictions on foreign ownership of Japanese securities. Most of the restrictions were relaxed in December 1980 and further liberalisation in 1984 effectively

Table 2.21   Foreign Investment in Japanese Stocks by Regions — all Stock Exchanges, 1982–1988 (¥ billion)

Region		1982	1983	1984	1985	1986	1987	1988
	Purchases	3,505	6,943	7,649	8,461	15,647	20,918	20,674
Total	Sales	3,342	6,206	9,583	9,276	19,408	27,841	20,562
	Net	416	737	−1,934	−815	−3,761	−6,924	112
	Purchases	549	931	1,021	1,213	2,288	3,179	2,988
United States	Sales	398	679	1,079	1,248	3,119	4,379	2,942
	Net	151	252	−58	−35	−831	−1,200	46
	Purchases	2,104	4,177	4,568	4,949	8,528	10,226	9,946
Europe	Sales	2,133	3,791	6,052	5,639	10,978	14,534	10,357
	Net	243	385	−1,484	−690	−2,450	−4,309	−411
	Purchases	738	1,358	1,359	1,475	3,420	5,359	5,109
Asia	Sales	714	1,316	1,543	1,517	3,792	6,545	5,124
	Net	24	42	−184	−42	−372	−1,186	−16
	Purchases	114	477	701	824	1,411	2,154	2,631
Others	Sales	96	421	909	873	1,519	2,383	2,138
	Net	17	57	−208	−49	−108	−229	493

Source: Tokyo Stock Exchange.
Note: Calculated on the basis of reports from 'integrated' securities companies.

permitted foreign investors to purchase Japanese stocks freely. However, there remains a foreign ownership limit of 20% for broadcasting companies, and non-residents are barred from ownership of KDD and NTT because these two companies are thought to represent some national interest.

NTT shares have become a source of concern for the MOF. Since the first tranche in February 1987, the share price of NTT has nearly halved due to the competitive business environment in the telecommunications industry and the firm's involvement in the Recruit scandal. The government is considering the postponement of the fourth tranche, scheduled for September 1989, and instead allowing foreign investors to become stable shareholders.

Available Research

Tokyo Stock Exchange Publications

TSE Fact Book
Business Regulations of the Tokyo Stock Exchange
Listing Regulations of the Tokyo Stock Exchange
TOPIX — Tokyo Stock Price Index

TOPIX Futures — Outline of the Tokyo Stock Price Index Futures
TOPIX Options
Japanese Government Bond Futures
TSE Monthly Statistics Report

Japan Securities Research Institute

Securities Market in Japan
Japanese Securities Laws
Report on Japan's Stock Price Level, October 1988

Other

Economic Survey of Japan (Economic Planning Agency)
Yoshio Suzuki, *The Japanese Financial System* (Oxford: Clarendon Press, 1987)
Martin Roth, *Making Money in Japanese Stocks* (Tuttie, 1989)
Aron Viner, 'Inside Japan's Financial Market', *The Economist*
Daniel Burstein, *Yen: The Power of Japanese Money*

3

TAIWAN

Introduction

Taipei has a vibrant, active stock market, with a higher daily turnover on some days than Hong Kong or even London. Its brokerage houses bear witness to the extraordinary 'boom' that has occurred in Asia's capital markets, with taxi-drivers and housewives being active participants.

The Taiwan Stock Exchange (TSE) was established in late 1961; actual trading began in February of the following year. The Exchange is organised in the form of a corporation, with NT$689.97 million (US$25 million) capital divided between government operated banks and enterprises (39%) and private banks and large corporations (61%). The Exchange is overseen by a 15-member Board of Directors and three supervisors, all of whom are representatives of leading financial institutions. The day-to-day management is left to the Chairman, the President, and other executive officers.

All aspects of the issuing and trading of securities in the Republic of China (ROC) are regulated by the Securities and Exchange Commission (SEC). The SEC was established on 1 September 1960, and is now under the administration of the Ministry of Finance (MOF). The SEC is overseen by eight commissioners, including the Chairman and Vice Chairman of the SEC and representatives from the MOF, Ministry of Economic Affairs, the Central Bank, and the Ministry of Justice.

All listed companies on the TSE are classified into three categories (A, B, and C) according to the company's total paid-in capital, profitability, and distribution of shares.

Category A: The largest and most profitable companies fall into this category. As of December 1988, there were 103 stocks listed under this category, accounting for approximately 85% of the total market capitalisation. To be listed as a category A share, a company must have a paid-in capital of at least NT$200 million (approx. US$7.1 million).

Category B: As of 31 December 1988, there were 60 Category B shares. A company needs a paid-in capital of NT$100 million (approx. US$3.6 million) to be listed in category B. While a number of companies found in category B perform poorly, these stocks are the most actively traded in the market.

Category C: This is a new type of listing which is reserved for high-technology companies and other small firms which do not meet normal Category B listing requirements.

In order to limit wild fluctuations in the market, no transactions are permitted at a price which is more than 5% higher or lower than the previous day's closing price. Following the October 1987

Note: US$1.00 = NT$25.48.

Figure 3.1 Taiwan Weighted-Price Index, Weekly, 1986–1989

Figure 3.2 New Taiwan Dollar vs US Dollar, Weekly, 1985–1989

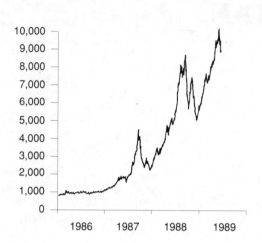

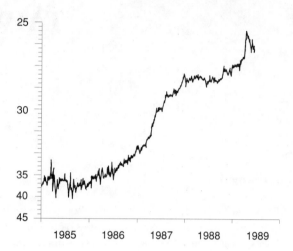

market crash, daily price limits were reduced to 3%; they were revised again to 5% in November 1988. The SEC is likely to continue to expand the limits with the aim of eliminating them as part of its market liberalisation campaign.

Although the Stock Exchange and the SEC try to ensure that companies seeking a listing have sound financial positions and meet certain minimum requirements, little effort has been made to de-list financially unsound companies.

At present, inward foreign exchange controls and laws against investment by foreign nationals prevent non-ROC residents from investing directly in the Taiwan stock market. Although Taiwan does not have immediate plans to open its market to foreign investment, the SEC has drawn up a three-stage plan for gradual liberalisation of the securities market:

Phase I: Indirect investment via investment funds.

Phase II: Direct investment by approved foreign companies.

Phase III: Direct investment by foreigners.

The first phase began in October 1983, with the launch of the *Taiwan (ROC) Fund* , a US$41 million mutual fund for foreign participation in the Taiwan stock market. The *Taiwan (ROC) Fund* is managed by the International Investment Trust Company Limited, a joint venture among 16 leading foreign and Taiwanese financial institutions. A second tranche of US$40 million was added in December 1984, bringing the fund to US$81 million.

Subsequently, three additional local firms were permitted licences to establish investment funds; all three launched US$25 million funds and started operation by 31 December 1986: Kwang Hua Securities Investment and Trust Company — the *Formosa Fund*; National Investment Trust Company — the *Taipei Fund*; and China Securities Investment Trust Company — the *Taiwan Fund Inc*.

There are plans to issue additional fund management licences in future, and it is also possible that existing funds might be permitted to increase in size.

The SEC has not given a set schedule for the implementation of phases II and III of its liberalisation plan, though government officials confirm that liberalisation will continue.

Historical Background

When the central government led by the Nationalist Party (the Kuomintang, or KMT) fled to Taiwan in 1949, the issuance and flotation of government 'Loyalty Bonds' encouraged the trading of securities. Although during the years of the Japanese occupation of Taiwan (1899–1945) Japanese brokers offered Japanese stocks for sale in Taiwan, a stock market did not come into existence until 1953 when the government issued land bonds and shares of four large government-owned enterprises (Taiwan Cement, Taiwan Paper, Taiwan Industry and Mining, and Taiwan Agriculture and Forest) to former large landowners in exchange for their land, which was allocated to small farmers under the 'Land to the Tiller' land reform programme.

Due to an initial lack of understanding of the value of stocks and the limited interest on the part of displaced landowners in holding them, many shares were offered for sale and sporadic markets and houses mushroomed to meet this demand for trading. The market was a rudimentary, unregulated, 'over-the-counter' market, and at its most buoyant there were 200–300 houses. After years of rampant price speculation and manipulation, investors lost all confidence in the stock market and it became apparent that if trading was to continue, a regulated and centralised market was necessary. In 1959, a group was therefore formed to study the establishment of a stock exchange, with the aim of promoting the nation's economic development while also protecting the investor. Based on the group's study and the report of an American adviser, the Securities and Exchange Commission was established in 1960 and a year later the Taiwan Stock Exchange came into being.

In 1968, the *Securities and Exchange Law* (a near clone of the 1934 US SEC Act) was passed to regulate the market.

The first Taiwan Stock Exchange Weighted Index was compiled in 1967, but it remained below 1,000 for 19 years before bursting through to 1,039.11 in 1986.

In 1973, the Taiwan stock market experienced unprecedented buoyancy when the index peaked at 514.85 as a result of the boom in textile exports. In 1974, however, the first oil crisis caused the index to plummet to 188.74. For the next four years, it drifted around 200 and 300 points before once again climbing on the back of the recovered economy to a new high of 688.52 in 1978. But the boom was short-lived, and the market, facing the second oil crisis, soon entered into a period of consolidation which was to last another four years.

From 1979 to 1982, when the market hovered around 400 and 500, many of the problems which had been hidden by the growing economy emerged, and a few companies which had sought listing at the time of the market boom suffered financial or operating difficulties; some even went to the wall. The fate of those that survived was not much better: as their share prices collapsed, investors accused the management of the stock exchange of incompetence and fraud. Faced with accusations that they had failed in their duty by not protecting the individual investor, and recognising that a complete collapse of confidence in the market would hinder future economic recovery, the Minister of Finance and the Chairman of the SEC were replaced, and a series of rescue and reform measures were implemented. These included short-term market rescue measures, such as a raising of the margin rate on the stock purchase, and more important long-term measures, such as making a start on the long-overdue revision of the *Securities and Exchange Law* and various other regulations. Other measures included a restructuring of the stock market, including stricter screening of listed companies, computerisation of stock trading to ensure a fair and orderly market, a clamp-down on insider trading, and encouragement of the establishment of more institutional investors in order to stabilise stock price movements, which had been heavily manipulated by individuals. Additionally, plans for the internationalisation of the market were laid with the announcement of the three stages of liberalisation.

In 1983, foreign investment was officially channelled into the market for the first time by the establishment of the first investment trust fund. The market responded to a recovery in the economy and the injection of foreign capital, rising to 765.71 in 1983 and 969.25 in 1984. After a cooling off on the back of a slower economy and the Cathay scandal, the market rallied again for two years. This period of tremendous turnover as a result of world economic recovery and abundant liquidity was interrupted only by the world stock market collapse in October 1987 and the local announcement of the reimposition of capital gains tax in September 1988. The highs of 1986, 1987, and 1988 were 1039.11, 4673.14, and 8789.78 respectively.

Table 3.1 shows that the Taiwan stock market has historically been a market of high turnover. In fact, even though the turnover rate is often near to 100% (meaning that each share changes hands once a year), the true turnover rate should be much higher as up to one-third of listed shares are held in very tight hands and therefore are rarely traded. With the local excessive liquidity rushing into the stock market in 1987 and 1988 due to the dearth of other investment outlets, shares changed hands at such a frantic pace that Taiwan ranked among the top three markets in the world in 1988 in terms of turnover.

Table 3.1 Taiwan Stock Exchange Turnover, 1980–1988

	TSE Weighted Index Closing	Listed Shares (bn)	Stock Turnover (bn shares)	Turnover Rate (%)	Turnover (US$bn)	Average Daily	Mkt Capitalisation (NT$bn)
1980	558.45	10.7	11.5	108	4.5	15	219.1
1981	551.03	12.8	13.2	103	5.5	19	201.3
1982	442.57	15.1	10.2	68	3.4	12	203.1
1983	761.92	16.7	23.9	143	9.0	31	306.0
1984	838.07	19.0	18.2	95	8.2	28	390.3
1985	835.12	21.3	14.5	68	4.9	17	415.7
1986	1,039.11	24.1	39.0	162	190.0	67	548.4
1987	2,339.86	28.7	76.9	267	193.4	325	1,386.1
1988	5,119.11	34.4	101.7	296	279.3	968	3,383.3

Source: W.I. Carr (Taiwan).

The Securities and Exchange Commission

Since its establishment on 1 September 1960, the Securities and Exchange Commission (SEC) has functioned as a watchdog, regulating every aspect of both the primary and secondary markets. The SEC is overseen by a committee consisting of nine commissioners, including the SEC Chairman and Vice Chairman, part-time representatives from the ministries of Finance, Economic Affairs, and Justice, and officials of the Central Bank of China and the Council of Economic Planning and Development of the Executive Yuan. Under the leadership of the SEC Chairman and Vice Chairman, there are four divisions responsible for market matters and four offices responsible for administration.

The major responsibilities of the four divisions are as follows:

Division I: Supervising public offering and listing of shares.

Division II: Supervising the TSE, securities companies, and securities trading.

Division III: Supervising margin financing, securities investment trust companies, securities investment consulting companies, and the OTC market.

Division IV: Securities market statistics, information, and investigation.

Stock Market Performance

The Taiwan Stock Exchange (TSE) is currently organised in the form of a corporation. At the end of 1988, its total assets were valued at NT$6,540 million (US$232 million) and it had a total equity of NT$2,166 million (US$77 million), of which 39% was invested by government-owned banks and enterprises and 61% by private banks and enterprises. However, in line with the *Securities and Exchange Law*, the corporate-formed Exchange will be replaced by a membership-formed Exchange when local securities firms are deemed by the government to be qualified to run the Exchange. The tenure of the TSE has been extended on a number of occasions, and it is believed that the government aims to convert it into membership form in 1992.

The Exchange is governed by a board of 15 directors and three supervisors. The major source of income of the Exchange is commission (10% of the total commission earned by the brokers), with only limited funds coming from listing fees.

The high turnover of recent years resulting from the computerisation of the trading system has led to significant increases in both brokers' commissions and the TSE levy.

Securities Companies

Before the 1988 revision of the *Securities and Exchange Law*, there were three kinds of securities company: the broker, the trader, and the underwriter; each was engaged solely in its designated business field. Before the liberalisations that commenced in mid-1988, there were 28 brokers (of which 14 were banks), 10 traders, and 22 underwriters, with no new licence applications approved with the exception of free entry for the unprofitable underwriting licence. The 1988 revision removed these restrictions and the Taiwan stock market, after being closed for over 20 years, entered a stage of free entry and competition. Any prospective securities company that meets the requirements will now be granted a licence. The major requirement for issuance of brokerage, trading, and underwriting licences, as well as for integrated licences (a combination of all three), is the minimum capital requirement of NT$200 million (US$7 million), NT$400 million (US$14 million), and NT$100 billion (US$35 million) respectively. To the end of 1988, 67 new brokerage firms and eight new integrated firms had joined the industry to give a total of 103 brokers (including 14 bank brokers), 18 traders, and 30 underwriters.

Since 1985, brokers have contributed over 99% of total turnover (see Table 3.2). Of these, non-bank brokers dominate the market, as they offer commission and bonus incentives to their salespeople compared to the rigid government-controlled payments in the banking sector. An interesting development in 1988 was the loss of market share by the old to the new. The market share held by bank brokers decreased from 23.56% in 1987 to 17.75% in 1988. Although the market share held by non-bank brokers increased from 76.27% in 1987 to 82.08% in 1988, the old brokers accounted for only 62.65%, with 19.43% going to the new brokers. It is expected that the new brokers will take up more market share in the future. Nevertheless, with a continuing high market turnover, any decrease in market share can still be an increase in overall business due to the expanding pie. In 1988, the whole market made US$326 million before-tax profit, with the number one broker, Jih Sun, making US$41.7 million. (The required capital was US$7 million.) It is expected that securities companies will continue to enter the fray while high turnover makes such profit levels possible.

Table 3.2 Market Share of Securities Firms, 1985–1988 (%)

	1985	1986	1987	1988
Non-bank Brokers	70.49	73.38	76.27	82.08)
Bank Brokers	29.02	26.42	23.56	17.75)
Total Brokers	99.51	99.80	99.83	99.83
Traders	0.49	0.20	0.17	0.17
Total	100.00	100.00	100.00	100.00

Source: W.I. Carr (Taiwan).

According to the *Securities and Exchange Law*, the market traders should be responsible for stabilisation of the market in the course of their trading. Traders tended, as a result, not to be too active in the market, buying or selling shares only upon government instructions when the market was considered too low or overheated. However, with the current trend towards increasing liberalisation, traders should have more freedom in the future.

Geographically, Taipei has been the centre of stock trading, with the percentage of transactions conducted in Taipei falling below 80% only since 1988 with the establishment of new and aggressive brokers outside the capital.

Dividends

Dividends distributed by the listed companies are in the form of cash, stocks, and/or free shares (from the capital reserve attributed from the revaluation/sale of assets, particularly land).

Up until three years ago, listed companies tended to distribute more cash dividends, as some small shareholders treated the cash dividend as a source of income and because of the SEC ruling that at least 50% of a dividend distribution be in cash. In recent years, however, a number of companies have taken the risk of upsetting their smaller shareholders by keeping more earnings in the company for expansion and tax-saving purposes, distributing dividends in the form of stock. (Dividends are taxable after paying corporate tax.) This move is becoming more popular and acceptable as investors realise that the future growth of a company, and hence the value of their shares, depends significantly upon expansion and improved competitive abilities.

TSE listed companies revalue their land and equipment based on the appreciation of those assets so as to increase the book value of total assets, and then distribute shares according to the increased amount. In the late 1970s and early 1980s, this practice was very popular in Taiwan, as it enabled a listed company to manipulate its share prices by announcing and distributing more shares to the shareholders, who mistakenly saw the additional new shares as an increase of wealth rather than a dilution of holdings.

In line with the efforts of the MOF and the SEC to rebuild the reputation of the stock market and restore the confidence of investors, strict restrictions have been imposed since 1982 on the issuance of shares based on the revaluation of assets, and now only 10% of the revaluated amount can be distributed in shares each year following the year of revaluation.

Price/Earnings Ratio

Price/earnings ratio (PER) was not commonly known or used in the Taiwan stock market prior to 1983 when gradually it was quoted and then suddenly became fashionable. Initially, the PERs were calculated by dividing an organisation's past year's average price or closing price by the past year's average earnings. The method then changed to the present market price divided by the previous year's earnings, before changing again to the present market price of a listed company divided by the estimated future earnings (prospective PER). PER remained a popular indicator until the share prices went up too high to be justified for a reasonable price level. Investors started to doubt the value of PER, as they failed to see that it can be used only as a reference for decision-making.

Table 3.3 shows the PER of the Taiwan stock market after adjustment for capital increases and weighted by the stocks' market capitalisation. There is no regularly published, market-accepted PER figure.

Table 3.3 Price/Earnings Ratio of the Taiwan Stock Market, 1984–1988

Year	Adjusted Simple Average		Weighted Average	
	w/Banks	w/o Banks	w/Banks	w/o Banks
1984	85.7	59.4	17.0	13.7
1985	91.1	66.5	15.8	13.8
1986	73.5	56.8	15.3	12.6
1987	39.5	29.4	28.7	16.5
1988	32.9	29.2	47.1	22.9

Source: W.I. Carr (Taiwan).
Note: The PER is calculated at closing on 29 December 1988.

The overall performance of the Taipei market is shown in Table 3.4. What is noteworthy is the appreciation of the local currency against the US dollar since 1987, and the positive impact this has had on the local capital market.

Table 3.4 Stock Market Performance, 1984–1988

Market Indicator	1984	1985	1986	1987	1988
Population (mn)	19.20	19.20	19.40	19.70	20.10
GNP (US$bn)	58.6	61.1	79.3	110.8	121.4
GNP Growth Rate (%)	10.6	5.1	11.7	11.9	7.3
No. of Listed Companies	123	127	130	141	163
Average Daily Trading Volume (US$mn)	28.00	17.10	62.40	289.80	956.90
P/E Ratio	13.85	15.80	15.30	28.70	68.90
Yield (%)	0.60	3.80	2.25	1.00	0.67
Inflation	(0.03)	(0.2)	0.70	0.50	1.30
Exchange Rates	39.47	39.85	35.50	28.55	28.19
Currency Appreciation vs US$	2.00	(1.0)	11.00	19.60	1.30

Source: W.I. Carr (Taiwan).

Stock Exchange Details

Address

7–10th Floors
City Building
85 Yang Ping South Road
Taipei
Tel: 2–311–4020
Tlx: 22914 TSEROC
Fax: 2–311–4004

Trading Days/Hours

The trading hours of the stock market are from 9 am to 12 noon from Monday to Friday, and 9 am to 11 am on Saturday.

Par Value

Since 1979, in order to standardise the form of stock certificates issued by listed companies, the SEC has governed the physical specifications of the certificates, the trading unit and set the par value of all the shares at NT$10.

Types of Orders

There are two types of orders: market orders and limit orders. Since the instalment of the computer-aided trading system, investors have tended to use the faster market order, as the limit orders often miss the market.

Trading System

Computer-aided trading system

The idea of using a computer-aided trading system (CATS) was initiated by the SEC in the early 1980s in an attempt to ensure fair and just trading operations, to reduce manual operational errors, and to increase the speed and accuracy of trading. Prior to the installation of the first computer to trade all Section II stocks in August 1985, trading in the TSE was all done manually. Almost all transactions except bond transactions are now carried out by computer, making the TSE the most automated exchange in the world.

Trading Procedures

When an order is received, whether by phone or in person, the broker inputs the information (volume, price, a/c number, ID number, margin trade signal) via a terminal connected directly with the TSE's CPU. All orders transmitted from the brokers' offices are processed and displayed on the TSE's matching terminals, where TSE trading clerks manually match the orders according to the price and time priority. As soon as the order is executed, a confirmation report is sent back to the broker, typically in five seconds; the broker then informs the investor that the order has been successful. Trading terminals are also available for traders, who can then place their own orders. The CATS can execute a maximum of 5,000 orders per minute — around 1 million a day.

Margin Transactions

Margin transactions were introduced in 1974 to upgrade the stock market and to promote its acceptability to investors. Initially, only three government banks — the Bank of Taiwan, the Bank of Communications, and the Land Bank of Taiwan — were authorised to finance the purchase of stocks at the margin rate, which was subject to adjustments approved by the SEC and the Central Bank depending on how active the stock market was. In 1980, Fuh-Hua Securities Financing Co. was established to be specifically responsible for all margin financing under the *Rules of Margin Financing*. The margin financing work of the three banks was transferred to Fuh-Hua, which also introduced securities lending for short selling soon afterwards. In line with the market liberalisation movement which began in mid-1988, Fuh-Hua's monopoly will soon change as new market participants are to be permitted to provide multi-function services of which margin financing will be one.

Unlike other countries where margin financing is designed for brokers, the mechanism of margin financing designed by Fuh-Hua is aimed at individual investors. An investor who wants to trade on margins has first to open an account with the broker, and will have to have a trading record of six months before being approved by Fuh-Hua to trade on margins upon application. The listed shares which are qualified to be traded on margin have to meet the eligibility criteria for margin trading stocks. In March 1989, 103 stocks out of the total of 163 qualified for margin trading.

On a margin purchase, the investor is required to put down a certain percentage of the purchased amount, with the rest to be financed by Fuh-Hua. The shares bought are held by Fuh-Hua as collateral. The rate of margin finance is subject to change depending on the stock market situation, with the SEC tightening or relaxing the rate as a measure to cool or heat the market. To short sell, the investor is requested to put up a certain percentage of the sale proceeds as a guarantee deposit, and the proceeds from the sale will be kept by Fuh-Hua until the stocks loaned are returned. The deposit rate for short selling is changed in the same way as that for margin purchases. In March 1989, 102 shares qualified to be short-sold. As the government is criticised each time it alters the margin rate, the SEC announced in November 1988 that the margin will change automatically according to the closing level of the TSE Index (Table 3.5). Naturally, this index-linked margin requirement table aroused a flurry of criticism.

Table 3.5 Margin/Short Sell Rate

TSE Index	% of Margin Financing		% of Short Sale Guarantee Deposit
	Sec. 1	Sec. 2	
2,700	70	60	120
4,500	60	50	110
6,000	50	40	100
7,200	40	30	90
8,100	30	20	80
9,000	20	10	70
9,600	10	0	60
10,2000	0	50	

Source: Taiwan Stock Exchange.

For each margin account, Fuh-Hua arbitrarily sets a maximum limit for margin purchases of NT$1.2 million or NT$3 million, depending on the creditability of the individual account. The limit is NT$50 million for traders. A complicated formula applies for short sale. The terms of margin financing, which can vary depending on the government's interpretation of the market situation, is one year for margin purchase and three months for short sale, renewable at the end of each term. Fuh-Hua is entitled to dispose of the shares or recover the short positions if investors do not respond to the margin calls. The interest rate charged will reflect the interest rate level prevalent during the time of financing — often the lower side of the short-term lending rate.

As the stock market has developed, the use of margin financing has become more popular. From the outstanding value of margin purchase and short sales shown in Table 3.6 it is obvious that with the large majority of investors long on stock investments, the outstanding value of margin purchases exceeds that of short sales. However, margin transactions are not a good barometer for measuring the short-term market sentiment as there is rampant illegal underground financing, with terms and rates much more flexible than those set by Fuh-Hua.

Table 3.6 Margin Transactions, 1980–1988 (NT$ million)

Year	Margin Purchases		Short Sale	
	New	Outstanding	New	Outstanding
1980	7,956	1,011	435	25
1981	2,131	2,190	1,966	126
1982	25,487	3,128	3,023	80
1983	48,545	3,752	5,568	273
1984	36,907	2,597	5,972	202
1985	36,789	4,824	4,158	48
1986	81,507	4,525	7,244	407
1987	155,580	10,449	12,903	386
1988	578,028	24,225	26,989	1,660

Source: W.I. Carr (Taiwan).

TSE Index

The Taiwan Stock Exchange Weighted Index (TSE Index) is the oldest and most popularly used barometer measuring the sentiment of the stock market. The index was first compiled in 1967 using the 1966 price as the base level. Although there are now two non-TSE indexes — the Economic Daily Index and the Commercial Times Index — which are calculated on a sample of 37 to 100 stocks unweighted by capital, the TSE Index is weighted, and based on almost all listed stocks, except those of government-owned companies and the stocks traded under the full delivery method. At the end of 1988, there were 142 stocks in the index.

Since 1981, other than the compositive TSE Index, Section I, Section II, and eight sector indices have been published to give the public a better view of the market. Moreover, in mid-1988, the TSE commenced publication of a bank-exclusive index in order to give investors a view of the market movement without the influence of the heavily capitalised — and consequently heavily weighted — bank shares, especially with bank share prices shooting through the roof. The weighting of the banking sector in the composition index reached 50% in mid-1988 before coming down to 45% by the end of the same year.

The computer-aided trading system and efficient telecommunications enable the index and trading volume to be calculated by the TSE and displayed in the user's terminal every five minutes.

The TSE is also planning to publish in 1989 another two indicators: the TSE 30-stock Average and the 20-stock Industry Average, which will be similar to the Dow Jones Average.

Unit of Trading

Round lot

Since 1979, in order to unify and standardise trading, the trading unit for the round lot was specified by the SEC to be 1,000 shares per certificate or its multiple. The SEC ruled that all trading carried out in the centralised market (TSE) should be carried out in round lots.

Odd lot

An odd lot is a certificate with less than 1,000 shares. They are normally issued by listed companies for stock dividends out of the current year's earnings or free shares out of capital reserve from asset revaluation calculated as proportion of the existing holdings. There is no trading market for odd-lot trading as there is in the United States.

The SEC requires each listed company to appoint one trader as its odd-lot share trader, and odd-lot certificates can only be sold to or bought by this designated trader. The trader can buy or sell the odd-lot from Monday to Friday after 10.30 am. The orders are input into the CATS system by the brokers before 10.30 am, which permits traders to make some profit out of the activity. Normally, the trader combines the odd lots to make round lots which he then sells to the market, and in an uptrend this adds to the profitability of the activity. In a downtrend, the reverse is true, as some traders refuse to buy odd lots from investors. The SEC has issued a warning that any trader who refuses to undertake his designated function will be in danger of losing his overall licence to trade.

Block transactions

A block transaction is the trading of 500 units (500,000 shares) or more, or when the par value of the trading exceeds NT$5 million. The rules for these transactions were changed in 1988. Every block trade now has to be submitted to the TSE after 2.30 pm on the day preceding the determined transaction day, at a price negotiated but within the ceiling and floor limit of the previous day's closing. With this new rule, a block trade may not be limited to a transaction between two definite parties, as the CATS is programmed to allow other investors to participate in the bidding/offering by time/price priority.

Price Limit

A daily floor and ceiling price limit operates to reduce speculation and to offer investors protection from wide fluctuation. At present, the daily limit has been set at +/-5% on the previous day's close for stock and +/-2% for bonds. As the market becomes more mature, and the daily limit gives investors expectations for higher or low prices rather than a measure of protection, the daily limit is expected to be broadened to 10% before eventually being revoked.

Settlement and Delivery

The clearing department of the TSE is responsible for handling all the settlements of securities transactions in the market. Buyers and sellers are required to make physical delivery of stock certificates or cash to the broker's office on the next business day (day 2) following the transaction day (day 1). The broker offsets the buying and selling of the same stock and settles the net with the TSE on transaction day 2. On the third business day following the transaction day (day 4), customers receive the proceeds or stock certificates from the broker. If investors do not wish to safekeep their stock certificates, Fuh-Hua Securities Financing Co. renders a safekeeping service at a low charge, and the custodial receipt can be used as the instrument for settlement with brokers. By 1991, it is expected that the book-entry settlement and central depositary system, which has been discussed and studied by the SEC and TSE, will be introduced to the market in order to improve the present system and reduce the settlement/delivery risks.

Disclosure

Although Taiwan is still a closed market, the disclosure requirements are somewhat stricter than those of some open markets. When applying for a listing, a company is required to produce a prospectus covering operational information for the past three years, such as product lines, production capacities, sales breakdown and sales to related subsidiaries, wide-range financial statements, and future sales and operational expansion plans. Since 1988, in an effort to safeguard the interests of the investor and make sure that the investing public understands fully the true value of a company before making an investment decision, the SEC requires every listed company to hold an open hearing for at least 500 of the general public, where the disclosed information, future plans, underwriter's report, fairness of the pricing, and evaluation of pricing method, etc, can be discussed. All listed companies are required to file periodic and non-periodic disclosures including monthly sales reports, quarterly financial reports, monthly reports on shares held by directors and supervisors, immediate reports of news or decisions which will have an impact on the operations of the company or the movement of its share price, semi-annual financial statements, yearly sales/earning forecasts, and an annual report which contains similar information to the pre-listing prospectus.

Furthermore, in order to make all the required disclosed information accessible to the public, the SEC has required the TSE, the Institute of Securities Market Development, and brokers to make all the above information readily available to the public.

Securities Investment Consulting Companies

According to the *Rules Governing Administration of Securities Investment Consulting Enterprises*, securities investment consulting companies (SICCs) are allowed to:

- provide research, analysis, or advice, on a commission basis, on matters related to securities investment
- publish information relating to securities investment activities
- conduct seminars in connection with securities investment
- engage in other relevant securities investment consulting activities as approved by the SEC.

As it is unheard of in Chinese society to pay directly for information, the SICCs are unable to make a living if the approved areas are rigidly kept to. Therefore, many locally owned SICCs, especially those with a connection to broker parents, secretly manage clients' portfolios, although the SEC clearly states that no physical handling is allowed. By the end of 1987, the *Point for Consultation on Foreign Funds by SIC Companies* was promulgated and some foreign-owned SICCs such as Jardine Fleming and Fidelity started publicly to promote their parent companies' funds in Taiwan after each fund had been approved. However, with more SEC-approved foreign funds and many non-SEC approved funds entering the market, the competition is fierce. At the end of 1988, there were 34 SICCs, of which 9 were foreign or foreign-related, and 52 foreign funds had been approved by the SEC. Although there are constant calls from the SICCs to legalise the private client portfolio management business, the SEC is still reluctant to do so.

Market Information System

Since the computerisation of stock trading, the use of computers has become popular among all the participants of the stock market, even down to individual investors. At present, the major market information available for the investing public via their PC terminals is a second-by-second view of stock prices, market turnover, number of unfulfilled buy/sell shares of each stock at ceiling/floor price, daily high/low points and price movement chart, and every five minutes an updated TSE Index and the number of accumulated buy/sell orders. The system used by brokers, traders, and fund managers is similar to that available to the public, with a slightly different screen display. Furthermore, some brokers develop their own information system based on the public information to fit their own or their clients' special requirements.

The Twenty Largest Stocks

The 20 largest quoted companies by market capitalisation are shown in Table 3.7.

Table 3.7   The 20 Largest Quoted Stocks by Market Capitalisation,
as at 31 December 1988

Company	NT$bn
China Steel	324.5
Int. Comm. Bank of China	244.9
Cathay Life	244.0
First Commercial Bank	179.2
Hua Nan Commercial Bank	171.8
Chang Hua Commercial Bank	170.7
Formosa Plastics	78.9
Nan Ya Plastics	77.2
Formosa Chemical & Fiber	75.1
Far Eastern Textiles	71.4
Evergreen Marine	58.00
Asia Cement	55.0
Yue Loong Motor	54.1
Taiwan Cement	50.6
Taipei Business Bank	49.7
Yuen Foong Yu Paper Manufacturing	39.5
Formosa Taffeta Co. Ltd	33.7
Cathay Construction	31.5
Teco Electric & Machinery	29.2
Taiwan Glass	28.0

Source: W.I. Carr (Taiwan).

Dealing Costs

Commissions

The general brokerage commission for all stock transactions is set at 0.15% for both buying and selling. For corporate and government bonds, the rate is 0.1%. Brokers are required to surrender 10% of their commission income to the TSE.

Securities Transfer Tax

The securities transfer tax is levied on sales of securities at 0.3% of the trading amount. The sale of government bonds, however, is exempted from the securities transfer tax.

Public Offering

Under Taiwan's company law, if the capital of a company reaches NT$200 million, it is required to go public by making its annual financial statements and annual reports available. (Firms which are at least 45% foreign-owned and whose setup was approved according to the *Statute for Encouraging Foreign Investment* are excluded from the above requirement.) In addition, all firms, no matter what size, are required to have at least 300 shareholders, each holding over 1,000 shares, before the SEC will give approval for an increase of capital. Although many companies avoid going public by keeping their capital under NT$200 million, the number of public but unlisted companies increases every year (Table 3.8).

Table 3.8 Public and Listed Companies, 1978–1988

Year	Public Companies No.	Total Cap. (US$mn)	Listed Companies No.	Paid-in Cap.	Mkt Cap. (US$mn)
1978	24	1,018	87	1,967	4,035
1979	24	1,300	96	2,444	4,963
1980	25	1,640	102	3,294	6,083
1981	54	2,343	107	3,596	8,086
1982	116	3,688	113	3,870	5,089
1983	130	4,790	119	4,211	7,598
1984	157	1,197	1232	4,926	9,888
1985	169	6,183	127	5,469	10,431
1986	182	7,414	130	6,841	15,449
1987	198	10,524	141	10,222	148,549
1988	226	12,140	163	12,513	120,102

Source: W.I. Carr (Taiwan).

Listing Criteria

Stocks

There are three sections of listed companies, and those seeking listing are required to meet the appropriate TSE listing criteria. The first section includes large capitalised and highly profitable firms; the third covers risk or high-tech ventures.

Financial companies, including banks and insurance companies, shipping companies, tourist hotels, and public utilities, are exempt from the capital structure requirements, and government-owned companies do not have to meet the distribution requirements.

A company in any section can be reclassified up if it meets higher section standards, or reclassified down if it fails to maintain the standards of its section.

In addition to the three formal sections, there is a section which is especially designed for the trading of a number of stocks which are not qualified for any of the three sections due to financial difficulties, bankruptcy, or reorganisation. While these firms should have been delisted, for bureaucratic reasons they continue to be traded. The stocks categorised in this section are restricted to trading under the 'Full Delivery Method', which requires advance payment and advance delivery of share certificates when traded, and no margin financing. Investors interested in such stocks are warned of the high risk. In 1988, in a measure to delist these stocks, the SEC promulgated a new rule setting out an automatic delisting procedure after the passage of a designated grace period during which improvements should be made. At the end of 1988, there are 19 such stocks, down from 22 in 1987 and 24 in 1986. It is planned to delist another 10 companies in 1989.

Listing Fees

While government bonds and corporate bonds are exempt from the listing fee for the purpose of promotion, listed companies are required to pay an original listing fee for the first-time listing and an additional listing fee for any listing of new shares. However, the annual listing fee calculated on a declining scale shall not exceed NT$300,000. Listing criteria are shown in Table 3.9.

Table 3.9 Minimum Standards for Listing

Capital Amount: Min. Cap. Stock	Category A NT$200mn	Category B NT$100mn	Category C High-tech NT$50mn	Others NT$100mn
Profitability: Min. Ratio of Income* Capital Stock	10% or 5% with income over NT$40mn for the past two years, *or* 10% in one	10% for the past year *or* 5% on average for the past two years	No requirement	Profit for the latest year and shareholder's equity per share shall be greater than
* Operating Income and Net Income Before Income Tax	of the past two years and 5% with income over NT$40mn in the other year			par value

Capital Structure:

Min. Ratio of Net Worth Assets	13 for the latest year	No requirement	No requirement	No requirement

Distribution of Shares:

(a) Minimum No. of Registered Shareholders	2,000	1,000	No requirement	No requirement
(b) Minimum No. of Public* Shareholders	1,000	500	No requirement	No requirement
(c) Minimum Public Shares	20% *or* 10 million shares	20% *or* 10 million shares	No requirement	No requirement

Source: W.I. Carr (Taiwan).
Note: * Each holding 1,000 to 50,000 or more.

Underwriting

Before a company is qualified to apply for listing, it must first be a public company. Often, the applicant firm combines the procedures for going public and for listing. The procedure for examining listing applications has been modified and strengthened by the SEC in order to ensure that full disclosure requirements are met and the company meets the required minimum standards. As it is mandatory to have at least 10% of total shares offered and held by the public prior to the listing (this can be reduced to a minimum of 5% for larger companies), the underwriters are entitled to fulfil their function by distributing the shares to the public. Although some underwriters claim to have underwritten a few issues on the stand-by basis, these were no different from issuance on the best-effort basis. However, with the capital gains tax reimposed from 1989, both the SEC and underwriters are seriously considering promoting the stand-by method to issuers who are concerned about investors turning away from the stock market because of the new tax.

The routing procedure for distributing shares publicly is to make an announcement in the major newspapers, with a brief introduction and summary prospectus on the issue. Hopeful subscribers clip the application forms and send them to the underwriter for the lucky draw. So as to give everyone an equal chance in the draw, the SEC will require from 1989 that all applications will be entered via brokers' terminals to the computer centre of the SEC. The success rate in the draw has historically been around 1–3%. Normally, two or three underwriters will underwrite an issue, with the leading one taking a higher market share.

Typically, it will take about three months before an application for listing is approved by the SEC after the TSE has submitted the case. The SEC reviews reports from the TSE, the auditor, and the underwriters, and occasionally undertakes inspections. From 1988, in order to alert the investing public to the disclosed information before the actual underwriting is carried out, the SEC has requested every applicant firm to conduct a public hearing where the company shall disclose all important factors which may influence decision-making, and where investors shall be given the opportunity to raise questions. The minutes of the hearing shall be submitted to the SEC to determine the public's opinion of the issue. Unfortunately, such public hearings have become a mere formality.

With the passage of the *Securities and Exchange Law* in 1988, the aforementioned approval method is not applied to the application of additional shares derived from earnings and capital reserves. The new rules allow an automatic registration form approval after a 30-day grace period from the filing date. This method has considerably shortened the time taken for applications to be approved and will be retained in future.

Size of the Market

It has been the government's long-term objective to enlarge the size of the stock market. As an inducement, for the last 20 years it has offered a 15% corporate tax deduction, but despite this tax break, and extensive promotion by the TSE and the SEC, not many companies have been listed. This may be due to a preference, common amongst the Chinese, for keeping business in the family and one's financial affairs secret, worries about shareholders' meetings, or the comparative ease with which financing can be obtained from banks and the kerb market.

This reluctance caused the number of listed companies to expand only very slowly until 1987, when changes in the general economic environment due to the stronger NT$ lost Taiwan its traditional competitive edge of cheaper labour. Forced to upgrade operations both domestically and internationally, to improve marketing, and especially to expand R&D and technology acquisition in order to compete in areas other than a bottom-line price, the manufacturing industry required the input of large amounts of capital. The extremely buoyant stock market since 1986 — evidenced by high turnover and a wider spread of participation by serious investors — convinced many companies of the real function and importance of the stock market as a steady source of large amounts of capital at a comparatively low cost, without the risk of jeopardising their financial structure. The number of newly listed reputable firms has thus increased dramatically since 1986, with a historically high 24 new listings in 1988 bringing the total number of listed firms to 165 (see Figure 3.3). It is expected in 1989 that an additional 40 firms will be added to the list. Furthermore, when share prices skyrocketed in 1987 and 1988, Taiwan became one of the top six markets in the world as market capitalisation reached US$120 billion. Banks are still a major part of the market (see Figure 3.4).

Liberalisation of the Market

As mentioned above, in 1982 the government initiated a three-stage plan to liberalise Taiwan's stock market, with the purpose of reviving the market and restoring investor confidence. The three stages of the plan were as follows:
1. Allow foreign investors to invest indirectly in Taiwan through investment trust funds.
2. Allow foreign institutional investors to invest directly.
3. Allow all foreign investors to invest directly.
The timetable was not determined when the plan was drafted and approved, as the completion of each stage would be dependent upon the future development of the stock market and the country's economy.

Figure 3.3 Total Market Value and Number of Listed Companies, 1966—1988

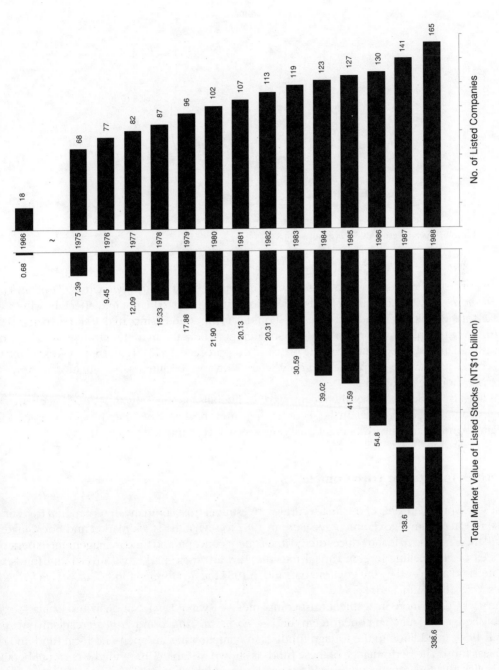

Source: Taiwan Stock Exchange.

Figure 3.4 Breakdown of Market Capitalisation by Sector, 1988

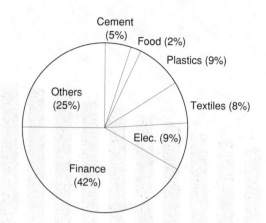

Source: Indosuez Asia Investment Services research.

The first stage was carried out in 1983 with the setting up of the *Taiwan (ROC) Fund* and later the *Formosa, Taipei,* and *Taiwan* funds. The second stage is yet to be put into effect, however, due to a lack of the capital demand and excessive liquidity in the country since mid-1986 and central bank control over the inflow of foreign funds in an attempt to limit the mounting foreign reserve which has resulted in the United States exerting pressure to appreciate the local currency. It is expected that the second stage will be implemented only when Taiwan's foreign reserve situation improves or there is a shortage of capital.

It must be understood that the recent wave of liberalisation in Taiwan is affecting all areas — social, economic, and political. In the securities field, new brokers have already been permitted, and margin financing and the investment trust business will continue to open up.

Securities Investment Trust Companies

The establishment in 1983 of the first securities investment trust company, International Investment Trust, resulted from a government measure in 1982 to revive the stock market and boost investor confidence. In a move to introduce foreign investment concepts and fund management experience, the idea of channelling foreign capital into the Taiwan stock market via investment funds was initiated and approved by the government, and in 1983 the first foreign fund, *Taiwan (ROC) Fund,* was successfully launched.

In 1986, three more investment trust companies — Kwang Hwa, National, and China — were established, each launching one foreign fund — *Formosa, Taipei,* and *Taiwan* respectively. As of March 1989, in addition to the foreign fund, each company has an open-end local fund and one overseas fund. The performance of these funds is shown in Table 3.10. With the current liberalisation policy, the government is expected to approve the establishment of more securities investment trust companies in 1989. (Table 3.11 includes the names of international shareholders in these investment trust companies.)

Table 3.10 Performance of International Funds, 1987–1988 (%)

	Taiwan (ROC)	Formosa	Taipei	Taiwan
1987 Annual Return	108.8	162.5	138.6	121.9
Standard Deviation on 1987 Monthly Return	20.3	22.2	20.5	19.4
1988 Annual Return	80.9	86.1	98.5	70.9
Standard Deviation on 1988 Monthly Return	14.0	14.4	13.3	13.4

Source: W.I. Carr (Taiwan).
Note: Return includes NAV's capital gains, dividend, and gains generated by NT$ appreciation.

Rules for Foreign Investors

Foreign Investment Restrictions

Foreign investors can invest in one local securities company, but the amount of investment cannot exceed 10% of the total capital of that securities company, and the total amount of investment made by a foreign investor in any securities company cannot exceed 40% of its total capital.

Foreign securities companies can establish their branch offices in Taiwan provided that Taiwanese securities companies are permitted to establish branch offices in those countries.

Foreign Exchange Control

Effective 15 July 1987, the controls over foreign exchange transactions conducted in or with the Republic of China (ROC) have been relaxed.

A ROC national or a foreigner living in the ROC with an alien resident certificate may remit into the ROC up to US$50,000 a year in the form of loans from abroad, gifts, and so on.

A ROC national, or a foreigner living in the ROC with an alien resident certificate or a registered business entity or non-business organisation, may remit out of the ROC up to US$5 million a year for such expenditures as repatriation of invested principal, remittance of profits, purchase of foreign real properties, purchase of corporate stocks and bonds, loans to foreign borrowers, and donations. Each remittance, however, should not exceed US$1 million.

Taxation

Transaction tax
A 0.15% transaction tax is currently imposed on sellers. This was reduced from 0.3% in 1989 as a government concession in the wake of opposition to the reimposition of capital gains tax.

Capital gains tax
In September 1988, the MOF announced the reimposition of capital gains tax on transactions of listed stocks effective from January 1989. The announcement so shocked the market that it entered a 19-day nosedive; the turnover was so small that few investors could get out at any price and many took

Table 3.11 International Funds in the Taiwan Market, 1989

Fund	Taiwan (ROC) Fund	Formosa Fund	Taipei Fund	Taiwan Fund
Manager	Int'l Investment Trust Co. Ltd	Kwang Hwa Sec. Inv. & Trust Co. Ltd	National Inv. Trust Co. Ltd	China Sec. Inv. Trust Corp.
Size	US$369mn	US$225mn	US$190mn	US$88mn
Launch Date	10/83 1st Tranche 12/84 2nd Tranche	3/86	5/86	12/86
Listing	New York	London	London	New York
Redemption Restriction	Already expired	Already expired	Already expired	Closed-end fund
Initial Sales Charge	2.75%	2.75%	2.75%	7.0%
Annual Mgt Fee	1.5%	1.5%	1.5%	1.5% + Performance adjustment
Local Partners	51% 10% Int'l Comm. Bank of China 8% Bank of Communication 8% Farmers' Bank of China 8% Central Trust of China 8% Bank of Taiwan 8% United Wld Chin. Comm. Bank 1% Ming Yu Co. Ltd	64% 48% Huei-Hong Inv. Co. Ltd 10% Kuo-Ling Inv. Co. Ltd 5% Rue-Tai Inv. Co. Ltd 1% Taiwan Fin. Econ. Consulting Co.	68.97% 30.82% National Group 9.91% Yuen Foong Yu Paper Mfg Co. Ltd 9.91% Bank of Communication 7.93% Chin. Auto Co. Ltd 2.97% Shih Feng Chemical Products Co. Ltd	65% 65% China Dev. Corp.
Foreign Partners	49% 7% Robert Fleming (HK) Ltd 7% Credit Suisse First Boston (Asia) Ltd 7% Vickers da Costa Int'l Ltd 7% Wardley Inv. Ser. Ltd 4% Citicorp Int'l Ltd 5% Gartmore (HK) Ltd 4% Lazard Bros & Co. Ltd 4% Nikko Int'l (Europe) Ltd 4% United Merchant Bank Ltd	36% 8% Federated Int'l (FE) Holdings Ltd 7% Interallianz Bank Zurich 6% Hoare Govett Asia Ltd 4% Govett Oriental Inv. Trust Plc. 4% Hambro Pacific Ltd 4% MNOPF Trustees Ltd 3% C'solidated Resources Ltd	29.13% 9.91% GT Mgt (Asia) Ltd 7.83% Prudential-Bache Sec. Inc. 7.43% BT Foreign Inv. Corp. Individuals: 1.88% K C Wang & Family	35% 15% Merrill Lynch Int'l Inc. 10% Bangkok Bank Ltd Sing Branch 5% Fidelity Int'l Ltd 5% Yamaichi Capital Mgt (Europe) Ltd

Source: W.I. Carr (Taiwan).

to the streets to protest. Politically unable to back down, the MOF decided to go ahead with its plan despite the protests, but offered a number of small concessions to placate investors.

Although the government faces difficulties in collecting the tax, the main essence is that every individual who sells stocks over NT$10 million a year shall incorporate any capital gains, after offsetting any losses from the transaction of other assets, into his annual income report. They will then be taxed at whatever tax bracket they fall into. The highest progressive income rate at present is set at 50%, although there has been some discussion about reducing the number of brackets and lowering tax rates in the future. If the stocks have been held for over a year, only half of the gain shall be taxed and no tax will be levied on the sale of shares purchased before 1989.

Taxation on dividends and interest

Under the *Income Tax Law*, income tax is chargeable on dividend and interest income from sources within the ROC. Cash dividends are subject to a 15% withholding tax for ROC residents or 35% for non-residents, which is reduced to 20% if the investment is approved under the *Statute for Investment by Foreign Nationals*. Stock dividends representing a distribution of capital surplus or an asset revaluation surplus are not subject to income tax, but stock dividends representing a distribution of earnings are subject to income tax, which is payable on receipt or, in certain cases, on disposal of the stock dividends. Interest income is subject to a 10% withholding tax for ROC residents or 20% for non-residents. Interest income from short-term bills is subject to 20% withholding tax at source for both residents and non-residents.

Dividends and interest may be included in the taxpayer's consolidated income with tax-exempt savings for a deduction up to NT$360,000. This tax-free income limit was initiated to encourage saving and investment at a time when the country needed savings to improve the economy. However, in recent years, this has resulted in a flood of liquidity which is used for speculation on the stock market, on property, and in underground lotteries. This tax incentive is likely to be phased out in the future.

Protection of Shareholders

Like other markets, Taiwan's stock market suffers from insider transactions. Although the *Securities and Exchange Law* prohibits insider transactions and lists severe penalties, legal loopholes make it difficult to enforce the law. The recent revision of the *Securities and Exchange Law* indicates the government's determination to put a stop to insider transactions by clearly defining insiders (directors, supervisors, managers, 10% holding major shareholders and their spouses, children under 20, and any other people whose names are used to hold stocks for the people stated above) and increasing the penalties.

In addition to tightening up the regulations, an overseeing mechanism has been installed, containing the personal data of all insiders of all listed companies. Computer matching of this data with trading data identifies any obvious insider trading. However, it is still relatively easy for insiders to cover their illegal tracks through the use of heads (names of friends or relatives, or rented names), or specially established investment companies. Furthermore, the SEC does not have the juridical power to investigate and a subpoena will be issued only upon formal request of the SEC to the court, which makes any investigation technically difficult and time consuming.

Available Research

The Status of Securities on the Taiwan Stock Exchange (monthly)
Stock Exchange Monthly Review (monthly)
Taiwan Stock Exchange Statistical Data (annually)
An Introduction to the Taiwan Stock Exchange (annually)
Taiwan Stock Exchange Trading Volume, Value and Stock Price Index (annually)
Taiwan Stock Exchange Factbook (annually)
Taiwan Stock Exchange Annual Report (annually)

4

SOUTH KOREA

Introduction

Koreans like to plan for the future on a grand scale. Like the magnificent Olympic complex, and the highway system on either side of the Han River, the Stock Exchange of Korea building on Yoido Island was built in the late 1970s to accommodate 500 brokers or 5,000 listings at a time when neither seemed possible. Yet, during the 1980s, the stock market has grown by a factor of almost ten-fold, with the number of listings now exceeding 500 (see Figure 4.3).

Despite Korea's new international standing since the 1988 Olympics, some characteristics of the 19th-century 'Hermit Kingdom' persist. This is very apparent in the attitude to foreign investors, who are still excluded from the market except through a handful of funds and convertible bonds. At the time of writing, the Ministry of Finance (MOF) in Seoul was still promising to open the market by 1992, but this date has been repeatedly postponed in the past.

Historical Background

The Korean Stock Exchange (KSE) was founded in 1956. The government held 68.19% of the share capital and the 25 member firms owned the remaining 31.41%* until 1 March 1988, when the government sold its shareholding to the member firms. The KSE is the only securities exchange in Korea. The Chairman and President are appointed by the President of Korea.

During its first four years of operation, the government did little to foster Korea's capital markets, but in 1961 General Park Chung Hee took power and introduced centralised state planning to promote the country's economic development.

The First Five Year Plan (1962–1966) stressed the mobilisation of savings for investment in industries, and steps were taken to develop the capital markets as part of a general effort to improve the nation's financial system. In 1962, the legal environment was also greatly improved with the enactment of the *Securities and Exchange Act* and the *Commercial Code*. In 1968, the government further stepped up its efforts to develop the capital markets by enacting the *Capital Markets Promotion Act* to provide tax and other incentives to both issuers and buyers of stocks.

In 1977, the regulatory system was reorganised with the establishment, as agencies of the MOF,

Note: US$1.00 = Won 670.

Figure 4.1 Korea (South) Composite-Price Index, Weekly, 1982–1989

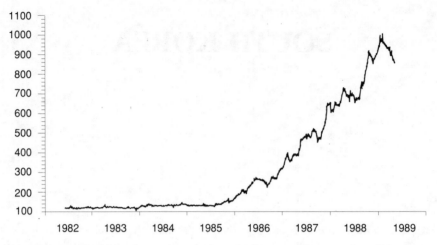

Source: Datastream.

Figure 4.2 Korean Won vs US Dollar, Weekly, 1982–1989

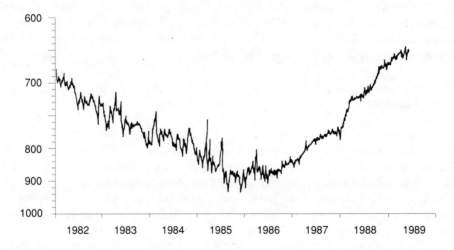

Source: Datastream.

of the Securities and Exchange Commission (SEC) to make policy and the Securities Supervisory Board to enforce it.

As a result of a stagnating economy and mounting foreign debt, the MOF announced in January 1981 that the capital markets would be gradually opened to foreign investors. The primary objectives of liberalisation were to access foreign capital through equity investments as well as bank borrowing and to help stimulate the depressed domestic capital markets. Two small offshore unit trusts, totalling US$30 million, were issued at the end of 1981.

Figure 4.3   Listed Companies, 1972–1987 (year end)

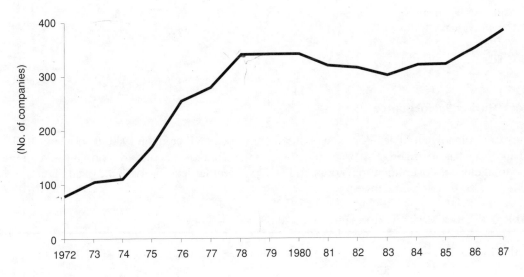

Source: Securities Market in Korea.

In June 1985, the government announced the *Measures for Fostering the Securities Market*, which encouraged insurance companies to expand their securities investments and promoted the establishment of pension funds that would invest in securities. The most recent development was the announcement of a liberalisation schedule by the MOF on 2 December 1988. Under this schedule, foreign investors will be permitted to invest directly in the Korean market, within certain limits, regardless of their CB holdings and Korean investors will be permitted to invest overseas, within certain limits, by 1992.

The Korean securities market is still closed to non-resident investors for direct investment without special permission from the MOF. However, foreigners who have been legal residents of Korea for more than six months can invest in the market. The investment vehicles for foreigners are limited to the following nine funds and four convertible bond issues:

Fund

1. Korea International Trust
2. The Korea Trust
3. The Korea Fund
4. Korea Growth Trust
5. Seoul International Trust
6. Seoul Trust
7. Korea Small Companies Trust
8. Korea Emerging Companies Trust
9. Korea Europe Fund.

Convertible bonds

1. Samsung Electronics
2. Daewoo Heavy Industries
3. Yukong
4. Goldstar.

Stock Market Performance

The extraordinarily rapid development of the Korean stock market in the 1980s is shown in Tables 4.1 and 4.2. It has been a broadly-based phenomenon, attributable not only to economic success but also to intelligent government direction, and is dependent far less on foreign capital than on the savings of Korean domestic investors.

Table 4.1 Stock Market Performance, 1985–1988

Market Indicator	1985	1986	1987	1988
Market Index (Seoul Composite)	163.37	272.61	525.11	907.19
Market Cap. (US$bn)	7.4	13.9	33.0	94.3
Market Cap./GNP (%)	8.9	17.3	30.0	57.0
No. of Investors (% of pop.)	1.9	3.4	7.4	10.0
Ownership of Institutional Investors (%)	19.0	24.0	27.0	30.0
Daily Trading Volume (US$mn)	14.2	38.0	89.0	250.0
No. of Listed Companies	342	355	389	502
Exchange Rate	890.2	861.4	792.3	684.1
Currency Appr. vs US$	−7.6	3.2	8.0	13.7

Sources: W.I. Carr; Indosuez Asia Investment Services research.

Table 4.2 Economic Indicators, 1985–1988

Indicator	1985	1986	1987	1988
GNP (Won T)	72.8	90.5	105.6	123.6
GNP Growth Rate (%)	5.4	12.9	12.8	12.2
PER (X)	12.0	12.8	19.8	26.9
Yield (%)	4.9	3.5	2.1	1.3
Inflation (%)	2.5	2.8	3.0	7.2
Exports (US$bn)	30.3	34.7	47.3	60.7
Imports (US$bn)	31.1	31.6	41.0	51.8

Source: W.I. Carr.

Stock Exchange Details

Address

Korean Stock Exchange
33, Yoido-dong
Youngdeungpo-gu
Seoul 150-010

Trading Days/Hours

The trading hours of the Korean Stock Exchange are from 9.40 am to 11.40 am and from 1.20 pm to 3.20 pm from Monday to Friday, and 9.40 am to 11.40 am on Saturday. No trading takes place on holidays and during the last five business days of the calendar year.

Trading Procedures

Orders are executed on the Exchange by individual auction, which is classified into single-price auction and multi-prices auction. The principles pertaining to the execution of orders are as follows:
1. Higher bids and lower offers take preference.
2. The first-come, first-served principle.
3. Priority is determined by the Exchange when bids and offers are made simultaneously.
    Quotation is made on the basis of one share in the case of stocks and beneficial certificates, and 10,000 Won at par value in the cost of bonds. In all cases, the quotation unit shall not be less than 10 Won.
    The trading units are:
1. Not less than ten shares for both stocks and beneficial certificates.
2. Not less than 100,000 Won for bonds (except for convertible bonds and bonds with warrant).
    A computerised on-line system for trading has been in operation since February 1983, enabling KSE members to send orders directly to the trading floor of the Exchange from their main and branch offices. The KSE is also developing a computer-assisted trading system which is expected to be operational by the late 1980s.

Kinds of Transactions

Depending on the time interval between the contract date and the settlement date, transactions on the Exchange are divided into 'spot transactions' and 'regular way transactions'. At present, all listed equity shares are traded under regular way transactions except for administration issues and bonds to be spot transacted. Bonds are traded on both a spot and regular way basis.
    Regular way transactions must be settled on the third business day from the contract date, while spot transactions are settled on the contract date. Issues designated as requiring administration by the Exchange must be settled within 14 days from the date of the contract.

Major Stock Market Participants

Overview

Individuals are the main participants in the market, holding 52% of all outstanding stock (see Table 4.3). However, perhaps as much as half of this stock is held by the controlling families and is never traded. Over the past 20 years, there has been a dramatic shift as the government has declined from being the largest shareholder to the smallest (see also Figure 4.4).

Table 4.3   Stock Market Participants, 1967–1987 (%)

Type of Investor	1967	1977	1987
Individuals	17.8	44.2	51.9
Other Institutions	10.2	16.2	38.2
Banks	6.9	5.7	5.0
Foreigners	0.1	1.5	3.5
Securities Firms	2.9	15.3	1.3
Government	62.1	17.1	0.2
Total	100.0	100.0	100.0

Note: 'Other institutions' includes corporations, insurance firms, investment trusts, and foundations.

Figure 4.4   Stock Ownership by Type of Investor, 1967 and 1987

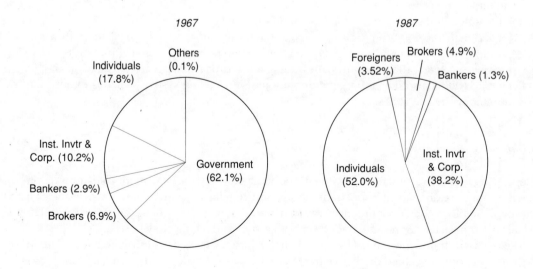

Securities firms

There are 25 securities firms in Korea. Only securities firms can join the KSE and broke securities. Securities firms dominate the underwriting and distribution of securities, although some other financial institutions are also licensed to engage in these businesses. Securities firms can and do invest in stocks for their own account. Regulations currently limit their own investments to 50% of their net worth, although this ratio has fluctuated from 0% to 100% depending on the government's interest in stimulating the stock market.

Since 1986, there has been a dramatic expansion in the capital, revenue, and staff of the securities industry, although the government has not permitted the establishment of new firms. Securities firms derive most of their profits from brokerage commissions. The big Korean business groups have been aggressive in moving into the brokerage business by acquiring smaller firms. All but one of the largest brokers are now part of large business groups.

Investment trust companies

There are only three investment trust companies in Korea: Korea Investment Trust Company, Daehan Investment Trust Company, and Citizens Investment Trust Management Company. Together, they manage about 10.1 trillion Won (US$12.8 billion). Their bond holdings are enormous: 8.6 trillion Won (US$12.8 billion). Their bond holdings are enormous: 8.6 trillion Won (US$10.9 billion), or 38% of the total bond market. Their equity investments are only 1.5 trillion Won (US$1.9 billion), or 6.6% of the value of the stock market.

Investment trust companies offer both equity and bond funds. Until 1988, they had a monopoly on the management of equity funds, but merchant banks are now permitted to offer equity funds in addition to bond funds. Investment trust companies provide both open and closed-end investment trust funds, but most are closed-end, with fixed termination periods. The beneficial certificates of closed-end trusts are traded on the Exchange.

Merchant banks

There are six merchant banks in Korea, all of which are joint ventures with major foreign financial institutions. Merchant banks can manage trust funds, as well as invest their own capital in the stock market. The total value of all securities (both stocks and bonds) was about 1 trillion Won (US$1.3 billion) at the end of 1987, the majority of which is believed to be invested in bonds. In November 1987, as part of a move to support the market, the government announced that it would allow merchant banks to manage equity investment trust funds in 1988, although none have yet done so.

Settlement/Delivery

Regulations on settlement

All transactions effected on the trading floor are cleared on the basis of net balance through the Korea Securities Settlement Corporation (KSSC) which is designated by the KSE as the sole agent for clearing transactions. Stocks and equity-related debt securities are settled two trading days after the trading date. Bonds, however, can be settled on an on-the-spot basis or on the second business day following the trading day.

Book-keeping entry settlement

In an attempt to expedite delivery of securities, the book-keeping entry clearing system was adopted in 1973. The KSSC functions as a central depository. This system mandates a securities company to open an account with the KSSC by depositing securities. Thereafter, the securities company can clear its transactions through book-keeping entries rather than through the physical delivery of certificates. Currently, all transactions of shares and bonds are cleared through this system, except in the case of the *Korea Fund* and the *Korea Europe Fund*.

If the *Korea Fund* places a bid, a broker physically delivers the purchased shares to the Citibank of Seoul, which currently acts as a sub-custodian bank to the *Korea Fund*. The same procedures are followed for the clearing of transactions by the *Korea Europe Fund*, except that a broker delivers the purchased shares to a custodian bank, the Bank of Seoul.

Transfer agent corporation

Any person who engages in registration of transfer shares as an agent shall be a stock corporation licensed by the MOF. A transfer agent corporation may engage in the business of paying dividends, interest, and redemption funds in connection with securities, and the business of issuing securities as an agent.

Reporting requirements

Any corporation offering its securities to the public through either a primary or secondary offering must file a registration statement with the SEC which is then made public. Once the registration statement becomes effective, the issuer must make a prospectus available. The prospectus must include a forecast of sales and earnings during the current year and the next two years.

Listed companies are required to file audited annual reports with the SEC and the KSE within 90 days after the end of the fiscal year. Unaudited semi-annual reports must be filed within 45 days of the end of the period. Both reports are made available to the public by the KSE. In addition, a summary of the income statement and balance sheet must be published in a major newspaper. Within 90 days of the end of the fiscal year, a shareholders' meeting must be held to discuss the results and declare dividends.

The audited annual reports must include an income statement, balance sheet, statement of appropriation of retained earnings, and a statement of changes in financial position. The semi-annual accounts do not have to include a statement of changes in financial position. To discourage fraud, the auditors are liable for any investment losses suffered if they are caused by misrepresentation of the accounts.

While the income statement and balance sheets can be more detailed than in the United States, the United Kingdom, or Japan, there are glaring weaknesses. Information on subsidiaries and affiliates is either scanty or non-existent. Current accounting standards recommend that companies that are more than 50% owned be consolidated into their parent, but this seldom occurs.

Moreover, it is practically impossible for an outsider independently to consolidate company accounts, since the parent company's financial statements rarely provide much financial information on affiliates; the affiliates themselves usually disclose little since they are typically unlisted companies. Furthermore, the 50% cutoff is inadequate and many business groups or individuals exercise tight control over companies with as little as a 15% holding through access to credit or group affiliation rather than by voting control.

Companies are required to make public through the SEC and KSE any event that has a material impact on the company. Certain events, such as the suspension of a bank account, the termination of a business operation, the dissolution of the company, and the filing of bankruptcy, must be reported immediately. However, companies have delayed disclosure by claiming that they are waiting for all the facts, and have not been penalised.

The Twenty Largest Stocks

The 20 largest quoted companies by market capitalisation and by turnover are shown in Tables 4.4 and 4.5 respectively, while the breakdown of market capitalisation is shown in Figure 4.5.

Table 4.4 The 20 Largest Quoted Stocks by Market Capitalisation, as at 31 December 1988

Company	Market Capitalisation (bn Won)	Price Range ('88) High	Low	Dividend (%)	PER
Lucky	4,800	24,800	15,000	12	15.4
POSCO	3,458	43,000	26,200	2	26.0
Hanil Bank	1,680	21,500	11,230	5	42.5
Bank of Seoul & Trust	1,558	20,500	11,000	4	58.6
Hyundai Eng. & Const.	1,280	32,500	13,290	10	53.4
Daewoo	1,271	31,800	13,810	10	41.2
Daewoo Securities	1,242	58,500	31,200	15	19.0
Goldstar	1,188	23,600	14,500	12	40.7
Samsung Elec.	1,116	38,600	28,800	18	11.4
Hyundai Motor	1,088	32,500	20,500	12	28.4
Yukong	1,085	38,000	25,000	15.8	19.8
Daishin Securities	990	53,800	29,000	15	21.5
Daewoo Elec.	756	22,700	12,650	10	37.4
Korean Air	696	30,700	16,500	12	20.8
Daewoo Heavy	608	23,000	12,060	8	80.1
Ssang Yong Cement	500	26,800	12,550	15	9.6
Han Yang Chemical	400	21,200	12,470	12	39.6
Kang Won Bank	280	30,300	16,500	7	31.5
Dong Ah Const. Ind.	266.6	32,000	13,600	10	51.5
Kolon	155	39,200	24,500	15	13.1

Source: Coryo Securities Corp.

There are a large number of active securities firms in Korea. Table 4.6 lists the largest brokers who publish research for international investors.

Brokerage Charges

Securities firms are free to establish their own commission rates. However, all brokers currently apply the same rates within the range of 0.3% to 0.5%, depending on total trading value.

For odd lots (less than ten shares), a 0.6% commission rate is applied to sales value.

Sales Value (unit: Won)	*Commission Rate*
Less 30 million	0.5%
30 million – 200 million	0.4% + 30,000
Over 200 million	0.3% + 230,000

The commission rate for bonds is 0.3% of trading value.

Table 4.5 The 20 Largest Quoted Stocks by Turnover, 1988

Company	Turnover (bn Won)
Daewoo	900
Bank of Seoul & Trust	419
POSCO	270
Goldstar	250
Daewoo Heavy	227
Daewoo Elec.	225
Hyundai Eng. & Const.	200
Lucky	193
Yukong	190
Dong Ah Const. Ind.	160
Hyundai Motor	140
Ssang Yong Cement	113
Daishin Securities	109
Samsung Elec.	101
Kang Won Bank	94
Han Yang Chemical	66
Daewoo Securities	58
Korean Air	54
Kong-A Pharm	38
Samsung	28

Source: Coryo Securities Corp.

Figure 4.5 Breakdown of Market Capitalisation by Sector, 1988

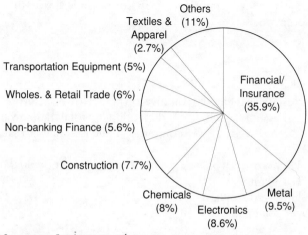

Source: Indosuez Asia Investment Services research.

Table 4.6 Principal Brokers

Securities Company	President	Cap. Stock (mn Won)	Telephone Number	Address of Main Office
Daehan	Chun-Sik Lee	20,000	785–1661	44–31, Youido-dong, Yongdungpo-gu, Seoul 150–010, Korea
Ssangyong	Byung-Woo Koh	60,000	771–12	198, 2-ga, Ulchiro, Chung-gu, Seoul 100–192, Korea
Hanshin	Suk-Nam Kong	30,000	784–3911 784–4911	44, Youido-dong, Yongdungpo-gu, Seoul 150–010, Korea
Daishin	Jae Bong Yang	66,000	784–1711/8	34-8, Youido-dong, Yongdungpo-gu, Seoul 150–010, Korea
Daewoo	Chang Hee Kim	76,050	784–8851	34-3, Youido-dong, Yongdungpo-gu, Seoul 150–010, Korea
Shinyoung	Byung Ryul Park	20,000	784–3701/10	34-8, Youido-dong, Yongdungpo-gu, Seoul 150–010, Korea
Korea	Kyu-Hong Um	15,300	785–4991	35–4, Youido-dong, Yongdungpo-gu, Seoul 150–010, Korea
Seoul	Hong-Yul Sul	20,000	785–1300	34–11, Youido-dong, Yondgungpo-gu, Seoul 100–021, Korea
Hanyang	Jae Hum Baik	20,000	785–2211	34–11, Youido-dong, Yongdungpo-gu, Seoul 150–010, Korea
Hanil	June Sik Choi	21,000	785–6611	34–10, Youido-dong, Yongdungpo-gu, Seoul 150–010, Korea
Kunsui	Hong Won Sohn	2,000	783–8541	43,Youido-dong, Yongdungpo-gu, Seoul 150–010, Korea
Lucky	Kun Joong Lee	63,000	784–7111	34–6, Youido-dong, Yongdungpo-gu, Seoul 150–010, Korea
Bookook	Jae Woo Lee	18,000	784–1010	34–2, Youido-dong, Yongdungpo-gu, Seoul 150–010, Korea
Shinhan	Chang-Ho Yim	21,050	777–1951/5	31–1, 2-ga, Myong-dong, Chung-gu, Seoul 100–022, Korea
Daeyu	Chang Mo Bae	21,000	782–7201/9	25–15, Youido-dong, Yongdungpo-gu, Seoul 150–010, Korea
Dongnam	Young Kyu Youn	21,000	783–5350/9	34, Youido-dong, Yongdungpo-gu Seoul 150–010, Korea
Hyundai	Nam-Chul Choi	45,000	757–6511	77, Mukyo-dong, Chung-gu, Seoul 100–170, Korea
Coryo	Hwa June Tohah	52,500	771–36	25–5, 1-ga, Chugmuro, Chung-gu, Seoul 100–011, Korea
Hanheung	Young Mo Ahn	27,200	757–1661	108, Da-dong, Chung-gu, Seoul 100–180, Korea
Dongsuh	In-Kie Hong	60,000	784–1211	34–1, Youido-dong, Yongdungpo-gu, Seoul 150–010, Korea
Korea First	Sang-Kuk Ahn	30,000	784–7233	44–11, Youido-dong, Yongdungpo-gu, Seoul 150–010, Korea
Shinheung	Dae Hyung Cho	8,000	776–8260/9	31–1, 2-ga, Myong-dong, Chung-gu, Seoul 150–011, Korea
Yuwha	Young Kyun Song	10,000	785–7951/60	35–2, Youido-dong, Yongdungpo-gu, Seoul 150–010, Korea
Tongyang	Dong-Woo Han	28,600	771–51	9–1, 2-ga, Yichiro, Chung-gu, Seoul 100–192, Korea
Dongbang	Yung-Moh Chung	30,000	553–2256/60	809–10, Yeoksam-dong, Kangnam-gu, Seoul 135–080, Korea

A transfer tax of 0.5% is levied on the total gross amount of each stock sale. Some transactions are exempt from the tax, such as when a securities investment trust sells stock, when the stock is trading below its par value, or when the stock is sold for a price below its initial offering price if sold within a year after the offering or before the record date of the first dividend after listing. The government increased the transfer tax in the spring of 1987 from 0.2% to 0.5% to cool off the market.

There are no stamp taxes or other charges.

Listing Criteria

Table 4.7 sets out the listing criteria for Korean stocks.

Table 4.7 Listing Criteria

Time since incorporation	Three years or more without suspension of business.
Capital stock	500 million Won or more.
Number of listed shares	50,000 shares or more.
Number of publicly offered shares	30% or more of the total outstanding shares. Must have performance of public offerings within six months prior to the date listing applied.
CPA's audit opinion	Either 'unqualified' or 'qualified'.
Debt ratio	Less than 500%, or less than 1.5 times the average of the same type of industry listed.
Return on paid-in capital	Equal to or exceeding time deposit interest rate during the latest two business years.
Capital impairment	No capital impairment during the latest business year
Valuation of equity	Asset value: exceeding 50% over par value.
Credit valuation	Profitability: higher than par value 60 points or more by KSDA standards.
Dishonour	No occurrence of dishonour during the previous one year.
Lawsuit	No pending lawsuit that affects management seriously.
Others	An applicant must not possess any reasons on which the exchange could see it as inappropriate for listing. Transfer contract between transfer agencies is required. Stock certificate must fit the standard size designated by the SEC.

When the Board of Directors of the Exchange decides to allow listing after the examination, it must be reported to the SEC for approval. When approval has been granted, the applicant company will be listed on the market upon conclusion of a listing agreement with the Exchange.

All companies are listed on the Second Section first. They can later move to the First Section if they satisfy certain requirements.

Listed companies are obligated to make disclosures revealing corporate information as required, in addition to regular reports.

The listing system is being improved to keep pace with the expansion of the securities industry

Table 4.8 Mutual Funds/Unit Trusts

	Korea International Trust	Korea Trust	Korea Growth Trust	Seoul International Trust	Seoul Trust
Date of Establish.	19 November 1981	29 November 1981	29 March 1985	19 April 1985	30 April 1985
Amount of Establishment	US$15mn (1.5mn units) *Additional tranche of US$10mn (16 Dec. 1983)	US$15mn (1mn units) *Additional tranche of US$10mn (12 Jan. 1984)	US$30mn (3mn units)	US$30mn (3mn units)	US$30mn units)
Objective	Long-term capital appreciation through investment in listed shares of Korean corporations.	Long-term capital appreciation through investment in listed shares of Korean corporations.	Long-term capital appreciation through investment in listed shares and bond markets of Korea.	Long-term capital appreciation through investment in listed shares and bond markets of Korea.	Long-term capital appreciation through investment in the securities and bond markets of Korea.
Type of Trust	An on-shore, contractual type open-end fund.	An on-shore, contractual type open-end fund.	An on-shore, contractual type open-end fund, listed on H.K. Stock Exchange	An on-shore, contractual type open-end fund.	An on-shore, contractual type open-end fund.
Basic Structure of Trust	*Investment mgr: Korea Investment Trust Co. Ltd *Trustee: Bank of Seoul and Trust Co. *Paying agent: Morgan Guaranty Trust Co. of London, Zurich and Frankfurt	*Investment mgr: Daehan Investment Trust Co. Ltd *Trustee: Bank of Seoul and Trust Co. *Paying agent: Citibank N.A.	*Investment mgr: Citizens Investment Trust Co. Ltd *Trustee: Bank of Seoul and Trust Co. *Paying agent: Morgan Guaranty Trust Co. of New York (Brussels)	*Investment mgr: Korea Investment Trust Co. Ltd *Trustee: Bank of Seoul and Trust Co. *Paying agent: Morgan Guaranty Trust Co. of New York (Brussels)	*Investment mgr: Daehan Investment Trust Co. Ltd *Trustee: Bank of Seoul and Trust Co. *Paying agent: Morgan Guaranty Trust Co. of New York (Brussels)
Lead Manager	Credit Suisse First Boston	Merrill Lynch International	Jardine Fleming (Securities) Ltd	Baring Brothers & Co. Ltd Vickers da Costa Ltd	Prudential-Bache Securities International
Life of Trust	Terminate in 2001	Unlimited	Terminate at the end of the accounting period on 31 March 2005	Terminate in the year 2005 unless extended.	Terminate at the end of the accounting period on 30 April 2005
Fund Size (US$mn)	251	198	207	216	204

and the internationalisation of securities companies. In October 1984, the *Commercial Code* was amended to grant listing of securities with pre-emptive rights, bonds with subscription warrant, and convertible bonds. The amendment also enabled the holding company and its subsidiary company to list shares without public offering of new issues, or outstanding securities in case either of them is listed, at the time of merger.

Mutual Funds/Unit Trusts

As the first step in the process of liberalisation, the Korean government authorised indirect investment prior to allowing direct securities investment by foreigners in the Korean capital market.

The Korea International Trust and the Korea Trust, both established in 1981, have posted remarkable performances. Additional trust funds established in 1985 were the Korea Growth Trust, the Seoul International Trust, and the Seoul Trust (see Table 4.8).

Rules for Foreign Investors

Foreign Investment Restrictions

Table 4.9 shows the proposed timetable for the opening of the Korean capital market, as published by the MOF in Seoul. This schedule should not be considered as precise and unalterable, however, since announced deadlines have frequently been postponed in the past.

Table 4.9 Capital Market Liberalisation Schedule

Year	Market Opening for Foreign Investors	Advance to the World Market (investment in the international market)
'89 Securities Market	Capital increase of existing funds for foreign investors (*Korea Fund*, etc). Free trade of converted stocks between foreigners in OTC markets. Expanding issuance of overseas securities (CB, BW, DR).	Establishment of overseas investment fund increases the range of domestic institutions participating in the international market.
Securities Industry	Increase the maximum equity stakes of foreign securities companies in domestic securities companies (one company 5% limit can be increased to 10%, total 10% limit can be increased to 40%). Additional establishment of foreign securities companies' branches in Korea.	Additional establishment of overseas branch offices of Korean securities companies. Allow Korean securities companies to expand international business.

Year	Market Opening for Foreign Investors	Advance to the World Market (investment in the international market)
'90 Securities Market	Establishment of *Matching Fund.*	Establishment of *Matching Fund*. Allow non-financial companies to invest in foreign markets.
'91 Securities Market	Allow foreigners to invest directly in Korean securities market. Foreign investors' reinvestment of their converted stocks into other Korean stocks.	
Securities Market	Allow foreign securities companies to establish their branches and joint-venture securities companies in Korea.	
'92 Securities Market	Expansion of foreigners' direct investment.	Allow all Korean individual investors to invest in foreign securities.

Foreign Exchange Control

Korean government approval is necessary for the offering and issue of bonds of a Korean company outside Korea and for the payment of principal, premium (if any), and interest to non-residents of Korea. The acquisition and sale of equity securities of Korean corporations by non-residents of Korea, and the repatriation of dividends and the proceeds of sale of such securities, also require approval of the Korean government.

Acting pursuant to his authority under the *Foreign Exchange Control Act* and related laws and regulations, the Minister of Finance has approved the offering and issue of bonds outside Korea on the terms and conditions set out therein. No further governmental approval is necessary for the subscription and issue of bonds in the primary market, or their sale and purchase in the secondary market, outside Korea or for the conversion of bonds into shares and delivery of the shares arising on conversion inside or outside Korea.

The payment of principal, premium (if any), and interest in respect of bonds in United States dollars outside Korea has been authorised in advance. The sole remaining approval must be obtained at the time of each actual payment from the company's designated Class A foreign exchange bank. The purpose of this approval is to ensure that the actual remittance is consistent with the terms of the approved transaction.

By virtue of the approval of the Minister of Finance for the issue of bonds, persons who have acquired shares as a result of the conversion of bonds may exercise their pre-emptive rights for new shares, participate in free share distributions, and receive dividends in shares without any further governmental approval. Under current law and regulations, a shareholder who is a non-resident of Korea does not require any governmental approval to transfer his shares to a resident of Korea, but may require approval to transfer them to another non-resident. It is a condition of the commencement of the conversion period that the necessity of obtaining any such approval (except when the transfer would cause any overall limit of general application on the percentage of the issued share capital of the company which may be owned by any particular non-resident to or by non-residents generally to be exceeded) should have been removed.

Dividends on shares will be paid in Won. No governmental approval is required for dividends, or the Won proceeds of the sale of shares, to be paid, received, and retained in Korea. Dividends paid on, and the Won proceeds from the sale of, shares held by a non-resident of Korea may be converted into a foreign currency and repatriated abroad subject to approval of a designated Class A foreign exchange bank in Korea. As before, the purpose of this approval is to ensure that the remittance is consistent with the approval given by the Minister of Finance. Any amount which is not repatriated must be deposited in a non-resident Won account and may be used for later repatriation abroad or for payment of the subscription price of new shares obtained through the exercise of pre-emptive rights.

The Minister of Finance may temporarily restrict the remittance of the proceeds of sale of shares by non-residents of Korea if he deems it necessary in the light of Korea's international balance of payments.

According to the current rules of the Korean SEC, no bond holder may exercise his conversion right if and to the extent that such exercise would result in any particular non-resident holding more than 3% of the shares of the company which were outstanding when the bonds were issued. If the result of a bond holder exercising his conversion right in full would be that his limitation was exceeded, the bond holder may have to convert his bonds by instalments, the shares resulting from conversion of the initial tranche of bonds being sold before further tranches are converted.

According to such rules, the company may not issue, or offer to non-residents, securities convertible into, or exchangeable for, or which carry rights to subscribe, shares amounting in the aggregate to more than 15% of the issued share capital of the company. The company will convenant in the trust deed not to issue any securities which would cause this limit to be exceeded. According to the current rules of the MOF, the percentage of the outstanding shares of the company (including shares which would be outstanding as a result of the conversion of convertible bonds, the exercise of warrants attached to bonds, and the exercise of pre-emptive right that may be held by non-residents generally, however they have acquired or may acquire their shares) is currently limited to 50%. The company will convenant in the trust deed to use its best efforts to maintain the ownership of its shares by non-residents at such a level that the conversion rights attaching to the bonds may at all times be exercised in full.

Taxation

Taxation of non-residents
The taxation of non-resident individuals and non-Korean corporations ('non-resident') depends on whether they have a 'permanent establishment' in Korea. Non-residents without permanent establishments are in general taxed at flat rates on their gross receipts from Korean sources. Non-residents with permanent establishments in Korea are taxed, like their Korean counterparts, at graduated rates on net income Korean sources.

The rate of income tax or corporation tax applicable to interest on bonds and dividends on shares for a non-resident without a permanent establishment in Korea is currently 25%. In addition, a tax surcharge called a residents' tax is imposed at the rate of 7 1/2% of the income or corporation tax (raising the total tax rate to 26 7/8%). Defence tax and education tax is not imposed with respect to non-residents without permanent establishments in Korea.

As the duty to withhold the tax is on the payer, Korean law does not entitle persons who have suffered the withholding of Korean tax to recover any part of the Korean tax withheld from the government, even if they subsequently produce evidence that they were entitled to have their tax withheld at a lower rate.

A non-resident without a permanent establishment in Korea is also subject to tax on his Korean source capital gains. Capital gains are taxed at the rate of 26 7/8% of the capital gain, or 10 3/4% of the gross realisation proceeds (before deduction of any allowance in respect of fiscal and sales charges), whichever is the lower.

Korean inheritance tax is imposed upon (a) all assets (wherever located) of the deceased if at the time of his death he was domiciled in Korea, and (b) all property located in Korea which passes on death (irrespective of the domicile of the deceased). Gift tax is imposed in similar circumstances to the above. The taxes are imposed if the value of the relevant property is above a certain limit, and vary according to the identity of the parties involved.

Under the Korean inheritance and gift tax laws, bonds and shares issued by Korean corporations are deemed to be located in Korea irrespective of where they are physically located or by whom they are owned.

The tax rates may be reduced by an applicable tax treaty, convention, or agreement between Korea and the country of the recipient of the interest, dividend, or capital gains. The relevant tax treaties are discussed below.

Tax on shares

Dividends, whether in cash or in shares, paid to a non-resident without a permanent establishment in Korea are subject to a withholding tax of 26 7/8%, unless reduced by an applicable tax treaty. Free distributions of shares representing a capitalisation of capital reserves are not subject to Korean withholding tax. A securities transaction tax of 1/5% is levied on sales proceeds from sales of shares in Korea (except where the share price is below par, in which case no tax is charged) and is payable by the seller.

Protection of Shareholders

Insider trading

As in the United States and Japan, insider trading is one of the chronic problems in Korea's securities market. Rumours about insider trading are abundant, but court decisions imposing civil or criminal liability for insider trading are extremely rare. Perhaps, buoyed in part by the recent surge of interest in insider trading in the United States and Japan, the securities authorities have strengthened the regulation of insider trading in the recent amendment to the SEL. Pursuant thereto, the SEC has carried out a series of investigations into rumoured incidents of insider trading and, as a consequence, a president of one listed company has been convicted.

The 1987 amendment to the SEL introduced a new insider trading provision into article 105, the general provision prohibiting unfair practices. Thus, in connection with any securities transaction, a person who has obtained non-public information on particular securities in the performance of his duty or by reason of his position in the corporation may not exploit, or have others exploit, the information. The exact reach of this provision will have to be determined hereafter by the courts. Any violation of this provision may give liability for damages.

Short-term profits

The SEL provides that directors, statutory auditors, employees, and major shareholders with not less than 10% of outstanding shares of a listed corporation or a registered corporation shall disgorge the profits gained from any purchase and sale transactions occurring within a six-month period through the use of non-public information obtained in the performance of one's duty or by reason of one's position in the corporation. The corporation itself, the SEC, or shareholders may enforce the insiders' obligation.

The SEL absolutely prohibits directors, statutory auditors, employees, and major shareholders of a listed corporation from effecting short sales of the shares of the corporation. Moreover, these insiders are required to file with the SEC and the KSE a report on their beneficial as well as direct shareholdings or any change thereof within ten days from the date when they become an insider or from the date of the change. Any insider who fails to meet this requirement is subject to criminal sanctions.

The control of insider trading is loose by Western standards, and there has been no criminal prosecution of an insider trading case in Korea. Current law makes it extremely difficult to prove insider trading since it has to be proved that the insider intended to misuse his privileged position, not just that he benefited from the misuse of nonpublic information. Moreover, the law exempts cases in which the security is held for more than six months.

Direct stock-market investments

In the past few years, foreign investors have been permitted only indirect stock investments through a handful of mutual funds such as the *Korea Fund*. But there has been wide recognition at home and abroad that the country cannot meet its development needs through borrowing alone, on which the government and the private sector have relied too heavily. Consequently, so as to respond to the new sources of funding at its highly leveraged conglomerates, the government decided to permit foreigners to invest directly in the Korean stock market by allowing its industrial giants to raise money on international bond markets through offerings convertible into stock. However, in the process of studying ways to allow foreigners to hold equity in Korean companies for the first time, the authorities became concerned over how to structure such investment, how much equity to allow, and the conditions the companies must meet to issue the instruments. To settle these problems, the MOF announced guidelines on 11 November 1985, which were adjusted on 27 July 1988 as follows:

*   Foreign investors will be allowed to hold up to a total of 15% of the paid-in capital of companies that issue convertible bonds. A single foreigner, however, will be allowed to hold only up to 3% of paid-in capital.
*   Bond-issuing companies must have assets of at least 50 billion Won.
*   Companies must meet certain rating criteria of Korean securities regulators.
*   The share price of potential issuers must exceed the weighted average share price of listed companies in the same industry.
*   Bonds may be converted into shares one and a half years after they are issued. But the government will be allowed to 'adjust' this period, a provision that could allow authorities to lengthen substantially the time a bond must be held before conversion to stock.

The MOF also announced guidelines for the issuance of depositary receipts, which will represent shares in Korean companies but will be traded elsewhere. Investors in Europe, for example, could buy and trade these receipts, but the stock they represent will be held by a trustee, either in Korea or elsewhere.

Companies issuing depositary receipts will face the same limitations on foreign ownership as convertible bond sellers. They also will have to meet the same requirements for assets and share prices.

The MOF also provided for exceptions. Companies that meet a certain test of internationally accredited rating agencies could waive the requirements.

An issue by Samsung Electronics Ltd opened the Euro-bond market to foreign investment in South Korean shares. In the equity linked market, investors took advantage of their first opportunity to buy direct stakes in South Korean companies, as Samsung found firm demand for its $20 million bond convertible into shares in 1985.

Overseas investors collectively can now hold as much as 15% of the market value of 14 large South Korean companies, while a single foreign investor's stake will be limited to 3%. Previously, foreign investment was confined to joint stakes, as in mutual funds.

In 1986, Daewoo Heavy Industries, the heavy engineering subsidiary of Daewoo, the Korean conglomerate, successfully completed its CB flotation (US$40 million), resulting in a great contribution to the internationalisation of the Korean securities market. Investors' expectations of a sharp appreciation in the Korean stock market were reflected in the bond's terms. The indicated conversion premium on the shares was set at 50%, a much higher level than is usual in the convertible market. The indicated coupon is 3% and the issue price par. The bond may be called from 1990 at 104% and then at declining premiums.

Yukong Ltd, the biggest oil refiner in South Korea, followed Daewoo Heavy Industries and designated Goldman Sachs International Corporation as the lead manager for its issuance in July 1986 of US$20 million of convertible bonds. Daiwa Securities Co. of Japan and SS Sangyong Investment and Securities Co. were named co-lead managers. Yukong supplies about 20% of South Korea's total energy requirements and is the third South Korean company to issue convertible bonds in the Euro-bond market.

Funds raised through the offering were supposed to be used for the company's overseas oil explorations in the Marib area, North Yemen, and in the Sudan . Bonds bear a 3% annual interest rate and the conversion price may be 160–170% of the average closing price of Yukong shares during a one-week period prior to the offering date.

In August 1987, Goldstar completed its CB flotation (US$30 million) as Korea's fourth CB issuer abroad. Foreign investment in Korean securities amounts to US$385 million at present.

During 1987, only one company, Goldstar, was allowed to float convertible bonds abroad because excessive money flowing into the nation due to the current account surplus caused havoc with monetary management.

5

HONG KONG

Introduction

Hong Kong is the only truly international city in Asia. It is the point where China meets the world, and where many Westerners first encounter Asia. Although the population is 98% Chinese, there are large communities of Indians, Filipinos, Americans, British, Australians, and many other nationalities.

With its low taxes (15%) and minimal government regulation, Hong Kong offers unique advantages as an international business centre. Although local labour costs and rents have risen steeply in recent years, Hong Kong still offers more convenience to Western-based multinationals than any other Asian city.

A large part of Hong Kong's trading activity is concerned with the People's Republic of China. As the only deepwater port on the coast of China and as the largest container port in the world, Hong Kong has unrivalled facilities for transshipment and re-export of China-made goods. In addition, it has a large and prosperous banking sector, dominated by The Hongkong and Shanghai Banking Corporation, as well as insurance and legal services, fund management, broking, and consultancy.

The Hong Kong stock market also reflects financial and trading activities, but a large part of its US$50 billion capitalisation is accounted for by the property sector, since real estate has been the most common source of wealth for Hong Kong investors. In addition, there are three listed utilities and a number of smaller manufacturing stocks.

In a sense, Hong Kong is China's capital market (see also Chapter 16). An investment in Hong Kong is an investment in China, and in its economic and political future. This provides both high rewards, and high risks, for international investors in the Hong Kong share market.

Historical Background

In Hong Kong, trading in equities began in 1866, a year after the first *Companies Ordinance* was passed. In 1891, the Association of Stockbrokers in Hong Kong, the first formal stock market in Hong Kong, was formed, changing its name to the Hong Kong Stock Exchange in 1914. A second exchange, the Hong Kong Sharebrokers' Association, was established in 1921 to give wider membership. In 1947, these two exchanges were merged to form a joint exchange under the name of the Hong Kong Stock Exchange Limited.

Note: US$1.00 = HK$7.8.

Figure 5.1   Hang Seng Index, 1966–1989

Figure 5.2   Hong Kong Dollar vs US Dollar, Weekly, 1982–1989

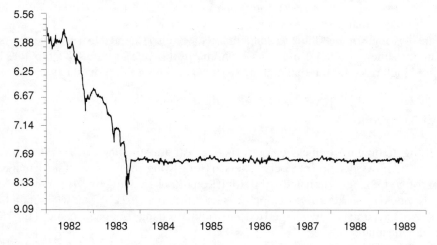

Source: Datastream.

The period from 1866, when equity trading began, to 1947, when the Hong Kong Stock Exchange (HKSE) was formed, was not one of marked economic growth for Hong Kong. The stockbroking industry, still operating under the shadow of Shanghai, saw little expansion, and a stock exchange with relatively few listings was adequate for its needs up until 1949. Bank lending continued to be the main source of finance for corporations, and in 1962 the HKSE still listed only 65 companies.

However, financial confidence in Hong Kong began to increase after 1968, when it became clear that the excesses of the Cultural Revolution would not affect the territory. The ensuing growth in the economy produced major changes in equity trading as the stock market became a more important source of finance for local industry, and an increasing number of privately owned companies decided to go public. Business on the stock market increased steadily. In 1965, average monthly turnover on the HKSE was US$4.1 million (HK$32 million). By 1969, this figure had increased to US$27.2 million (HK$212 million) and there were now 73 companies listed on the Exchange.

In 1969, the first London overseas member was admitted to the Exchange. An even more significant development that year was the opening of the Far East Exchange, which commenced business on 17 December. This had a dramatic effect on trading which had previously been conducted in Cantonese and was thereafter more international in character. Listings increased in number and became fairly easy to obtain.

With the amendation of the *Companies Ordinance* in February 1979, the Governor in Council was empowered to recognise stock exchanges for certain limited purposes connected with the offering in writing of shares to any member of the public. Many local businessmen became stockbrokers. Stocks were priced at levels attractive to ordinary investors, and stock exchange activity became a matter of interest to the man in the street.

On 15 March 1971, the Kam Ngan Stock Exchange commenced business, and on 5 January of the following year, the Kowloon Stock Exchange Limited began trading, signifying the continued growth of the stockbroking industry. It would have been impossible for any other territory in the world as small as Hong Kong, with a population of only 5.7 million, to have possessed four stock exchanges, as the colony did until 1986.

The First Crash, 1973–1974

The expansion of the stock exchange brought its problems. In the early 1970s, the stockbroking industry was far removed from the professionalism of today, and it became apparent that it lacked the expertise and sophistication to meet the new demands made upon it.

Housewives, amahs, and hawkers packed the public gallery of the stock exchanges, known as goldfish tanks. Listing rules were so loose that new listings came to the market every week and their shares were snapped up indiscriminately. Research on listed companies was totally inadequate, a situation which was exploited by market manipulators, and frauds were not uncommon. Forged scrips, or share certificates, also made their appearance about that time.

In the run up to the crash of 1973, research was regarded as superfluous since fundamentals were ignored — shares were trading at 100 times earnings.

With effect from 8 January 1973, the four stock exchanges, the Far East Exchange, the Hong Kong Stock Exchange, the Kam Ngan Stock Exchange, and the Kowloon Stock Exchange agreed to standardise their trading sessions. Their membership now totalled more than 1,000 brokers. Trading was buoyant, and in March of that year, the Hang Seng Index reached a record high of 1,775 points, a point not reached again until July 1981.

The Stock Exchange, however, was completely unprepared for the crash which followed in

March 1973. The Hang Seng Index plummeted, and by December stood at 437 points. It continued to fall, and in December 1974 reached a low of 150 points, a fall of over 90% from its peak.

The crash was a painful lesson for both the industry and the public. As the public began to demand more information before they would make an investment, research became an important part of any stockbroking business.

Up until 1973, only one Chinese financial newspaper was available to the public, and the *South China Morning Post* was one of the few newspapers with a business page. Financial news was carried by local Chinese newspapers in the main news section. However, by the late 1970s, the demand for economic and business news was such that all the four major Chinese newspapers — *Sing Tao Jih Pao, Ming Pao, Sing Pao,* and the *Oriental Daily* — had a financial page. Now whole sections spanning two to four pages were devoted to economic and business news. Besides the *Hong Kong Economic Journal*, the fledgeling *Hong Kong Economic Times* was also devoted to servicing the financial sector. Even the government-run television station, RTHK, started to run a financial programme once a week reflecting public interest.

Following the crash, a series of measures were taken to control the Stock Exchange and to protect shareholders. In early 1973, a Commissioner for Securities had been appointed to head a Securities Advisory Council. Although the Council had no statutory power, it was set up to help prepare the way for statutory provisions to be imposed later.

Progress Towards Stock Exchange Unification

In February 1973, the establishment of stock exchanges was effectively controlled with the enactment of the *Stock Exchange Control Ordinance*. The Ordinance imposed heavy penalties on anyone operating a stock market which was not recognised under the Ordinance, and the government announced that it was mandatory for all companies seeking listing to have their prospectuses registered with the Registrar of Companies. It now became apparent that more wide-reaching measures were necessary.

In October 1974, Part VI of the *Securities Ordinance* and the *Securities (Dealers, Investment Advisers and Representatives) Regulations 1974* were brought into force, requiring all dealers (whether or not they are members of the stock exchanges), investment advisers, and their representatives, to register with the Commissioner for Securities.

During 1975 and 1976, continued steps were taken to formalise stockbroking procedures, and in August 1975 the Securities Commission approved the *Code on Takeovers and Mergers* for Hong Kong. In December of the same year, the Securities Commission also approved a statutory rule prohibiting directors of a listed company incorporated in Hong Kong from issuing shares — other than on a pro-rata basis to existing shareholders — without the prior approval of shareholders. Also, under the *Securities (Stock Exchange Listing) Rules 1976* (August), a listed company should appoint a member of the Federation of Share Registrars to be its registrar.

As has been mentioned, the four stock exchanges had standardised their trading sessions in 1973, and a year later they formed a consultative body, the Hong Kong Federation of Stock Exchanges. Now, in May 1977, considerable progress was made towards the formation of a unified stock exchange in Hong Kong in place of the existing four. A working party was established by the government, under the chairmanship of the Commissioner for Securities, to study the question of unification. As a result of that working party's investigations, and discussions with all four stock exchanges, a bill was drafted to provide for unification, which would not come into effect until 1980. Prior to that act of unification, many other changes were made in the Hong Kong Stock Exchange.

These changes included the setting up of an Insider Dealing Tribunal in December 1977 and the reduction of stamp duty on securities dealing from 0.8% to 0.6% with effect from 6 March 1978.

The formation of the first 22-member Council of the Exchange in October 1979, together with the first Nominating Committee of the Exchange on 7 November, signified the Exchange's move towards greater maturity. The admission of the more professional overseas stockbrokers as full members helped to speed up the process. In 1979, notwithstanding strong opposition among local brokers to the admission of overseas members as full members, the Far East Exchange had admitted a representative of a Canadian stockbroker as a full member, and in 1980, the local director of Vickers da Costa (an overseas member of the Hong Kong Exchange) was admitted as a full member of the Far East Exchange. Full membership soon followed for those overseas members of the Hong Kong and Kam Ngan Stock Exchanges who desired it. By 1983, several members of the exchanges were connected with banking interests in Hong Kong and overseas.

Thus, well before the time of unification, the four stock exchanges were composed of a variety of members, ranging from the locally based sole trader members (representing the vast majority of the membership in volume) to large domestic broking firms, overseas members, and members connected with banks.

Despite the enactment of many new measures, and the inclusion of overseas members, the trading volumes on the exchanges did not revive significantly. It became a widely held view that only unification of the four exchanges could raise trading volumes and boost confidence in the stock market.

The Stock Exchange of Hong Kong Limited was incorporated on 7 July 1980, and on 31 March 1981 it was recognised by the Securities Commission as the Exchange Company, for the purposes of the unification. In October 1981, the first committee members of the Stock Exchange of Hong Kong Limited were elected.

The Securities Commission in January 1981 adopted a trigger point of 35% as the maximum percentage shareholding in a listed company that any group or individual could hold without making a general offer for all the remaining shares. There was a creeper clause which allowed anyone currently holding between 35% and 50% to increase their shareholdings by not more than 3% in any 12-month period without making a general offer for all the remaining shares.

The Second Crash, 1981–1982

In spite of the new legislation and unification of the four exchanges, trouble hit the stock market again in 1981, when the property crash coincided with a further steep decline in the stock market. The year was characterised by the famous *Carrian* case which became the most expensive case in the legal history of Hong Kong in respect of the widespread consequences and the number of people involved. It is difficult to ascertain whether Carrian's demise brought about the stock market crash in the early 1980s or vice versa. It is probably fair to say that the uncertainty regarding the political future of Hong Kong after 1997, and the Sino–British negotiations, aggravated the situation. (The rapid decline of the overheated property market was also a major factor.)

The 1982 visit of Mrs Thatcher to China provoked a further crisis of confidence in 1983, when the Hong Kong dollar crashed from 5.6 to 9.6 to the US dollar in a matter of months and the Hang Seng Index fell to 750.

After the collapse of the Exchange following the *Carrian* case, further controls were implemented. The *Code on Takeovers and Mergers* was revised in March 1983 to the effect that bids involving less than 35% of a company's voting shares were not subject to control, but other partial bids were subject to the consent of the Takeovers Committee.

1986: The New Unified Exchange

The year 1986 was a memorable one for the Hong Kong stock market, both at home and internationally. In that year, the four exchanges were finally unified into the new Hong Kong Stock Exchange in its smart, technologically equipped new premises in Exchange Square (one of the most modern office complexes in Asia).

Although the unification of the four exchanges had been recognised as far back as March 1981, it was not until 27 March 1986 that they finally ceased trading as the Hong Kong Stock Exchange, the Far East Exchange, the Kam Ngan Stock Exchange, and the Kowloon Stock Exchange, at the close of business on that day. With effect from 2 April 1986, the Stock Exchange of Hong Kong Limited commenced trading, and had the exclusive right to establish, operate, and maintain a stock market (the 'Stock Exchange') in Hong Kong. On the same day, the Hong Kong Index was inaugurated, and set at 1,000. There were 45 constituent stocks.

On 22 September 1986, the Exchange became a full member of the Federation Internationale des Bourses de Valeurs (FIBC), the international federation of stock exchanges which promotes closer collaboration between stock exchanges.

The official opening of the Stock Exchange of Hong Kong took place on 6 October 1986. The growth of the unified exchange can be seen in Table 5.1, with the dramatic increase in both daily trading volume and total market value. However, the number of companies listed grew more slowly, both as a result of political uncertainty over Hong Kong's future, and also because few of the smaller manufacturing companies performed well. Nonetheless, two or three major companies came into the market, among them Hong Kong Telecommunications with the largest quoted stock, and Cathay Pacific, in May 1986.

The Great Crash of October 1987

In the four years from 1983 to 1987, the Index had risen to a peak of nearly 4,000 by October 1987. Reaching a new historical high, the Hang Seng Index closed at 3,949.73 on 1 October, while the Hong Kong Index closed at 2,614.18 on 5 October. The value of turnover on 2 October also reached a new high of HK$5.4 billion (approximately US$700 million) before collapsing in a more spectacular fashion than any other world stock market. The market fell 12% on Monday, 19 October, as the Hang Seng Index and the Hong Kong Index plunged 420.81 and 293.36 respectively, and world stock markets started to crash. Following Wall Street's steep decline, which took place, owing to the 12-hour time difference, at night, it was unanimously resolved at 4 am by the then Chairman of the Stock Exchange, Ronald Li, and the General Committee of the Stock Exchange of Hong Kong, with the agreement of the Financial Secretary, Piers Jacobs, to close the Stock Exchange for the next four days from 20 to 23 October. Trading was also suspended in Hang Seng Index Futures for the same period.

This controversial decision did not avert disaster, however: the following Monday, 26 October, the market reopened and the greatest one-day fall was recorded. The Hang Seng Index lost 1,120.70, representing a 33.33% decrease, and the Hong Kong Index lost 739.22, representing a 33.41% decrease, in a single trading session.

The Hong Kong Government, together with several leading financial institutions, raised a rescue fund of HK$4,000 million to enable the Hong Kong Futures Guarantee Corporation Limited to finance its obligations to members of the Futures Exchange. With effect from 29 October 1987, a levy of HK$30 per Futures Exchange transaction and a special levy of 0.03% on transaction value of securities dealings were collected to repay the interest and principal of the rescue package.

Mr Ray Astin, Chairman of the Takeovers Committee, announced on 26 October that the Committee had decided that for a period of one month, the trigger point, or creeper provision, under the Hong Kong *Code on Takeovers and Mergers*, would be waived.

The limit of compensation payable out of the Exchange Fidelity Fund, or a member's guarantee for the default of a defaulting member, would be increased from HK$500,000 to HK$2,000,000, subject to the availability of funds, with effect from the commencement of trading on 9 November.

Following these events, a thorough reorganisation of the Hong Kong Stock Exchange was undertaken, with special attention to the Futures Exchange, and the Securities Review Committee was established on 16 November.

A new Securities and Exchange Commission was set up under Mr Robert Owen. The market had completely recovered within a year, and international investors returned to buying Hong Kong shares without much concern. Today, the Hong Kong market is now as well regulated as any Western market.

The China Crisis, June 1989

Despite the effectiveness of all these new regulations and the restoration of Hong Kong's reputation for clean and efficient dealing, the stock market was to suffer yet another bout of volatility following the eruption of student demonstrations in Peking in May 1989. At first, observers in Hong Kong were optimistic about the outcome, as it appeared that the chances for more liberal and democratic reforms in China were good.

These hopes were rudely shattered, first by the declaration of Martial Law on 15 May when shares fell by 20%. Two weeks later, on 4 June, the Tiananmen massacre deeply shocked an already emotional Hong Kong populace, and the Hang Seng Index fell a further 20% to reach a low of 2,100, compared to nearly 3,300 in early May. In the weeks and months that followed, confidence slowly returned, despite the sombre political mood, as it appeared that some shares in the market, such as utilities, had become unreasonably cheap. Judging by the 20-year history of the Hong Kong market, one of its main features has been not only volatility, but also a sturdy resilience in the face of recurrent crisis.

It is surprising to many visitors to find that there is no noise, no bustle, no apparent movement at all on the floor of the Exchange. All is silent, efficient, computerised: brokers sit quietly at their terminals and feed in buy-and-sell orders to the central console. A large electronic flashboard gives minute-by-minute the movements of the Hang Seng Index (which has historically been one of the most volatile indices in the world, as a glance at the 20-year chart will reveal). Hopefully, under the influence of the new regulations, it has not lost the fast-moving pace which has always made it an exciting and rewarding place to invest.

Stock Market Performance

Exchange Rate

The Hong Kong dollar is pegged to the US dollar at 7.8. On 31 December 1988, the prime leading rate was 10%. Because of the peg, it follows the trend in the United States.

Table 5.1 Stock Market Performance, 1985–1988 (year end)

Market Indicator	1985	1986	1987	1988
Market Index (HSI)	1,752.45	2,568.3	2,302.75	2,687.44
Growth (%)	45.99	46.55	–10.3	16.7
Listed Companies	279	253	276	304
Total Market Value (US$mn)	34,553	53,754	53,796	74,407
Average Daily Trading Volume (US$mn)	39	64	194	103
Year-end PER	16.53	19.04	12.15	12.51
Market Capitalisation/GNP (%)	103	139	114	136
Dividend Yield (%)	3.5	2.92	4.44	4.5

Source: Indosuez Asia Investment Services research.

Stock Exchange Details

Address

The Stock Exchange of Hong Kong Limited
Main Floor
One and Two Exchange Square
8 Connaught Place
Central
Hong Kong
Tel: 5-221122
Telex: 86839 STOEX HX
Fax: 5-8104475

Trading Days/Hours

The trading hours of the HKSE are from 10 am to 12.30 pm and 2.30 to 3.30 pm, Monday to Friday.

Settlement

Settlement on the HKSE is made on a 24-hour basis. Share certificates in board lots, together with attached transfer deeds, must be delivered on the day following the transaction. Payment is due against delivery. For overseas institutions it is essential to have stocks registered in the nominee companies of local banks and, when purchasing, for payment to be authorised against advice of execution. Similarly, it is essential for stocks to be physically available for delivery in board lots when selling, and for the client to telex release instructions to his bank immediately upon advice of execution. The buying broker can, and will, 'buy-in', unless this procedure is observed rigorously.

The Twenty Largest Stocks

For many years, the Hongkong and Shanghai Banking Corporation was the largest quoted company on the stock exchange, with over 15% of market capitalisation. The total finance sector now accounts for only about 11% of the market (Table 5.2). However, since 1987, when Cable and Wireless listed the local telephone company, Hong Kong Telecommunications, this new utility stock represents almost 10% of the market (see Table 5.3). The old *hongs*, or trading houses — Jardine Matheson, Swire, and Hutchisons — are also still important and active counters. The most important point for overseas investors to comprehend is the visible (and often invisible) influence of the property market on the stock market. Property visibly accounts for around 40% of listed shares, but much of the banks' lending is in the form of mortgages, and many trading and manufacturing houses make a large part of their profits from real estate.

Table 5.2 The Hong Kong Market by Sector

Classification	Turnover (HK$mn)	% of Total
Finance	19,808.27	10.74
Utilities	14,015.06	7.60
Properties	71,960.45	39.03
Consolidated Enterprises	50,245.50	27.26
Industrials	20,722.26	11.24
Hotels	7,344.86	3.99
Others	255.34	0.14
Total	184,351.74	100.00

Source: Hong Kong Stock Exchange
Note: Turnover in warrants, debt securities, and unit trusts is not included.

Table 5.3 The 20 Largest Quoted Stocks by Market Capitalisation, as at 31 December 1988

Company	Market Cap. (HK$mn)	% of Market Total
Hong Kong Telecommunications	53,154.64	9.16
Hongkong Bank	33,541.35	5.78
Swire Pacific	28,390.19	4.89
Cathay Pacific Airways	26,639.96	4.59
Hutchison Whampoa	26,029.12	4.49
Hong Kong Land	23,354.68	4.03
Hang Seng Bank	19,810.27	3.41
China Light	18,800.64	3.24
Sun Hung Kai Properties	18,650.70	3.21

Company	Market Cap. (HK$mn)	% of Market Total
Cheung Kong (Holdings)	17,690.33	3.05
New World Development	15,633.31	2.69
Wharf (Holdings)	15,163.97	2.61
Hong Kong Electric	12,849.70	2.22
Cavendish International	9,204.28	1.59
Jardine Matheson Holdings	9,072.60	1.56
World International (Holdings)	8,962.22	1.54
Henderson Land	8,698.14	1.50
Dairy Farm International	7,783.07	1.34
Hong Kong & China Gas	7,673.50	1.32
New Town (NT) Properties	7,660.32	1.32
Total	368,762.99	63.54
Market Total	580.378.02	100.00

Source: Hong Kong Stock Exchange.

Major Types of Investors

It is very difficult to get a precise idea of share ownership in Hong Kong, owing to the nominee system, but the breakdown in Table 5.4 represents a fair estimate as agreed by well-informed observers. There is about US$50 billion funds under management in Hong Kong, and while this is not all invested in local equities, it is partially included in local institutions and local syndicates. Despite the influence of large local investors, the Hong Kong market is certainly more open to international investors than any other Asian market.

Table 5.4   Estimated Share Ownership, 1988

Investors	Breakdown (%)
Locally managed institutions	30
Foreign managed institutions	30
Local syndicates and individuals	20
South-East Asian investors (variable)	10
China-related organisations	10
Total	100

Source: Indosuez Asia Investment Services research.
Notes
1.   No official breakdown or estimate of different investor type.
2.   Widespread use of nominees makes task virtually impossible.
3.   Since 19 October, investor mix has changed as activity by foreign managed institutions has eased. Prior to that date, foreign managed institutions may have accounted for over 50% of activity.

Dealing Costs

Brokerage/Stamp Duty

The following brokerages and fees are applied to each securities transaction:

Brokerage
Stockbrokers should charge a brokerage of not less than 0.25% and not more than 1% of the value of the transaction to either a buyer or a seller. The minimum charge for brokerage is HK$25.

Ad valorem stamp duty
An *ad valorem* stamp duty is levied on each transaction at the ratio of HK$3 for every HK$1,000 or any part thereof on the value of the transaction, on both the buyer and the seller.

Transaction levy
The HKSE charges a transaction levy of 0.025% on the value of the transaction, payable by both the buyer and the seller.

Special levy
In addition to the transaction levy, a special levy of 0.03% of the amount of the consideration for each purchase or sale of securities recorded on the Exchange is payable by both the buyer and seller to the HKSE.

Transfer deed stamp duty
Independent of the quantity of shares traded, the government levies a transfer deed stamp duty of HK$5, payable by the registered holder of the pertaining share certificate(s), ie the seller, on each new transfer deed.

Transfer fee
Independent of the quantity of shares traded, the registrar of each listed company levies a transfer fee of HK$2 per board lot of shares from the registered holder, ie the buyer, for each new certificate issued.

Major Securities Houses

There are nearly 1,000 members of the Hong Kong Stock Exchange, of whom about 600 are active traders. The list below includes only the largest brokerage houses, mainly international firms with a good research product.

Baring Securities (Hong Kong) Limited
8th Floor, Three Exchange Square
8 Connaught Place
Hong Kong
Tel: 5-214192
Tlx: 89271
Fax: 5-295730

James Capel (Far East) Limited
39th Floor, Two Exchange Square
Central
Hong Kong
Tel: 5-8439111
Tlx: 75100
Fax: 5-202945

W.I. Carr (Far East) Limited
21st Floor, St George's Building
2 Ice House Street
Central
Hong Kong
Tel: 5-255361
Tlx: 73036
Fax: 5-8681524

Cazenove & Co. (Overseas)
Suite 3601, Two Exchange Square
Central
Hong Kong
Tel: 5-261211
Tlx: 74355

Barclays de Zoete Wedd (Asia) Limited
15th Floor, Alexandra House
Central
Hong Kong
Tel: 5-8415148
Tlx: 62422
Fax: 5-8680092

Jardine Fleming Securities Ltd
46th Floor, Jardine House
Central
Hong Kong
Tel: 5-8438888
Tlx: 85608
Fax: 5-8105411

Schroder Asia Securities (HK)
26th Floor, Two Exchange Square
Central
Hong Kong
Tel: 5-211636
Tlx: 75682
Fax: 5-8681023

Sun Hung Kai Securities Limited
3rd Floor, Admiralty Centre
18 Harcourt Road
Wanchai
Hong Kong
Tel: 5-8225621
Tlx: 74782
Fax: 5-8225664

Smith New Court Far East Limited
30th Floor, One Exchange Square
Central
Hong Kong
Tel: 5-8190338
Tlx: 81678
Fax: 5-8101042

S.G. Warburg Securities Far East Limited
20th Floor, Alexandra House
Central
Hong Kong
Tel: 5-246113
Tlx: 83495
Fax: 5-296316

Peregrine Securities Limited
16th Floor, New World Tower
18 Queen's Road Central
Hong Kong
Tel: 5-8456111
Tlx: 69251
Fax: 5-8459411

Citicorp Scimgeour Vickers (Hong Kong) Limited
43rd Floor, One Exchange Square
8 Connaught Place
Central
Hong Kong
Tel: 5-8435777
Tlx: 74562
Fax: 5-8459304

Mutual Funds/Unit Trusts

Mutual funds and unit trusts open to international investors are listed in Table 5.5.

Table 5.5 Hong Kong Unit Trusts Registered with the Securities Commission

Baring Hong Kong Fund
CEF Hong Kong Trust
Citicorp CI Hong Kong Equity
Colonial Securities Hong Kong Fund
Dao Heng Hong Kong Fund
G.T. Hong Kong Fund
GAM Hong Kong Inc.
Gartmore Hong Kong Fund
JF Hong Kong Trust
Mansion House HK Trust
NM Hong Kong Fund
NM Portfolio Selection Hong Kong Fund
Old Court Hong Kong Fund
Schroders Asia Hong Kong Fund
SHK Hong Kong Equity Fund
Thornton Hong Kong & China Gateway Fund
Wardley Global Selection HK Equity

Source: Hong Kong Unit Trust Association.

Listing Criteria

Before a listing can be obtained, the company must comply with the *Securities (Stock Exchange Listing) Rules 1986* ('the Statutory Rules') and the relevant provision of the *Companies Ordinance.* The *Exchange Listing Rules*, the *Statutory Rules*, and the provision of the *Companies Ordinance* should be read and considered together as constituting the requirements to be observed by public companies seeking or having access to the securities market of Hong Kong.

Application for listing shall be approved by the Listing Committee of the Exchange at its absolute discretion.

General regulations regarding the initial listing of securities are as follows:

1. A company applying for listing must be a public company and must continue to be a public company to remain listed.
2. There must be sufficient public interest in the subject matter of the business of the company or group.
3. The application for listing must be sponsored by a member of the Exchange.
4. All information to be released before listing must be approved by the Listing Department.
5. An initial listing fee of HK$100,000 must be paid by companies applying for listing. Monthly listing fees are payable by companies already listed in accordance with the prescribed scale. The criteria for securities listing are as follows:

1. The usual minimum initial aggregate market capitalisation for securities to be listed is HK$50 million.
2. In general, a minimum of 25% of any securities intended to be listed should be in the hands of the public. Such securities refer to the issued portion of the subject securities.
3. The company applying for listing of its securities must have a trading record of adequate duration.
4. Normally, no more than 10% of the securities to be offered may be offered to employees and past-employees of the company or its subsidiaries.
5. Accounts to be delivered should be made up to a statutory and accounting standard acceptable to the Listing Committee and be audited by a qualified auditor.

Rules for Foreign Investors

There are no restrictions on foreign portfolio investment in Hong Kong, nor are there limitations regarding ownership of domestic securities by foreigners. Several of the major Hong Kong quoted companies have listings on exchanges outside Hong Kong.

Foreign Exchange Control

There are no exchange control regulations operating in Hong Kong and investors have total flexibility in the movement of capital and the repatriation of profits. Funds invested in Hong Kong can be repatriated at will; dividends and interest are freely remittable.

Taxation

The standard flat rate of individual income tax is 15%, while corporate income is taxed at 16%.

Dividends are regarded as having been paid out of taxed profits and are thus not subject to further taxation. In particular, there are no Hong Kong taxes imposed on foreign shareholders receiving Hong Kong dividends and there are no withholding taxes on dividends paid by Hong Kong companies. There is no tax on capital gains.

Hong Kong has not entered into any double taxation agreements with other countries because only income arising in, or derived from, Hong Kong is subject to Hong Kong tax. There is provision for partial double tax relief for income which has been taxed in another Commonwealth country, providing the legislation in the other country also provides for similar relief. The United Kingdom is not regarded as a Commonwealth country for this purpose.

The absence of double taxation agreements means that any non-resident investor investing through Hong Kong would suffer withholding tax on dividends from foreign equities, certain fixed-interest securities, and certain bank deposits.

Investment in Hong Kong securities is not subject to withholding tax, capital gains tax, or income tax.

Available Research

Memorandum and Articles of Association
Member List
Rules of the Exchange
Rules Governing the Official Listing of Securities
List of Stock Code
The Weekly Report (Annually)
The Securities Bulletin (Monthly)
The Securities Bulletin (Annually)
Monthly Market Statistics
Market Summary (Quarterly)
All Sales Record (Quarterly)
Market Summary and All Sales Record (Quarterly)
Fact Sheet (Quarterly)
Fact Book (Annually)
Companies Handbook

6

SINGAPORE

Introduction

Singapore is a paradox. To the visitor it appears a perfectly organised, modern, technocratic city-state. Its 2.6 million people inhabit an island of only 620 sq km. Yet beneath the smooth façade lie the origins of the freewheeling port founded in 1819 by a buccaneering but visionary Englishman, Sir Stamford Raffles. To this free port flocked Malays, Indians, Jews, Britons, and, above all, Chinese settlers from the southern Chinese provinces of Fujian and Guangdong. They formed the backbone of a population that is today 77% Chinese, 15% Malay, and 6% Indian. Singapore is still today, as at its foundation, a melting pot and a natural trading centre for the surrounding nations, especially Indonesia and Malaysia, whose wealth is based on oil, rubber and palm oil plantations, and property and trading interests.

The Singapore stock market presents a true reflection of the city. Open to international investors, its smooth, efficient organisation is dominated by a small number of powerful Chinese groups. Dominant in the capitalisation of the market are the bankers — OCBC, UOB, OUB, and DBS — which also have brokerage subsidiaries. The rubber plantations are less important than in the old days, but are still represented through joint listings of major Malaysian conglomerates such as Sime Darby. Of the 317 companies listed on the Stock Exchange of Singapore, 183 are Malaysian incorporated entities which make up 50% of the market's total capitalisation.

The twin listing of Singaporean and Malaysian entities on each other's exchanges dates back to the 1930s when the two British colonies operated a joint exchange. That arrangement came to an end in 1973, but the problems and varying ambitions of one can still spill over on to the other. In 1986, for example, the collapse of the Singapore-incorporated Pan-Electric Industries listed on both exchanges pushed Kuala Lumpur to follow Singapore's example and impose an unprecedented three-day cessation in trading. In late 1986, another cloud appeared on the horizon when the MAS described the exchange system of fixed brokerage commissions as 'anachronistic' and called instead for the negotiated fees more befitting an international financial centre. With government appointees outnumbering brokers on the committee which runs the Singapore Stock Exchange, the proposal seems likely to be implemented eventually. Many Malaysian brokers, however, are against adopting such arrangements, and failure to obtain their compliance would mean the delisting of Malaysian stocks on the Singapore Stock Exchange.

Note: US$1.00 = S$1.97.

Figure 6.1 Straits Times Industrial Index, 1982—1989

Source: SBCI.

Historical Background

The Singapore Stock Exchange dates back to the late 1920s, when European traders opened their own kerb exchange in Singapore and began to transact business in overseas issues. In the 1930s, a stock association was organised, but it was only in June 1973 that the Stock Exchange of Singapore Ltd (SES) was incorporated. Prior to that date, Singapore shared a common stock exchange with Malaysia and the two trading rooms are linked by direct telephone lines. With the termination of the currency interchangeability arrangement between the two countries in 1973, the stock exchange was separated and the majority of listed companies, whether incorporated in Singapore or Malaysia, were listed on both stock exchanges in their respective currencies. The SES, which handles a greater volume of turnover than the Kuala Lumpur exchange, is a self-regulatory body administered by a nine-member committee comprising five non-broker members and four elected representatives from the stockbroking members. As the executive body of the SES, the committee has extensive

Figure 6.2 Singapore Dollar vs US Dollar, Weekly, 1982–1989

Source: Datastream.

authority in fulfilling the objectives and policies of the SES.

Since 1975, listed companies have been assigned into one of two sections: the First Trading Section or the Second Trading Section. To be classified under the First Trading Section, certain criteria have to be met. The committee may, however, exempt a company which is unable to comply with any of the criteria, after taking into consideration its overall performance. Listed companies which don't meet the criteria for the First Trading Section are classified under the Second Section.

Stock Market Performance

The Singapore Exchange, as can be seen in Table 6.1, suffered a setback in 1985–1986, but has since made steady progress, although the tight regulations imply that the number of listings has grown rather more slowly than elsewhere.

Table 6.1 Stock Market Performance, 1984–1988

Market Indicator	1984	1985	1986	1987	1988
Market Index (Straits Times)	812.61	620.04	891.3	823.58	1,038.62
Market Cap. (S$bn)	56.1	70.6	85.3	85.4	103.6
Daily Trading Volume (S$mn)	32.6	26.3	33.3	93.7	52.8
No. of Listed Companies	308	316	317	321	327
Exchange Rate	2.1780	2.1050	2.1750	1.9985	1.9462
Currency App. vs US$	–2.4	3.4	–3.3	8.1	2.6

Source: Indosuez Asia Investment Services research.

After the recession of 1985, exports started to grow rapidly in 1986 and 1987 (see Table 6.2). Meanwhile, tight monetary control has enabled Singapore to keep its inflation rate below that of its competitors.

Table 6.2 Economic Indicators, 1985–1988

Indicator	1985	1986	1987	1988
PER (X)	16.6	35.2	21.3	20.9
Yield (%)	5.8	3.0	3.2	2.7
CPI (%)	0.5	−1.4	0.5	1.6
Exports (S$bn)	50.2	58.7	66.0	87.1
Imports (S$bn)	57.8	64.4	70.6	90.4
GNP (S$bn)	39.9	39.6	43.7	49.8
GNP Growth Rate (%)	−1.8	1.8	8.8	11.0

Source: Indosuez Asia Investment Services research.

Stock Exchange Details

Address

Stock Exchange of Singapore Ltd
1 Raffles Place
#24–00 OUB Centre
Singapore
Tel: 535 3788
Tlx: RS 21853

Trading Days/Hours

Trading sessions are held from Monday to Friday between 10 am and 11 am, 11.15 am and 12.30 pm, and 2.30 pm and 4 pm.

Transactions on the Stock Exchange

Transactions include purchase and sale of shares, debentures, bonds, warrants, loan stocks, and convertible stocks. Listed stocks are classified into seven industry sections: Industrial and Commercial, Finance, Hotel, Property, Plantations, Mining and Debentures, Bonds, and Loan Stocks. The Stock Exchange uses the 'post system', which is similar to that used in New York and Sydney where all trading is done by open outcry. Only the highest bid and the lowest offer are recorded on the monitor screen.

In 1961, the Exchange instituted the scoreboard system of trading, but in July 1982 this system was replaced by electronic trading boards. However, under the new trading system introduced in July 1988, 96 television monitors located at six trading posts replaced the huge electronic scoreboard.

Instead of telephones, a dealer or remisier (accredited broker's representative) keys in an order through a computer terminal, which is transmitted to the stockbroking firm's administrative booth on the trading floor. There the order is printed out on a special order card which the firm's runner then takes to the authorised trading-room clerk for execution. With order routing introduced in this system, broking firms can now comply with the *Securities Industry Act* requirement for orders to the floor to be time-stamped.

Where a bid or offer is made at the same price, priority is given to the clerk whose trading number is displayed. When a bid and offer matches, a transaction is completed.

For all stocks, trading is done in lots of 1,000 shares. For stocks priced above S$10, trading may also be done in lots of 500 or 100 shares.

Settlement

Ready Market
The only market traded on the trading floor, the Ready Market comprises the main volume of trading on the Exchange. The settlement period is seven days, after which time the seller must deliver his scrip to the broking firm and the buyer must pick up his or her scrip. After this settlement period, the Exchange buys the promised shares using the Buying-in Market.

Cash Market
The Cash Market allows immediate liquidation of positions. The seller must deliver the promised shares by 5 pm the same day, and the buyer must pay and collect the shares on the same day.

Buying-in Market
The Exchange uses the Buying-in Market to 'buy-in' shares for which trades were previously done but no timely settlement made. The seller must deliver his shares on the same day as the trade is transacted.

Odd-lot Market
Traders in this market can trade in odd-sized blocks of stocks. Settlement rules are the same as for the Ready Market.

Disclosure

For many years, Stock Exchange policy has required companies whose securities are traded on the Exchange to make prompt and adequate public disclosure of material developments in their affairs. A company which lists its shares on the Exchange in effect invites the public to invest in those securities. Thus, the Exchange considers that a company has an obligation to disclose to the public the information necessary to make informed investment decisions even when, as is frequently the case, the disclosure entailed must be more prompt and comprehensive than is required by the securities laws.

Immediate public disclosure of material information
A listed company is required to make immediate public disclosure of all material information concerning the following: its affairs, financial condition, and prospects; mergers and acquisitions; and dealings with employees, suppliers, customers, and others; as well as information concerning

a significant change in ownership of the company's securities owned by insiders or representing control of the company.

Thorough public dissemination

A listed company is required to release material information to the public in a manner designed to obtain its fullest possible public dissemination.

Clarification or confirmation of rumours and reports

Whenever a listed company becomes aware of a rumour or report, whether true or false, that contains information that is likely to have, or has had, an effect on the trading in the company's securities or would be likely to have a bearing on investment decisions, the company is required publicly to clarify the rumour reports as promptly as possible.

Response to unusual market action

Whenever unusual market action takes place in a listed company's securities, the company is expected to make enquiries to determine whether rumours or other conditions requiring corrective action exist, and, if so, to take appropriate action. If, after the company's review, the unusual market action remains unexplained, it may be appropriate for the company to announce that there has been no material development in its business and affairs not previously disclosed, nor, to its knowledge, any other reason to account for the unusual market action.

Unwarranted promotional disclosure

A listed company should refrain from promotional disclosure activity which exceeds that necessary to enable the public to make informed investment decisions. Such activity includes inappropriately worded news releases, public announcements not justified by actual developments in a company's affairs, exaggerated reports or predictions, flamboyant wording, and other forms of overstated or overzealous disclosure activity which may mislead investors and cause unwarranted price movements and activity in a company's securities.

Insider trading

Insiders should not trade on the basis of material information which is not known to the investing public. However, insiders should refrain from trading, even after material information has been released to the press and other media, for a period sufficient to permit thorough public dissemination and evaluation of the information.

The Twenty Largest Stocks

Tables 6.3 and 6.4 list the 20 largest quoted companies in Singapore by market capitalisation and by turnover, while Figure 6.3 shows the breakdown of market capitalisation by sector.

Table 6.3 The 20 Largest Quoted Stocks by Market Capitalisation, as at 31 December 1988

Company	Market Capitalisation (S$mn)
SIA	7,808.0
OCBC	4,502.8
Sime Darby	3,211.0
DBS	3,182.6
UOB	2,185.6
Harrisons Asia	2,047.3
SPH	1,848.7
K L Kepong	1,533.8
M Banking	1,389.1
City Dev	1,271.3
Gentings	1,267.7
F & N	1,226.0
Cons Plant	1,185.0
OUB	1,020.5
Rothmans Asia	977.9
Straits Trading	938.5
Esso	934.2
Perlis Plant	872.1
Public Bank	814.0

Source: Stock Exchange of Singapore.

Figure 6.3 Breakdown of Market Capitalisation by Sector, 1988

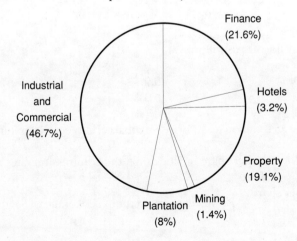

Source: Indosuez Asia Investment Services research.

Table 6.4 The 20 Largest Quoted Stocks by Turnover, 1988

Company	Turnover Units (mn)
DBS Land	910.42
Sime Darby	859.99
KKC	450.75
Amal Steel	391.31
DBS	381.50
Public Bank	380.02
Cons Plant	368.82
Keppel Corporation	293.24
K L Kepong	261.66
OCBC	235.78
SIA	190.42
Gentings	166.56
City Dev	148.01
UOB	145.40
Inchcape	131.18
K Banking	128.58
F & N	124.02
Straits Trading	75.33
Harrisons Asia	73.99
SPK	63.66

Source: Stock Exchange of Singapore.

Dealing Costs

Brokerage

The brokerage charges payable are as follows:

On the first S$250,000	:	1.0%
On the next S$250,000	:	0.9%
On the next S$250,000	:	0.8%
On the next S$250,000	:	0.7%
On amounts exceeding S$1 million	:	Negotiable, subject to a minimum of 0.5%.

For contracts at prices below S$1 per share or stock unit, the commission rates are:

Under 50¢	:	1/2¢ per share
50–99¢	:	1¢ per share

} Subject to a minimum brokerage of S$5 per contract.

Clearing Fees and Stamp Duties

In addition to brokerage, there is a clearing fee of 0.05% on the value of the contract, subject to a maximum of S$100. A contract stamp duty of S$1 per S$1,000 or part thereof is also charged.

A transfer stamp duty of 0.2% of the value of the contract is payable when shares are sent for registration.

Transaction Fees

Besides the usual brokerage payable, a transaction fee of 1/4%, with a maximum of $4 per 1,000 shares or part thereof, will be charged by the approved banks with whom members have opened their Central Provident Fund (CPF) Investment Account.

Major Securities Houses

BT Brokerage & Associates Pte Ltd
50 Raffles Place
#21-03/04 Shell Tower
Singapore 0104
Tel: 2249233
Tlx: RS 26413
Fax: 2249180

DBS Securities Singapore Pte Ltd
DBS Securities Building
22 Malacca Street
Singapore 0104
Tel: 5339688
Tlx: RS 20438
Fax: 5357785

Fraser Roach & Co. Pte Ltd
10 Collyer Quay
#27-01 Ocean Building
Singapore 0104
Tel: 5359455
Tlx: RS 21433
Fax: 5351745

G K Goh (Stockbrokers) Pte Ltd
50 Raffles Place
#33-00 Shell Tower
Singapore 0104
Tel: 2251228
Tlx: RS 26624 20024 43329
Fax: 2251522 2246906

Hoare Govett Summit Securities Pte Ltd
65 Chulia Street
#22-01 OCBC Centre
Singapore 0104
Tel: 5333388
Tlx: RS 20763 55508
Fax: 5326333

J Ballas & Co. Pte Ltd
#06-01 Straits Trading Building
9 Battery Road
Singapore 0104
Tel: 5358111
Tlx: RS 21425
Fax: 5322331

J M Sasson & Co. (Pte) Ltd
1 Raffles Place
#44-00 OUB Centre
Singapore 0104
Tel: 5352888 2866
Tlx: RS 21288 26508
Fax: 5337956

Kay Hian Pte Ltd
1 Bonham Street
#22-01 UOB Building
Singapore 0104
Tel: 54332936 5353036
Tlx: RS 26128
Fax: 5326919

Kim Eng Securities Pte Ltd
5 Shenton Way
#13-00 UIC Building
Singapore 0106
Tel: 2209090/9575
Tlx: RS 25871 20426
Fax: 2258746

Morgan Grenfell Asia & Partners Securities Pte Ltd
65 Chulia Street
#26-01 OCBC Centre
Singapore 0104
Tel: 5331818
Tlx: RS 23147 28325 28326 23705
Fax: 5327211

OCBC Securities Pte Limited
18 Church Street
#06-00 OCBC Centre South
Singapore 0104
Tel: 5352882
Tlx: RS 42570
Fax: 5322768

Ong & Co. Pte Ltd
76 Shenton Way
#06-00 Ong Building
Singapore 0207
Tel: 2239466
Tlx: RS 22071 55106
Fax: 2240253

OUB Securities Pte Ltd
50 Collyer Quay
#01-01 Overseas Union House
Singapore 0104
Tel: 2251166
Tlx: RS 42576
Fax: 2256884

Paul Morgan & Associates (Securities) Pte Ltd
11 Collyer Quay
#18-01 The Arcade
Singapore 0104
Tel: 2219991
Tlx: RS 20225 26081
Fax: 2259948

Philip Securities (Pte)
95 South Bridge Road
#11-17 South Bridge Centre
Singapore 0105
Tel: 5336001
Tlx: RS 20188 43176
Fax: 5353834

Tat Lee Securities Pte Ltd
63 Market Street
#12-06/07 Tat Lee Bank Building
Singapore 0104
Tel: 5339666
Tlx: RS 43125
Fax: 5336989

Tsang & Ong Stockbrokers (Pte) Ltd
11 Collyer Quay
#16-00 The Arcade
Singapore 0104
Tel: 2245877
Tlx: RS 28142
Fax: 2246632

UOB Securities Pte Ltd
1 Bonham Street
#11-00 UOB Building
Singapore 0104
Tel: 5356868
Tlx: RS 36237
Fax: 5331747

Mutual Funds/Unit Trusts

A complete list of all unit trusts registered for sale and managed in Singapore appears in Table 6.5.

Table 6.5 Singapore Listed Funds

Singapore Unit Trust	*OUB Investment Management*
The Commerce Fund	Union Global Fund
The Savings Fund	Union Singapore Fund
Singapore Progress Fund	Union Gold Fund
Singapore Security Fund	
Singapore Investment Fund	Diamond Singapore Fund (US$)
Singapore Equity Fund	Diamond Singapore Fund (S$)
Asia Unit Trust	*DBS Bank*
Malaysia Investment Fund	Shenton Growth Fund
Malaysia Progress Fund	Japan Growth Fund
Malaysia Security Fund	Shenton Thrift Fund
Malaysia Berjaya Fund	
Malaysia Equity Fund	*UOB Management*
Malaysia Commercial Fund	Unifund
	Unibond
Royal Trust Security Asia	
RT Singapore Growth Fund	*Others*
RT Asia-Pacific Growth Fund	Asean Fund
	Daiwa Japan Fund
OCBC-SIMBL Investment	Thai Prime Fund
Savers Capital Fund	ADEF
	Alpha Fund

Source: Banque Indosuez, Singapore.

Table 6.6 includes a selection of international funds invested in Singapore and Malaysian equities and managed mainly from Hong Kong, while Table 6.7 provides a broader selection of equity funds invested in South-East Asian markets, or ASEAN (Singapore, Malaysia, Thailand, Indonesia, the Philippines, and Brunei).

Table 6.6 Singapore/Malaysia Equity Funds Available to International Investors

Baring Malaysia and Singapore Fund
Bridge Singapore and Malaysia Trust
GAM Singapore Malaysia Inc.
Gartmore Singapore and Malaysia Trust
NM Portfolio Selection (Singapore and Malaysia)
NM Singapore and Malaysian Fund
Wardley Global Selection (Singapore Equity)

Source: Hong Kong Unit Trust Association.

Rules for Foreign Investors

Foreign Investment Restrictions

In Singapore, apart from the *Banking Act* and the *Newspapers Act*, which specifically stipulate the restrictions on foreign ownership, there is no legislation governing this matter. However, some government companies in sensitive industries (such as the airline industry) can incorporate a foreign ownership restriction clause in their Companies' Memorandum.

Foreign Exchange Control

There are no foreign exchange controls on the trading of securities by non-residents. There are also no restrictions on the acquisition of securities by foreign investors. Foreign ownership is restricted only in certain companies. Foreigners face no limitations on the repatriation of income, capital gains, and capital.

No restrictions exist on the acquisition of foreign securities by residents, but dividends received from abroad are subject to income tax.

Taxation

Capital gains are not taxed, and capital losses are not deductible. Although no withholding tax is applied to corporate dividends, tax at the corporate income tax rate of 33% is deemed to have been deducted at source. In the hands of the recipient, dividends are to be included in taxable income.

Protection of Shareholders

According to the Singapore *Code on Takeovers and Mergers*, all persons privy to confidential price-sensitive information concerning an offer or contemplated offer must treat that information relating to the potential offer as secret. No person who is privy to such information should make any recommendation to any other person as to dealing in the relevant securities. All such persons must conduct themselves so as to minimise the chances of an accidental leak of information.

Save in so far as appears from the Code, it is considered undesirable to fetter the market. Accordingly, all parties to a takeover or merger transaction (other than to a partial offer) and associates are free to deal, subject to daily disclosure to the Stock Exchange, the Council, and the press (not later than 12 noon on the dealing day following the date of the relevant transaction) of the total of all shares of any offer or the offeree company purchased or sold by them or their respective associates for their own account on any day, during the offer period in the market or otherwise, and the prices paid or received.

Available Research

Stock Exchange of Singapore Annual Fact Book
Stock Exchange of Singapore Fact Sheet
Annual Companies Handbook

Table 6.7 ASEAN Equity Funds Available to International Investors

Baring Octopus Fund
CEF Emerging Pacific Market Trust
Federated Asia Trust
Fidelity South-East Asia Trust
GT Asean Fund
Hambro-Pacific South-East Asian Fund
Indosuez Asian Growth Fund
JF Asean Trust
JF Eastern Trust
Schroders Asian Fund
Scimitar Asian Smaller Markets Equity Fund
SHK Middle Kingdom Fund
SHK Oriental Emerging Economies Fund
SHK Oriental Growth Fund
Thornton Little Dragons Fund
Thornton Tiger Fund
Wardley South-East Asia Trust

Source: Wyatt Report.

Investment Analysis in Singapore (1985)
Securities Regulations in Singapore and Malaysia
Securities Market in Singapore (2nd ed. 1985)
The SES All-Share Price Indices 1975–88

7

MALAYSIA

Introduction

The Federation of Malaysia covers a total area of 330,434 sq km and comprises the 11 states of Peninsular Malaysia and the two states of Sarawak and Sabah in northern Kalimantan, or Brunei. The Malay Peninsula represents almost 40% of the total land mass of Malaysia.

In mid-1985, the total population of Malaysia was estimated to be 15.68 million, compared with the 1980 Census figure of 13.75 million. From 1970 to 1980, the average annual rate of increase of the overall population was 2.2%, while the percentage of people living in urban areas increased to 37% for the Malay Peninsula and to 34% for the country as a whole.

The 1980 Census also reported that approximately 55% of the population of Malaysia were Malays, or Bumiputras, 'the sons of the soil', 33% were Chinese, and 8% Indian. The Malaysian government estimates the total population of Malaysia in 1988 to be approximately 16.96 million.

The official language of Malaysia is Malay (Bahasa Malaysia); however, English and Chinese are also widely used. The official religion of Malaysia is Islam, with other religions being practised freely.

Malaysia is essentially a constitutional monarchy. The head of state and Supreme Commander of the Armed Forces, the Yang di Pertuan Agong, is elected every five years from among the Conference of Rulers which comprises the hereditary rulers of the nine states, known also as Sultans. The States of Malacca, Penang, Sabah, and Sarawak are headed by governors appointed for a term of four years.

The framework of government is determined by a constitution adopted at the time of independence from Britain in 1957. The Parliament consists of two houses, a Senate and a House of Representatives. The Senate comprises 32 senators who are appointed by the Yang di Pertuan Agong and 26 members elected by the 13 State Legislative Assemblies. The 177 members of the House of Representatives are elected by general election every five years. Each state also has its own elected legislative assembly, which deals with matters not covered by the Federal Parliament.

The judiciary is constitutionally independent of executive and legislative control. Judges are appointed by the Head of State, on the advice of the Prime Minister, while magistrates are appointed by state rulers. The Prime Minister serves as the head of government and presides over a Cabinet selected by himself from among members of Parliament.

The present ruling coalition of Malaysia is the Barisan Nasional, comprised of 13 political parties. While a vocal opposition continues to exist, it has never been successful in gaining sufficient popular support to challenge the Barisan Nasional. In the most recent federal elections in August 1986, the Barisan Nasional won some 84% of the seats in the House of Representatives. The next elections for Parliament are scheduled to be held in 1991.

Note: US$1.00 = MR2.7.

Figure 7.1 Kuala Lumpur Composite-Price Index, Weekly, 1986–1989

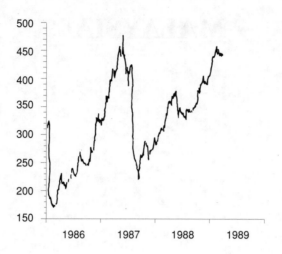

Source: Datastream.

Figure 7.2 Malaysian Ringgit vs US Dollar, Weekly, 1982–1989

Source: Datastream.

Economy

With its abundant natural resources, Malaysia is the world's leading exporter of tin, rubber, and palm oil. It is also a principal exporter of tropical hardwoods and has large reserves of petroleum and natural gas. The average annual rate of increase in Malaysia's GDP, measured in real terms, was 7% during the period 1961–1976, rising to 8.5% in the period of the third Malaysia Plan from 1976 to 1980. More recent economic indicators are shown in Table 7.1.

Table 7.1   Economic Indicators, 1985–1988

Indicator	1985	1986	1987	1988
GDP (MR bn)	55.8	58.3	61.1	65.7
GDP Growth Rate (%)	−1.0	1.2	5.2	8.5
PER (X)	18.6	26.4	30.6	21.0
Yield (%)	5.8	3.5	3.0	3.4
Inflation (%)	0.4	0.6	1.1	2.5
Exports (MR bn)	37.4	36.4	43.9	57.3
Imports (MR bn)	29.8	28.1	30.2	43.2

Source: W.I. Carr (Far East) Limited.

Malaysia's present economic development is concentrated on resource-based, consumer, and export-oriented industries. It is actively seeking foreign capital, and the rise in foreign investment from Japan, Taiwan, and Singapore is an important factor in the country's move towards industrialisation.

With a domestic market of only 16.9 million people, the economy is directed towards exports. The commodity sector will remain the core of the Malaysian economy for many years to come, but it is unlikely to be able to generate sufficient employment. The manufacturing sector, which has performed well since 1986, has been the most dynamic sector since Independence. As a result, the Malaysian economy has recorded positive and successively strengthening real GDP growth since 1986.

In 1987, growth in real GDP began to improve, partly as a result of commercial restructuring in 1986. Capital investment and economic growth increased further in 1988 as a result of firmer commodity prices, improved manufactured exports, and a stronger domestic market generated by greater consumer spending. Real GDP growth reached 7.3% in the first quarter of 1988 and 10.6% in the second quarter. Malaysia registered an overall growth rate for 1988 of 8.5%.

Initially, this economic recovery was led by external demand for electronic products and commodities, but subsequent growth appears to have been broader-based. Total new direct foreign investment in the first seven months of 1988 amounted to approximately US$383 million, compared with US$298 million in the whole of the previous year.

Tourism is another important economic activity. Promotional campaigns are increasing, while preparations are also underway for 'Visit Malaysia Year' in 1990.

The construction sector is also experiencing rapid growth. The government's emphasis on private home ownership, coupled with commencement of work on the US$1.31 billion North–South Highway project and US$500 million natural gas pipeline project, will stimulate growth in this sector.

In its October 1988 budget, the government reduced corporate income tax by 5% to 35% and expressed the intention to abolish gradually the 5% development tax. The 3% excess profits tax was repealed in 1987. Liberalisation of foreign ownership policies should attract more foreign investors to Malaysia.

Historical Background

In colonial times, the stock markets of Malaysia and Singapore started as one entity. The origin of the Kuala Lumpur Stock Exchange (KLSE) can be traced to the Singapore Stockbrokers' Association of the 1930s, and later to the Malaysian Stock Exchange and the Stock Exchange of Malaysia and Singapore in the 1960s. Following the withdrawal of Singapore from Malaysia in 1965 and the termination of currency agreements between the two countries, the present KLSE Bhd was incorporated in 1976 under the *Securities Industry Act 1973*.

Consequently, the KLSE still retains listings of major Singapore incorporated companies and some UK incorporated companies. Over the years, with the promotion of the National Economic Policy (NEP), the number of Malaysian incorporated listings has increased substantially over that of foreign companies through new listings of Malaysian companies, the separation of Singapore companies into separate entities, and the repatriation of UK-domiciled Malaysian companies. A second board was introduced in late 1988 to accommodate the listing of smaller companies.

In March 1986, the government announced a Corporatisation Policy whereby approved financial institutions, including foreign brokers, were permitted to acquire up to 30% of local broking houses. In July 1987, this limit was increased to 49% (with certain requirements). So far, only one local broker, Seagroatt & Campbell, has a foreign partner, in Banque Indosuez's W.I. Carr. There are 53 broking members of the KLSE, including six wholly bank-owned brokers.

Stock Market Performance

Five-year market trends for the period 1985–1988 are shown in Table 7.2.

Table 7.2   Stock Market Performance, 1985–1988

Market Indicator	1985	1986	1987	1988
Market Index (KL Composite)	233.46	252.26	261.19	357.38
Market Cap. (MR bn)	58.3	64.5	73.8	99.1
Daily Trading Volume (MR mn)	26	14	38	26
No. of Listed Companies	284	289	291	295
Exchange Rate	2.4265	2.6030	2.4928	2.7153
Currency App. vs US$	–0.06	–7.27	4.23	–8.93

Source: W.I. Carr (Far East) Limited.

Figure 7.3 shows the breakdown of the economy between agriculture (mainly plantations) and manufacturing, now the largest sector comprising 32% of GDP. By contrast, the stock market is dominated by industrial/manufacturing companies, accounting for over 51%, whereas palm oil and rubber plantations represent only 13% of the total and banks over 21% (see Figure 7.4).

Figure 7.3 GDP Breakdown, 1988

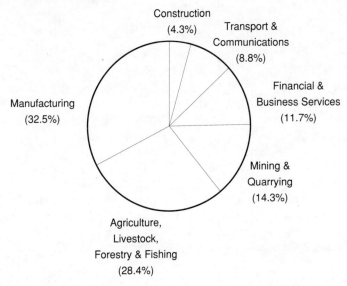

Source: Kuala Lumpur Stock Exchange.

Figure 7.4 Breakdown of Market Capitalisation by Sector, 1988

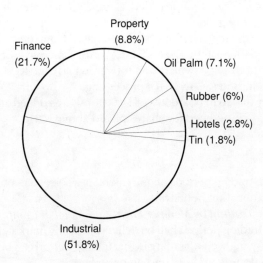

Source: Kuala Lumpur Stock Exchange.

Stock Exchange Details

Address

The Kuala Lumpur Stock Exchange
3rd and 4th Floors, Block A
Komplek Bukit Naga
Off Jalan Semantau
Damansara Heights
50490 Kuala Lumpur
PO Box 11023
50732 Kuala Lumpur
Tel: 03-2546433/2546815
Tlx: KLSE MA 30241
Fax: 03-2557463

Trading Days/Hours

Trading is on Mondays to Fridays (other than on market holidays). Each market day is divided into two sessions: 10 am to 12.30 pm and 2.30 pm to 4 pm.

Transactions on the Stock Exchange

Various securities, including ordinary shares, preference shares, loan stocks, debentures, warrants, bonds, and notes, can be traded on the KLSE. Trading in ordinary shares dominates. Buying and selling of shares on the trading floor of the KLSE is by the open-outcry system. Each member company has authorised trading-room clerks to carry out transactions on the trading floor. The clerks receive and execute buy/sell orders from stockbrokers and remisiers (accredited brokers' representatives) through the direct telephone system provided. Buy/sell orders are called to the board, where they are recorded by KLSE posting clerks.

Securities are sold to the highest bidder and purchased from the lowest offeror. Real-time prices are transmitted to subscribers of the KLSE's 'MASA' price dissemination service. All transactions are recorded on trading-room slips which are forwarded to the KLSE clearing house, Securities Automated Network Sdn Bhd (SCANS), for processing.

Shares are normally traded in board lots of 1,000 for shares priced at MR10 or below. Smaller lots (500 or 100 shares) may be allowed for shares priced above MR10.

Settlement

The year is divided into trading periods of one calendar week each. A trading period consists of five market days (other than market holidays).

Under the *Rules for Trading by Member Firms and Member Companies*, all shares/stock traded on ready contacts in a trading period shall be delivered on any market day but no later than 3 pm on Wednesday of the following week. Trading in one trading period can be set off in that trading period but not against transactions in another trading period.

The buyer pays in settlement to the seller after delivery. Shares delivered before 12.30 pm on any market day shall be paid for before 11 am on the second market day following. The rules for delivery and payment are less specific. It is stated that a buying client should make payment promptly on delivery of the debit note or on being duly notified that the securities purchased on his behalf are ready for collection. In practice, the buyer is given three days to make payment.

Disclosure

Interim report
An interim report is submitted to the Exchange within three months of the expiration of the first six months of each financial year. This report, compiled by the directors of the company, concerns the company's activities and profits and, where applicable, the group's activities, for such period.

The report should state the percentage relationship compared with the corresponding period of the preceding year of profitability and turnover or sales, and any material factor and/or exceptional circumstances affecting the earning capacity and profits of the company.

Final results
Companies listed on the Exchange are required to notify the Exchange, immediately after the board meeting at which the accounts for the preceding financial year have been approved, of the net profit or loss of the company and of its subsidiaries for each financial year, stating whether such final results are audited or subject to audit.

No announcement shall be made after the end of the company's financial year of any dividend, bonus or rights issue, closing of books, capital return, passing of a dividend, or sales turnover unless accompanied by the foregoing information.

KLSE queries
Subsequent to any announcement being made in the Interim Report or Final Results, the Exchange may request such explanation or clarification as may appear necessary regarding any omission or ambiguities appearing in any statement.

Circulars
At the time of any bonus issue, rights issue, or capital return, the company shall indicate:
- any expected change in profitability compared to the previous financial year; and
- any expected change in the amount of dividend to be paid on the new capital.

Explanations and qualifications
Where any audited accounts differ materially from announced unaudited accounts or any prospectus, or when any auditor has qualified his report, an announcement of such difference or full details of such qualification shall be given to the Exchange immediately for public release upon its receipt by the company.

Custodial Services

Foreign investors have access to custodial services from Malaysian and Singaporean banks.

The Twenty Largest Stocks

The 20 largest quoted companies in terms of market capitalisation are shown in Table 7.3.

Table 7.3 The 20 Largest Quoted Stocks by Market Capitalisation,
as at 31 December 1988

Company	Market Capitalisation (MR mn)	Turnover (MR mn)
Sime Darby	4,433	3,367.2
MISC	3,475	1,383.8
HMPB	2,834	523.1
MAS	2,328	1,577.5
KLK	2,140	277.7
Malayan Banking	1,921	N/A
Genting	1,763	402.7
Cons Plant	1,665	620.0
Rothmans (M)	1,356	628.8
Esso (M)	1,307	938.0
Perlis Plant	1,205	415.
Public Bank	1,128	540.13
MMC	1,091	524.7
ASM	1,054	585.1
Guinness (M)	1,011	255.2
Hi & Lo Plant	858	127.37
MUI	799	312.8
Shell	780	1,130.7
Asiatic Development	744	69.0
Inchcape Bhd	700	N/A

Source: W.I. Carr (Far East) Limited.

Dealing Costs

Brokerage

Brokerage commissions applicable to Malaysian shares are shown in Table 7.4.

Clearing Fee

A clearing fee of 0.05% of the transacted value is payable for services provided by the clearing house, SCANS.

Table 7.4   Stocks, Ordinary Shares, and Preference Shares

Price (MR)	Ready Contracts	Other
<0.50	MR0.005	MR0.005
0.50–1.00	MR0.015	MR0.015
>1.00	1.0%	1.5%

Source: W.I. Carr (Far East) Limited.

Stamp Duty

Stamp duty is payable as follows:
- Contract notes: MR1 for MR1,000 of value or fraction thereof.
- Shares certificates: MR2 per certificate.
- Transfer: MR3 per MR1,000 of value of Malaysian or UK incorporated companies with a Malaysian Branch Registrar or fraction thereof; MR2 per MR1,000 value of securities of Singapore incorporated companies or fraction thereof.

Major Securities Houses

There are 53 member stockbrokers throughout Malaysia. The major companies are as follows:

Kuala Lumpur

Antah Jardine Fleming Sdn Bhd
19th Floor, Pernas International
Jalan Sultan Ismail
50250 Kuala Lumpur

Tel: 03 2618255
Tlx: 31094

Ariffin & Low Securities Sdn
Lot No 22.02, 22nd Floor
Menara Promet
Jalan Sultan Ismail
Kuala Lumpur
Tel: 03 422088
Tlx: 30991

Charles Bradburne & Co. (1930) Sdn Bhd
2nd Floor, President House
Jalan Sultan Ismail
Kuala Lmpur
Tel: 03 485411 485418
Tlx: 33186 CEEBEE MA

G.P. Securities Sdn Bhd
Lot 264, 2nd Floor
Jalan Raja Chulan
Kuala Lumpur 04-04
Tel: 03 413533
Tlx: 31072 GP MA

H.A. Securities Sdn
301–3 Wisma S I A
Jalan Dang Wangi
Kuala Lumpur
Tel: 03 927016 927276
Tlx: 32107 AZAM MA

K. & N. Kenanga Sdn Bhd
901–4, 9th Floor
Wisma Lim Foo Yong
86 Jalan Raja Chulan
Kuala Lumpur
Tel: 03 420355 421501
Tlx: 31070 KEN MA

Kris Securities Sdn Bhd
4th Floor, Pertama Complex
PO Box No 11106
Kuala Lumpur
Tel: 03 917713 917527
Tlx: 31796 KRISMA MA

Leong & Co. Sdn Bhd
4th Floor, Wing On Building
16 Jalan Silang
Kuala Lumpur 01-19
Tel: 03 223308 220115
Tlx: 31363 SHABON MA

Malayan Traders & Co. Sdn Bhd
6th Floor, Menara Tun Razak
Jalan Raja Laut
PO Box 10310
Kuala Lumpur
Tel: 03 935088

Othman & Ng Sdn Bhd
3rd Floor, MUI Plaza
Jalan P Ramiee
Kuala Lumpur 04-01
Tel: 03 485355 485586
Tlx: 30848 MA

Rashid Hussain Securities Sdn Bhd
10th Floor, Menara Tun Razak
Jalan Raja Laut
Kuala Lumpur 50350
Tel: 03 2934166
Tlx: 31791 RHS MA

Seagroatt & Campbell
Wisma Hamzah — Konw Hing
7th Floor, No 1 Leboh Ampang
Kuala Lumpur 50100
Tel: 03 2327122
Tlx: 32816 SEAGRO MA

W.I. Carr (Far East) Limited
14th Floor, Menara Boustead
Jalan Raja Chulan
50200 Kuala Lumpur
Tel: 03 2436411
Tlx: MA 32424

Zalik Securities Sdn Bhd
9th Floor, Menara Apera-ULG
84 Jalan Raja Chulan
Kuala Lumpur
Tel: 03 436544 436584

Selangor

Apex Securities
Halim Securities

Johore

Hamid & Chua Securities

Penang

A.A. Anthony & Co.
Thong & OH Securities

Listing Criteria

Companies seeking to list on the KLSE must meet a series of requirements laid down by both the KLSE and the Capital Issues Committee (CIC). In practice, the KLSE requirements are superseded by stricter requirements established by the CIC.

KLSE listing requirements include:

- Minimum paid-up capital of MR2 million.
- Minimum outside ownership of at least MR750,000 (par value) or 25% of paid-in capital, whichever is higher, held by no less than 500 persons, none of whom holds either more than 10,000 or less than 500 shares each.
- Shares must be issued in registered form, with those registered in the names of the nominee companies not to exceed 5% without disclosure of beneficial owners.

- Capital represented by preference shares may not exceed the capital represented by ordinary shares.

The Capital Issues Committee

Established in 1968, and under the authority of the Minister of Finance, the CIC oversees the issuance of securities and their listing on the KLSE. All companies which intend to issue or offer securities to the public, or to list such securities on a Malaysian securities exchange, must obtain the CIC's approval. The CIC also determines the offering price of a new issue of securities.

The CIC evaluates and decides upon proposals in accordance with its own guidelines. The CIC is not under any obligation to disclose the reasons supporting its decision. Applicants may, however, appeal within one month decisions of the CIC to the Minister of Finance, whose decision will be final.

CIC guidelines for new issues include the following:
- unimpaired paid-up capital >MR5 million;
- acceptable earnings record over five (exceptionally three) years;
- good prospects of future profits adequately supported by ordinary income from principal activities; and
- reasonable external board representation.

Procedures for takeover bids are covered by the *Companies Act*. A formal *Code on Takeovers and Mergers* is administered by the Takeovers Panel.

Mutual Funds/Unit Trusts

There are currently 26 mutual funds and unit trusts listed in Malaysia. There are also three international closed-end 'country funds' investing in Malaysia that are open to foreign investors (see Table 7.5). See also Table 6.6 in the Singapore chapter, which lists Singapore and Malaysian equity unit trusts managed in Hong Kong.

Table 7.5 Malaysian Funds Available to International Investors

Fund	Manager	Inception Date	Listing	Size (US$mn)
Malacca Fund	Indosuez Asia Investment Services Limited	Jan. 1989	London	35
Malaysia Fund	Merrill Lynch	Mar. 1987	NYSE	80
Malaysia Fund	Morgan Stanley	Dec. 1987	NYSE	84

Rules for Foreign Investors

Foreign Investment Restrictions

Under the National Economic Policy, Bumiputras should own at least 30% corporate equity, with 40%

held by other Malaysians and not more than 30% by foreigners. However, foreign investors can own up to 100% of a company's capital provided that the company's products are wholly destined for export.

Furthermore, regulations and procedures established by the Malaysian government virtually deny foreign investors access to subscriptions for new listings.

Any transactions which result in the transfer to foreign ownership of substantial fixed assets; control through joint venture; 15% of company voting power by any single foreign interest, or 30% in aggregate; or assets or interests exceeding MR5 million in value, must be approved by the Foreign Investment Committee.

Foreign Exchange Control

In practice, there are no foreign exchange controls which would prevent foreign investors from freely repatriating principal, realised capital gains, and all dividends and interest received. The official guidelines are as follows:

- Foreign investors are required to notify Bank Negara (the central bank of Malaysia) when making remittances exceeding MR5,000.
- Foreign investors require the approval of Bank Negara when making remittances exceeding MR2 million in a single transaction. These approvals are given as a matter of course.
- Malaysian companies wishing to open bank accounts outside Malaysia require the approval of Bank Negara.
- Malaysian banks outside Malaysia cannot extend Ringgit loans without the approval of Bank Negara as the central bank does not wish to internationalise the Ringgit.

Taxation

Interest and dividend income are subject to income tax in Malaysia. A non-resident shareholder will receive the full amount of dividend less income tax at 35%. Recovery of income tax deducted may be possible depending on double taxation agreements with the country of residence of the shareholder. For a resident shareholder, an amount corresponding to income tax deducted is treated as a tax credit when an individual files a tax return. Dividends paid by companies granted pioneer status by the Ministry of Trade and Industry are tax-exempt.

Interest on a non-approved loan is subject to 20% withholding tax for non-residents.

There is no tax on capital gains derived from transactions of securities in Malaysia.

Protection of Shareholders

The authority to regulate the Malaysian securities industry is vested primarily in the Register of Companies (ROC) and the Capital Issues Committee. In addition, the KLSE regulates the organisation and conduct of its members and has established standards for listing securities.

Existing statutes grant the ROC power to regulate the contents of prospectuses; to license dealers, investment advisers, and their representatives; to enforce prohibitions against fraud, market manipulation, and short selling; and to require that dealers disclose certain conflicts of interest.

Local companies must maintain a share register and disclose changes in holdings of directors and persons holding 5% or more of their shares. The ROC monitors trading on the KLSE and, in connection with annual licence renewals, reviews the financial condition of dealers. In addition, civil remedies are available for violation of prohibitions against trading on material, non-public information and for misleading or incomplete disclosures in a prospectus.

Available Research

Investors Digest (Monthly)
Daily Diary
Annual Companies Handbook
The KLSE Memorandum and Articles of Association and Rules Relating to Member Firms and Member Companies, Rules for Trading by Member Firms and Members Companies
Listing Manual (Main Board)
Listing Manual (Second Board)
Location of Share Registers
Manual on Compilation of KLSE Sectoral and Composite Indices
KLSE Monthly Volume and Value (from 1973)
KLSE Weekly Volume and Value (from 1973)
KLSE Monthly Average Indices (from 1970)
KLSE Monthly Closing Indices (from 1970)
KLSE Weekly Closing Indices (from 1970)
KLSE Daily Closing Indices (from 1970)
KLSE Monthly Market Capitalisation (from 1974)
Fact Sheet
Fact Book
Going to the Stock Exchange
Types of Securities

8

THAILAND

Introduction

The Kingdom of Thailand is a nation wedged like a keystone into the heart of South-East Asia. The population is approaching 55 million, of which the majority are Buddhists. The climate is tropical, and the major agricultural products are rice (of which Thailand is the largest exporter in the world), tapioca, maize, and rubber. The country has become a favoured tourist destination, with four million visitors in 1988.

Thailand has the distinction of being the only Asian country, apart from Japan, never to be colonised. Despite invasions from Burma, and the Khmer empire, Siam retained its independence through the 19th century as a buffer kingdom between the British and French colonial empires. It survived the Second World War, and subsequent conflicts in the Indochina peninsula, with its borders intact. Today, Thailand combines growing economic prosperity with sufficient military strength to maintain its independence.

The greatest guarantee of Thailand's political stability is the devotion of the Thai people to their monarchy, of which King Bhumibol Adulyadej is the living symbol, having reigned since 1946 despite numerous *coups d'état* since the peaceful 1932 'revolution' which saw the transition to constitutional monarchy. After eight years in office, the Prime Minister, General Prem, stepped down in 1988 to be replaced by General Chatichai.

Economy

Thailand has the advantage, compared with other Asian NICs, of a balanced economy with a strong agricultural sector, a growing manufacturing base, and an increasingly successful service sector headed by the booming tourist industry. Thailand's basic GNP growth rate is around 7% per annum and it is estimated that, at this rate, the per capita GNP will surpass US$1,575 by 1993. The domestic market, comprising a total population of 54 million, is growing rapidly as living standards improve. In this respect, Thailand in the period 1988–1993 is expected to mirror the economic development of Korea and Taiwan in the last five years.

The remarkable shift in the pattern of Thailand's exports is reflected in Figure 8.3. Agriculture, especially rice and tapioca, accounted for nearly 50% of exports as recently as 1980. However, by 1987, manufactured exports comprised approximately 60% of the total (see Table 8.1). This figure is predicted to be 75% by 1990.

Note: US$1.00 = Baht 26.

Figure 8.1 Stock Exchange of Thailand (SET) Monthly Index, 1977–1989

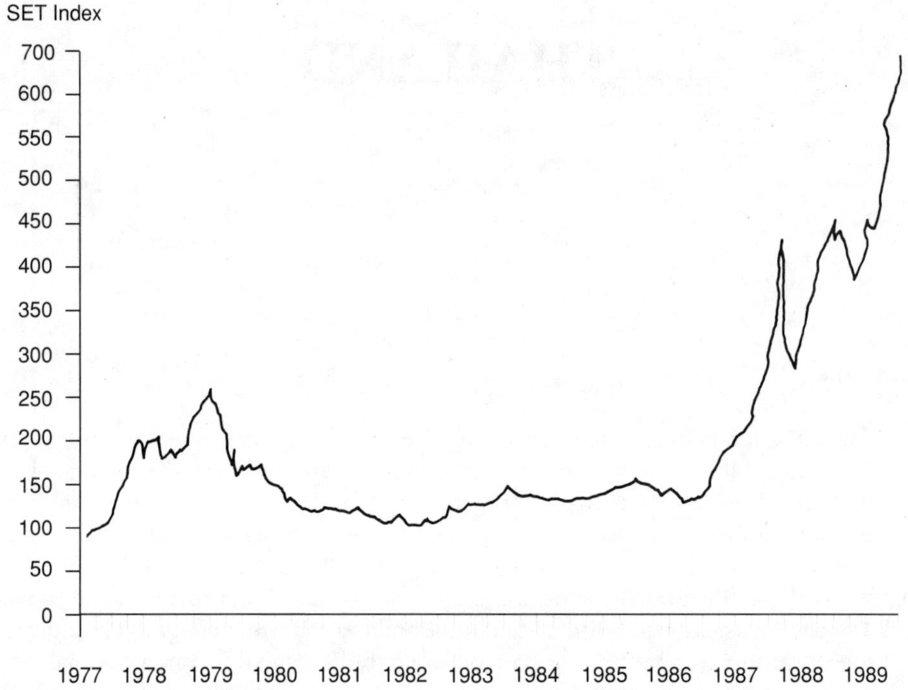

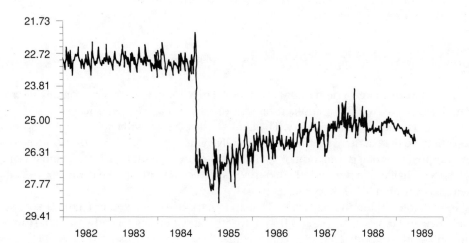

Source: Indosuez Asia Investment Services research.

Figure 8.2 Thai Baht vs US Dollar (Period Ave), Weekly, 1982–1989

Source: Datastream.

Figure 8.3 Sectoral Shares of Exports, 1980 and 1990E

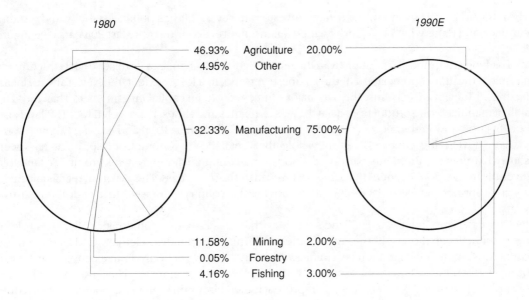

1980		1990E
46.93%	Agriculture	20.00%
4.95%	Other	
32.33%	Manufacturing	75.00%
11.58%	Mining	2.00%
0.05%	Forestry	
4.16%	Fishing	3.00%

Table 8.1 Top 10 Manufactured Exports, 1988

Commodity Group	Export Value (Baht mn)
Garments	38,275
Jewellery and gemstones	26,000
Integrated circuits	16,500
Canned seafood	13,650
Textile products	12,950
White sugar	7,480
Shoes	6,500
Canned pineapple	3,920
Furniture	3,750
Rubber products	3,550

Source: Department of Business and Economics, Thailand Ministry of Commerce.

Foreign Investment in Thailand

The attractions of Thailand to the foreign investor are several. It has political stability and a stable currency, the Baht, which has hardly varied against the US dollar over the last 20 years (see Figure 8.2).

Thailand is currently benefiting from the recent significant change in its relative cost structures as a result of the rapid appreciation of the Japanese yen and, to a lesser extent, the New Taiwan dollar. Japan and Taiwan are currently the two major sources of foreign capital investment in Thailand. The shift of manufacturing production, in such areas as textiles and shoes, has accelerated. Thailand also benefits from low labour costs compared to, say, Japan (less than 10%) and Taiwan (about 25%).

As a developing country, it is inevitable that Thailand's economic development has been somewhat uneven. Problems with roads, ports, and communication systems are understandable given the tremendous changes that have occurred in the last few years. The government has allocated a significant percentage of its budget to improving the country's infrastructure over the next five years.

Of greater importance to Thailand's future within Asia, as well as internationally, is its role of mediator between the neighbouring countries of Burma, Kampuchea, Vietnam, and Laos. As these countries strive to revitalise their economies, Thailand will serve not only as an example of what can be achieved, but also as adviser, bank, and a source of technology transfer. Thailand's neutral stance towards both East and West enables it to represent its neighbours in both hemispheres — what could be described as 'the Domino Theory in Reverse' (Figure 8.4). During the Vietnam War, the Pentagon expected the South-East Asian nations to topple like dominoes before the advance of communism. Now it is the success of the free nations such as Thailand that may win over its neighbours by peaceful means.

Historical Background

The Bangkok Stock Exchange was established in 1962. However, there was very little activity and the Exchange was disbanded soon after. In 1974, the Securities Exchange of Thailand (SET) was created; by 1976, it was operating with the listing of 14 companies and two government bonds.

In 1978, the SET had its first bull market. The index reached 266.18 and then crashed almost immediately following the collapse of a highly speculative finance company. From 1979 to 1981, interest in the stock market was minimal, dampened by the government's tight monetary policy, high interest rates worldwide, and declining corporate earnings. In September 1981, the SET Index hit a low of 103.19.

By 1982, declining oil prices and lower interest rates began to stimulate the market, and prices moved higher on a steadily improving volume. Despite a devaluation in the currency in November 1984, the SET Index closed the year at 142.29.

In 1985, a healthier trade account and the announcement of increased foreign investment through the *Bangkok Fund* (launched by Merrill Lynch) spurred the index to a high of 158.08 in July. Trading was then slow until June 1986, when the market embarked upon its present bullish trend, fuelled by a series of interest rate cuts and an upturn in the economy. The launch of the US$30 million *Thailand Fund* (Morgan Stanley) in December 1986 gave a further boost to the market.

Figure 8.4 The Domino Theory in Reverse

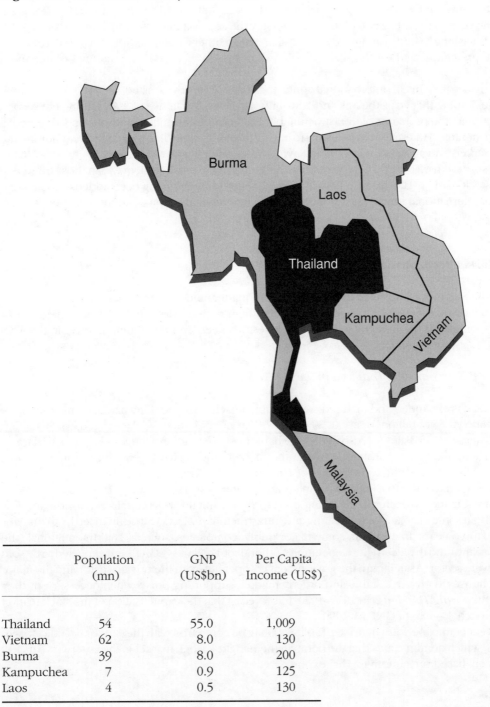

	Population (mn)	GNP (US$bn)	Per Capita Income (US$)
Thailand	54	55.0	1,009
Vietnam	62	8.0	130
Burma	39	8.0	200
Kampuchea	7	0.9	125
Laos	4	0.5	130

Source: Indosuez Asia Investment Services research.

In early 1987, fund managers around the world discovered Thailand and wanted to invest there. Despite the crash in October of that year, the market was still one of the world's best-performing, ending the year up 68%. The end of the year also saw the creation of the foreign board, designed for foreigners wishing to trade foreign-registered shares with other foreigners. This enabled previously unofficial premiums paid for the scarce foreign shares to be recorded, and trading became more orderly.

In early 1988, a major international fund, the *Siam Fund,* was listed on the London Stock Exchange. During that year, the SET Index went from 280 to 391, a rise of 39%. During the second half of the year, the problems of infrastructure became more apparent to investors, and a change in government caused international investors to pause, resulting in the disappearance of liquidity in the money markets and a rise in interest rates. Savings rates on deposits went from 6.5% to 10.5% in the space of six months. To many local investors, these rates were more attractive than those offered in the dull stock market. The year ended with some US$600 million having been added to the market by way of international funds, and an increase in market capitalisation of about 20%, from US$7.5 billion to US$9 billion.

Stock Market Performance

In 1989, the SET Index improved by 28% in the first quarter, and market capitalisation has reached US$11.3 billion (see Figure 8.1). The premium on foreign-registered shares has gone as high as 40% on some companies, demonstrating overseas investors' keen and continuing interest in the Thai market.

The Securities Exchange of Thailand in the 1990s

The market has expanded and matured considerably, reaching a mid-1989 market capitalisation of approximately US$12 billion, or about 20% of GNP. Turnover in mid-1989 averaged US$30 million per day. There are 145 issues listed, of which the banking shares and cement shares are the two largest sectors. There are 34 Thai brokers active in the market, and a growing number of international brokerage houses have offices in Bangkok. The quality of information has also improved as Thai companies learn to cater to the needs of international investors.

The stock market is increasingly being used to raise capital for economic expansion and it is expected that some major civil engineering and infrastructure projects will be financed by this means in the next two years. In addition, some major public companies, such as Thai International (the national airline) and the Electricity Generating Authority of Thailand (EGAT), are expected to be sold to the private sector. As in Japan, the government co-operates with the private sector and the major financial houses to ensure a stable and orderly market, supporting prices when necessary, as they did with the *Krung Thai Fund* in 1979–1980. It is forecast that the capitalisation of the stock market may approach 30–40% of GNP by 1990.

Five-year market performance (see Table 8.2) may be compared with the economic indicators in Table 8.3, which demonstrates that the boom in the Bangkok stock market in the past two years has been largely based on a boom in Thai exports.

Table 8.2 Stock Market Performance, 1985–1988

Market Indicator	1985	1986	1987	1988
Market Index (SET)	134.95	207.20	284.94	386.73
Market Cap. (US$bn)	1.86	2.90	5.40	8.80
Daily Trading Volume (US$mn)	2.30	3.84	19.17	25.00
No. of Listed Companies	97	92	102	122
Exchange Rate	26.65	26.13	25.07	25.24
Currency App. vs US$	1.84	1.95	4.06	-0.69

Source: Indosuez Asia Investment Services research.

Table 8.3 Economic Indicators, 1985–1988

Indicator	1985	1986	1987	1988
GNP (Bt bn)	996.8	1072.2	1211.4	1440.4
GNP Growth Rate (%)	3.5	4.7	8.0	10.9
PER (X)	9.6	12.3	9.3	14.1
Yield (%)	8.2	4.3	3.9	3.8
Inflation (%)	2.4	1.9	2.5	4.5
Exports (Bt bn)	189.2	229.9	290.8	401.3
Imports (Bt bn)	247.8	243.0	333.4	492.2

Source: Indosuez Asia Investment Services research.

Stock Exchange Details

Address

Securities Exchange of Thailand
2nd Floor, Sinthon Building
132 Wireless Road
Bangkok 10500
Tel: 250–0001/8 250–0010/15
Cable: SECEXTHAI
Tlx: 20126 BEJARA TH
Fax: 254–3040

Trading Days/Hours

Trading hours are from 9.30 am to 11.30 am, Monday to Friday.

Stock Market Indices

Four different market indices are calculated on a daily basis: the SET Index, the TISCO Index, the Book Club Index, and the CMRI Index. The SET and Book Club indices both incorporate all quoted securities, are weighted for market capitalisation, and are adjusted for capital changes and changes in the number of components. There are certain differences, however, in the ways the SET and Book Club indices assume prices for untraded securities and adjust for capital changes.

The TISCO Index is unweighted for market capitalisation but is adjusted for capital changes. The CMRI Index is weighted according to turnover value. In addition to the four market indices, there are daily sectoral indices for the banking, financial, commercial, construction, and textiles sectors.

Trading is conducted on three separate boards: the main board, the special board and the foreign board. The main board is for regular trading. Trading is done by 'open auction', whereby members post their bids and offers. The special board is for big and odd lots. The foreign board is for trading in foreign-registered stocks which are available for shares to be owned and registered in the name of foreigners.

Rules and Regulations

The rules and regulations for trading on the stock market are as follows:
1. Bid price shall be made at not less than four spreads from the last sale or the last highest bid of the previous day, whichever is higher.
2. The offer price shall be made at not more than four spreads from the last sale or the last lowest offer of the previous day, whichever is lower.
3. A member may not trade more than 20 board lots for an order. If he wants to trade more than the limit, he must post his number below that of other members.
4. The price is not permitted to move higher or lower than 10% of the closing price of the preceding day.
5. Any single transaction exceeding 10 million Baht or 10% of the capital of any listed company is categorised as a big lot. It must be traded on the special board and have the approval of the SET.

Settlement

Settlement in Thailand takes four days. All transactions on the trading floor are cleared through the SET on the third business day following the trading day. On the afternoon of the trading day, the local broker telexes confirmation of the number of shares purchased or sold, the price, the total cost (including the fixed brokerage fee of 0.5%), and the payment date. Upon receipt of the confirmation telex, instructions are sent to the client and to the custodian bank. Since many clients do not have Thai baht accounts, settlement is mostly in US dollars. Funds should reach the broker in Thailand on the third day following the transaction so that the delivery of shares can take place on the fourth day.

Disclosure

The SET places great importance on the ready availability for public investors of any company news which may influence the prices of securities, so such information must always be disclosed accurately, promptly, and impartially. Disclosure measures arranged by the SET are shown in Table 8.4.

Table 8.4 Disclosure Measures

Type of Information	Time Period
1. Financial Statement: Quarter	Within 45 days from the end of each quarter of performance period.
Annual	Within 60 days if the financial statement of the fourth quarter had not been submitted before, and within three months if the financial statement of the fourth quarter had been submitted.
2. Information on operations and financial structure which might affect trading shares and interests of shareholders	Prompt disclosure.

Source: Securities Market in Thailand, 1988.

Custodial Services

It is possible to export share certificates by means of an Exchange Control (EC) form. However, this is a rather complicated procedure and is not to be recommended. Share custodial facilities can be provided by finance companies, Thai banks, and branches of foreign banks in Thailand.

It is possible for foreign investors to register shares in the name of a local nominee or 'street name'. Nominee services are provided by most finance companies. It is an offence for shares that are beneficially owned by a foreigner to be registered in the name of a local nominee with the intention of circumventing legal foreign ownership limits, and both the foreign beneficial owner and the local nominee are liable to be fined.

At present, it is not always possible to ascertain with accuracy the margin available for the registration of new foreign shareholders in a given company. Consequently, foreign investors can sometimes be placed in a false position if they buy shares on the local board in good faith and find, subsequently, that they are unable to register the shares because the foreign ownership limit has unexpectedly been reached. In such cases, the Bank of Thailand has been known to allow foreign beneficial owners to keep shares registered in a local nominee account for up to a year without imposing any restrictions on eventual repatriation of funds or dividends.

The Twenty Largest Stocks

Table 8.5, showing the 20 largest quoted companies, includes current foreign shareholdings as compared with the limit allowed in each.

Table 8.5 The 20 Largest Quoted Stocks by Market Capitalisation, as at 31 December 1988

Company	Market Capitalisation (Baht bn)	Maximum-allowed Foreign Holding (%)	Latest (%)
Siam Cement	35.05	25.00	24.99
Bangkok Bank	17.46	25.00	25.00
Siam City Cement	16.56	30.00	20.32
Thai Farmers Bank	11.07	25.00	24.96
Siam Commercial Bank	6.34	25.00	24.99
Bank of Ayudhya	7.28	25.00	25.00
Siam Pulp & Paper	6.51	20.00	7.18
Padaeng Industries	7.42	40.00	24.84
Thai Plastics	5.72	49.00	42.40
Thai Military Bank	5.41	20.00	3.54
First Bangkok	3.77	25.00	1.03
Thai Securities	3.51	40.00	40.00
CP Feedmills	5.01	40.00	21.54
Siam City	3.37	25.00	0.50
Oriental Hotel	3.64	49.00	49.00
Dusit Thani	3.31	30.00	30.00
Bangkok Insurance	2.88	25.00	3.40
Saha Union	2.62	20.00	20.00
East Asiatic	2.37	49.00	49.07
American Standard	2.45	100.00	69.76

Source: National Finance.

Table 8.6 shows the 20 largest quoted companies in terms of turnover.

Major Types of Investors

The Mutual Fund Company

There are currently nine country funds for foreign investors, worth approximately US$710 million, or 6.5% of market capitalisation. Six of these funds, as well as the five local mutual funds, are run by the only authorised fund management company, the Mutual Fund Company. It is estimated that as much as 15% of the market may be controlled by the Mutual Fund Company.

Table 8.6 The 20 Largest Quoted Stocks by Turnover, 1988

Company	Daily Average (Shares)
CP Feedmills	166,750
SCIB	124,926
Padaeng Industries	53,195
Bangkok Bank	41,242
FBCB	51,865
Saha Union	35,285
Oriental Hotel	26,210
Thai Farmers Bank	22,824
Thai Plastics	12,100
Bank of Ayudhya	10,285
Thai Military Bank	10,094
Jalaprathan Cement	8,617
Siam Commercial Bank	8,138
Thai Securities	7,380
Bank of Asia	6,280
Siam Cement	5,504
Bangkok Insurance	3,793
Siam City Cement	3,182
East Asiatic	1,465
International Cosmetics	1,442

Source: National Finance.

Individual Investors

Local businessmen are also very active in the market; often they are short-term players and participate in one or two stocks at a time. Their support, or lack of it, can cause dramatic fluctuations in a stock's price.

Foreign Investors

The foreign investor is limited in his activities on the SET and is rarely an important influence on daily fluctuations. The foreign board records a daily volume equal to roughly 11% of that of the SET, but as deals are rarely done during normal trading hours they have little influence on local prices. The trading in local shares for foreigners (not permitted except when the foreign limit in a stock is not reached) is fairly important, although impossible to measure. It may be about half of that recorded on the foreign board, or 6% of the total.

Dealing Costs

Brokerage

Commission paid to brokers for buying or selling securities is standardised, as shown in Table 8.7.

Table 8.7 Standard Brokerage Charges

Common stock, preferred stock, or unit trusts	0.5% of value traded (min. 50 Baht)
Government bond, debenture	0.1% of value traded (min. 50 Baht)

Source: Securities Exchange of Thailand.

Stamp Duty

Transferors of share certificates, debentures certificates, and bonds must pay stamp duty according to the value of the paid-up shares or the value of the transfer instruments, whichever is the greater, at the rate of one Baht for every 1,000 Baht or fraction thereof. The exceptions are:
* transfers of listed or authorised securities with the SET as registrar; and
* transfers of government bonds and the mutual fund company's unit trusts.
  A foreigner who is transferring shares must pay stamp duty at the same rate as a domestic investor.

Major Securities Houses

Thai Securities Co. Ltd
7th Floor, Boonmir Building
138 Silom Road
Bangkok 10500
Tel: 2339885–93

Nava Finance and Securities Co. Ltd
422 Phyathai Road
Bangkok 10500
Tel: 2150969–98

Phatra Thanakit Co. Ltd
Phatra Thanakit Building
183 Sukhumvit Road
Between Soi 13–15 Bangkok 10110
Tel: 2530121

Asia Securities Trading Co. Ltd
333 Bangkok Bank Building
Silom Road
Bangkok 10500
Tel: 2350733–40   2353230–1

Cathay Trust Co. Ltd
Cathay Trust Building
1016 Rama IV Road
Bangkok 10500
Tel: 2330421–9 2500350–2

Securities One Ltd
12th Floor, Maneeya Center Building
518/5 Ploenchit Road
Bangkok 10500
Tel: 2551388

Asia Credit Ltd
320 Rama IV Road
Bangkok 10500
Tel: 2351477

National Financial and Securities Co. Ltd
15th, 16th Floors, MBK Tower
444 Phyathai Road
Bangkok 10500
Tel: 2179595 2179622

General Finance & Securities Co. Ltd
62 Soi Langsuan,
Ploenchit Road
Bangkok 10500
Tel: 2513141–50   2535934–8

The Book Club Finance and Securities Co. Ltd
9th Floor, Amarin Tower
500 Ploenchit Road
Bangkok 10500
Tel: 2569113   2569118

Bangkok First Investment & Trust Ltd
300 Silom Road
Bangkok 10500
Tel: 2334150

Union Asia Finance Ltd
Ruamsermkij Building
136 Silom Road

Bangkok 10500
Tel: 2367511

Mithai Europartners Finance and Securities Co. Ltd
10th Floor, Boonmir Building
138 Silom Road
Bangkok 10500
Tel: 2331966–7

Dhana Siam Finance and Securities Co. Ltd
2nd Floor, Sinthon Building
132 Wireless Road
Bangkok 10500
Tel: 2500250–9

First Pacific Asia Securities Co.
6th Floor, Asia Building
11 Sathorn Road
Bangkok 10120
Tel: 2132681–8

Listing Criteria

Trading on the SET is restricted to listed and authorised securities. Listing criteria for each category are shown in Table 8.8.

Table 8.8   Listing Criteria

Qualification	Listed	Authorised
1. Capital is in the form of ordinary shares	20 million Baht	— 10 million Baht for small-size firm or restructuring firm — or 20 million Baht for newly established firm
2. Number of small shareholders*	300	50
3. Distribution of shares to small shareholders*	30% of paid-up capital	10% of paid-up capital
4. Specifications of equity shares	(a) registered shares (b) par value of no more than 100 Baht each, with the exception of shares of a juristic person established under a special law or of a limited public company	
5. Financial position	Sound, appropriate, and satisfactory past performance and/or good potential and/or sound future plan	
6. Main business	Economically and socially beneficial to the nation	
7. Transfer of shares	No restriction	

Source: Securities Exchange of Thailand.
Note: *A small shareholder is one who holds shares of not less than one board lot but not more than 5/1,000 of the paid-up capital.

Mutual Funds/Unit Trusts

Because of the increasing popularity of the Thai market and the scarcity of shares, the closed-end 'country' funds have become extremely popular. There are presently nine 'country' funds, managed or started up by foreign institutions, and four local mutual funds. The advantage of investing in these funds is that they offer a diversified portfolio that might otherwise be impossible to acquire. The disadvantage is that often, with the exception of the small local funds, these 'country' funds trade at a premium to net asset value.

There are three types of Thailand 'country' funds open to foreign investors: foreign onshore investment funds, foreign offshore investment funds, and domestic investment funds. All of these funds are open to foreign investors without any limitation and receive certain tax benefits. In accordance with the Ministry of Finance's preference for closed-end funds, most Thailand 'country' funds are closed-ended or redeemable only after a grace period.

All of the foreign investment funds, with one exception, are listed on foreign stock exchanges and thus provide foreign investors with a convenient means of acquiring a broad exposure to the Thai market without the need to go through Thai exchange control formalities.

Foreign Onshore Funds

The foreign onshore funds (see Table 8.9) have the benefit of Thai investor status, which means that they can hold local-registered stocks without restriction and do not have to buy on the foreign board. This obviates the need to pay foreign board premiums and facilitates the acquisition of those stocks which are in short supply on the foreign board.

The foreign onshore funds are managed jointly by their overseas managers and the partly state-owned Mutual Fund Company, which has the only investment management licence issued to date by the Ministry of Finance. The Mutual Fund Company enjoys sub-broker status on the stock exchange and pays only 0.3% commission, compared to the standard rate of 0.5%.

Table 8.9 Foreign Onshore Funds

Thai Fund Inc. (closed-ended)	Year launched:	1988
	Year of maturity:	2013
	Issue amount:	US$115 mn
	No. of units:	9.6 mn
	Invest. status:	Foreign onshore
	Listing:	New York
	Tax status:	12.5% capital gains tax. 10% withholding tax on dividends.
	Managers:	Morgan Stanley Asset Management Mutual Fund Company
	Invest. policy:	Emphasis on blue chips. Cannot invest in finance and securities companies.
Thailand Growth Fund (closed-ended)	Year launched:	1988
	Year of maturity:	2013
	Issue amount:	US$50 mn
	No. of units:	5 mn

	Invest. status:	Foreign onshore
	Listing:	Unlisted
	Invest. status:	Nil capital gains tax. 10% withholding tax on dividends.
	Managers:	Nikko International Capital Management Mutual Fund Company
	Invest. policy:	25% blue chips, 25% new listing. Up to 50% can be in debentures, government bonds, and the money market.

Thai Prime Fund (closed-ended)		
	Year launched:	1988
	Year of maturity:	2013
	Issue amount:	US$155 mn
	No. of units:	15.5 mn
	Invest. status:	Foreign onshore
	Listing:	Singapore
	Tax status:	Nil capital gains tax. 10% withholding tax on dividends.
	Managers:	Nomura Capital Management Mutual Fund Company
	Invest. policy:	75% in leading equities, 25% in new listings or unlisted securities.

Thailand Fund (open-ended)		
	Year launched:	1986
	Year of maturity:	2001
	Issue amount:	US$30 mn
	No. of units:	3 mn
	Invest. status:	Foreign onshore
	Listing:	London
	Tax status:	12.5% capital gains tax. 10% withholding tax on dividends.
	Managers:	Morgan Stanley Asset Management Mutual Fund Company
	Invest. policy:	To invest in a broad spectrum of stocks. 10% can be in unlisted equities, debentures, and other instruments.

Thai-Euro Fund (closed-ended)		
	Year launched:	1988
	Year of maturity:	2038
	Issue amount:	US$75 mn
	No. of units:	7.5 mn
	Invest. status:	Foreign onshore
	Listing:	London
	Tax status:	No capital gains tax. 10% withholding tax on dividends.
	Managers:	Lloyds Investment Managers Mutual Fund Company
	Invest. policy:	To invest in a broad spectrum of stocks. 10% can be in unlisted equities, debentures, and other instruments.

Thai International Fund		
	Year launched:	1989
	Year of maturity:	2018
	Issue amount:	US$100 mn
	No. of units:	10 mn
	Invest. status:	Foreign onshore
	Listing:	London
	Tax status:	No capital gains tax.
		10% withholding tax on dividends.
	Managers:	Fidelity International
		Mutual Fund Company
	Invest. adviser:	Phatra Thanakit
	Invest policy:	To invest in a broad spectrum of stocks. 10% can be in unlisted equities, debentures, and other instruments.

Foreign Offshore Funds

Foreign offshore funds (see Table 8.10) are obliged to buy foreign-registered stocks in companies which have already reached their foreign ownership limits, although premiums paid for foreign-registered stocks are ignored for the purposes of calculating NAVs. This means, in effect, that NAVs of foreign offshore funds are understated at times when overseas demand pushes foreign-registered shares to premiums. There is, however, an attendant downside risk that NAVs will be overstated if foreign board prices fall to a discount to the main board, as they did in the wake of the October 1987 crash. This element of the hidden foreign board premium/discount clearly has a distorting effect on the foreign offshore funds' own premiums/discounts to NAV.

Foreign offshore funds have investment advisers in Bangkok, but investment decisions are generally made by overseas managers (except for the *Bangkok Fund*).

Table 8.10   Foreign Offshore Funds

Bangkok Fund (open-ended)		
	Year launched:	1985
	Year of maturity:	2035
	Issue amount:	US$42.7 mn
	No. of units:	2.5 mn
	Invest. status:	Foreign offshore
	Listing:	London
	Tax status:	Nil capital gains tax.
		20% withholding tax on dividends.
	Manager:	Merrill Lynch/Bangkok First Investment Trust.
	Invest. policy:	No funds or unlisted companies.
Siam Fund (closed-ended)		
	Year launched:	1988
	Year of maturity:	2038
	Issue amount:	US$80 mn
	No. of units:	8 mn
	Invest. status:	Foreign offshore

	Listing:	London
	Tax status:	Nil capital gains tax.
		20% withholding tax on dividends.
	Managers:	Indosuez Asia Investment Services
	Invest. adviser:	Asia Securities
	Invest. policy:	Few restrictions except a maximum of 10% of assets can be invested in one company.
Thai Investment Fund (closed-ended)	Year launched:	1988
	Year of maturity:	2038
	Issue amount:	US$30 mn
	No. of units:	3 mn
	Invest. status:	Foreign offshore
	Listing:	London
	Tax status:	25% capital gains tax.
		20% withholding tax on dividends.
	Manager:	Yamaichi Capital Management
	Invest. policy:	Broad spectrum of Thai securities.

Domestic Funds

The three *Sinpinyo Funds* (numbers 3, 4, and 5), the *Ruam Pattana Fund*, and *Subthawee 2* are all listed on the SET and are actively traded by locals, although foreign interest has remained sporadic. *Sinpinyos 1* and *2* and *Subthawee 1* were liquidated on reaching maturity. The *Sub-Somboon Fund* is an unlisted, open-ended fund.

The five domestic funds are all managed by the Mutual Fund Company (see Table 8.11).

Table 8.11 Domestic Funds

Subthawee 2 (closed-ended)	Year launched:	1988
	Year of maturity:	1997
	Issue amount:	US$19.8 mn
	No. of units:	50 mn
	Invest. status:	Domestic
	Listing:	Bangkok
	Tax status:	Tax exempt
	Manager:	Mutual Fund Company
	Invest. policy:	Listed securities.
Sub-Somboon (open-ended)	Year launched:	1986
	Year of maturity:	Undated
	Issue amount:	Unlisted
	No. of units:	Unlimited
	Invest. status:	Domestic
	Listing:	Unlisted
	Tax status:	Tax exempt
	Manager:	Mutual Fund Company
	Invest. policy:	Listed securities.

Ruam Pattana	Year launched:	1987
(closed-ended)	Year of maturity:	1993
	Issue amount:	US$39.6 mn
	No. of units:	120 mn
	Invest. status:	Domestic
	Listing:	Bangkok
	Tax status:	Tax exempt
	Manager:	Mutual Fund Company
	Invest. policy:	Listed equities. Established after the October 1987 crash to improve market liquidity.

Sinpinyo 4	Year launched:	1987
(closed-ended)	Year of maturity:	1997
	Issue amount:	US$11.9 mn
	No. of units:	30 mn
	Invest. status:	Domestic
	Listing:	Bangkok
	Tax status:	Tax exempt
	Manager:	Mutual Fund Company
	Invest. policy:	Listed equities. Slight bias towards special situation.

Sinpinyo 5	Year launched:	1987
(closed-ended)	Year of maturity:	1997
	Issue amount:	US$47.5 mn
	No. of units:	120 mn
	Invest. status:	Domestic
	Listing:	Bangkok
	Tax status:	Tax exempt
	Manager:	Mutual Fund Company
	Invest. policy:	Listed equities. Slight bias towards special situations.

Rules for Foreign Investors

Foreign Investment Restrictions

Essential to an understanding of the Thai market is the difference between foreign and local shares. Thai companies are permitted by law to be up to 49% foreign owned — although percentages are lower in the finance sector and higher in the manufacturing sector. Companies can, and do, choose to allow even less to be available to the non-Thai investor, the consequence being that shares permitted to be held by the foreign investor are rare — and expensive. A foreign board was created in September 1987 to distinguish the trading in foreign shares from local shares, often at a considerable premium.

Foreign Exchange Control

All inward remittances of foreign exchange are documented by means of the Bank of Thailand's E.C. 71 form. Whenever it is desired to repatriate proceeds from sales or dividend payments, this form must be produced to prove that shares were originally purchased with legally imported foreign exchange.

There is no restriction on the number of buying and selling transactions that can be made with funds imported via a single E.C. 71 form. In practice, however, a large number of transactions can lead to a slight delay on final repatriation of funds as the history of the transactions must be traced. Repatriation of funds is effected by means of an E.C. 31 form.

The time required to complete exchange control formalities for repatriation of funds is on average between seven and ten days. The notorious delays in repatriation of funds which were experienced after the October 1987 crash are unlikely to be repeated as the Bank of Thailand has improved its procedures in this area. Local brokers' back offices are also now more adept at handling documentation required for foreigners' transactions.

Taxation

Dividends are subject to a withholding tax of 20% in the case of foreign corporate investors and 15% for foreign individuals. Capital gains are liable to withholding tax at the rate of 25% in the case of foreign companies which are not residents of a jurisdiction that has a double taxation treaty with Thailand. Foreign individuals are not liable to tax on capital gains.

The following countries have double taxation treaties with Thailand:

Austria	Italy
Belgium	Japan
Canada	Malaysia
China (PRC)	Norway
Denmark	Pakistan
Germany (GDR)	Philippines
Finland	Poland
France	Singapore
Holland	South Korea
India	Sweden
Indonesia	United Kingdom

Most of these jurisdictions benefit from total exemption from capital gains tax.

Available Research

Securities Market in Thailand, 1988
Exchange Control in Thailand — A Guide for General Readers on Foreign Investment

9

THE PHILIPPINES

Introduction

Until the late 1960s, the Manila Exchange (together with the Makati Exchange) was a larger and more active market than Hong Kong. During the long economic decline of the Marcos years, the market also fell into the doldrums: there was a growing flight of capital, as well as a 'brain drain'.

With the removal of Ferdinand Marcos, and the arrival of President 'Cory' Aquino in February 1986, the Philippine Stock Exchange recovered dramatically. However, continuing doubts about the political and economic stability of the country meant that there was little follow-through to this rebound.

By early 1989, the Philippine economy was once more firmly on a growth path (indeed, many observers were predicting it would be the next 'Tiger' economy), foreign direct investment had begun to flow in again at a rate of more than US$2.5 billion a year, and the stock market had at last begun to stir from its torpor. Multiples were at 6.3 times, the peso had stabilised, real estate prices were booming, and many of the large Philippine companies were reporting good earnings growth.

Historical Background

The Manila Stock Exchange (MSE) was incorporated on 10 August 1927 as a voluntary, non-profitmaking organisation patterned after the New York Stock Exchange. It is one of the oldest stock markets in Asia. Securities transactions were not regulated until 1936, when the Securities and Exchange Commission (SEC) was set up.

The first stock market boom occurred in 1934, when the devaluation of the US dollar increased gold prices to US$35.00 per ounce. Other periods of activity were associated with the rise in copper prices in 1989 and oil prices in the 1970s.

The Makati Stock Exchange was established in 1964 as a rival to the MSE. Now, however, they are practically unified. For example, listing on one exchange automatically guarantees listing on the other. There is also a joint listing approval committee that is comprised of members from both exchanges. At present, there are about 140 listed companies. However, as not all companies have both 'A' and 'B' shares (foreigners are only allowed to own 'B' shares, while Filipinos can own both), the total listed shares amount to about 230.

Note: US$1.00 = Ph. P21.3.

Figure 9.1   Manila S.E. Composite-Price Index, Weekly, 1987–1989

Source: Datastream.

Figure 9.2   Philippine Peso vs US Dollar, Weekly, 1982–1989

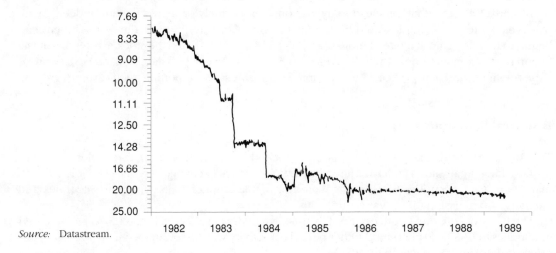

Source: Datastream.

Total turnover on the exchanges averages approximately US$2 million per day. The shares listed under the Commercial-Industrial Index account for 75% of the market capitalisation. The present market capitalisation is roughly US$4.6 billion.

Until the 1986 'People's Revolution', interest in the Philippine stock market was mainly domestic, with excitement in the market being generated by genuine and speculative rises in the prices of gold, copper, and oil. The revolution gave the Philippine stock market (and economy) a new lease of life. Domestic and foreign interest surged. In fact, for the first 12 months of the Aquino government, the Manila Composite Index (see Figure 9.1) grew over 230%. (The same index rose 570% for the first

18 months after the overthrow of Marcos.) GDP growth, led by pent-up consumer demand, was 2% in 1986, 5.7% in 1987, and 6.7% in 1988. In stock market terms, this spectacular turnaround in the economy meant that investors' focus was now on the commercial and industrial sector, the favourites of foreign investors being San Miguel and Philippine Long Distance Telephone.

With the economic recovery almost three years old, the question is: can it continue? The available statistics indicate that it can. The most significant of these is the Board of Investments' announcement that it had registered, in January 1989, investment projects worth over US$1 billion, 58% more than for the whole of 1988. Estimates now call for the investments segment of GDP to grow by over 26% in 1989. In fact, the recently approved International Monetary Fund (IMF) package of reforms calls for GDP growth averaging 6% over the next five years.

This renewed confidence in the Philippine economy (to a certain extent also influenced by the relative political stability) implies that the country's stock market will increasingly be at the forefront of international investors' attention. The rapid growth in the volume of activity on the MSE in the past two years is shown in Figure 9.3.

Figure 9.3 Volume Turnover, 1978–1988

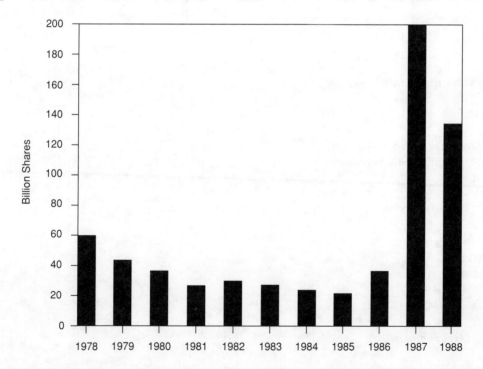

Source: Manila Stock Exchange.

Stock Market Performance

Table 9.1 demonstrates the dramatic recovery of both the Philippine economy and the stock market, following the political crisis of early 1986. The currency has remained fairly stable (see Figure 9.2), and the tourism industry has grown steadily.

Table 9.1 Stock Market Performance, 1984–1988

Market Indicator	1984	1985	1986	1987	1988
Real GDP Growth (%)	-6.80	-3.80	2.00	5.70	6.70
CPI (%)	50.30	23.10	0.80	3.80	8.80
Comm. & Indust. Index	106.00	161.00	548.00	813.00	847.00
Market Capitalisation (peso bn)	16.50	12.70	41.20	61.10	88.60
PER	5.84	4.91	3.84	7.93	6.70
Exchange Rate (peso/US$)	19.76	19.03	20.53	20.80	21.33
Visitor Arrivals ('000)	817.00	773.00	781.00	795.00	1,010.00

Source: Indosuez Asia Investment Services research.

Stock Exchange Details

Addresses

Manila Stock Exchange
Prensa St. Cor Muelle de la Industria
Binondo
Manila
Tel: 471125 408860

Makati Stock Exchange
Ayala Avenue
Metro Manila
Tel: 887871 886411
Cbl: MAKATSTOCK

Trading Days/Hours

Trading at the Makati and Manila stock exchanges is from 9.30 am to 12.10 pm, with a 20-minute extension to 12.30 pm during which time transactions are done on the basis of the closing prices at 12.10 pm. There are two ten-minute intervals, at 10.20 am and 11.30 am. Trading is from Monday to Friday, except for legal and special holidays.

Transactions on the Stock Exchange

Transactions on the Makati and Manila stock exchanges must be made through an approved stockbroker. However, some local banks are also permitted to provide these services. Common, preferred, convertible, and also over-the-counter shares are available for investment to the public.

Trading is done by board lots ranging from five to 200,000 shares depending on the price range of a particular stock and whether it is common or preferred stock. Trading on odd lots, or stocks transacted for less shares than the minimum board lot, is done by brokers on a board specifically assigned for odd-lot trading.

Trading is done by the open outcry system using blackboards where 'bid' and 'asked' prices are posted in the appropriate columns.

Two types of common stock are available in the Philippines: Class A common stock, which is exclusive to Filipino citizens; and Class B common stock, which can be owned by both Filipino and foreign investors alike. Both classes have the same privileges and receive the same dividends. Shares are classified in this way in order better to monitor the Filipino and foreign equity ownership of a company engaged in the exploitation and development of natural resources (such as mineral or oil properties), or the operation of public utilities.

Transactions for Non-residents

Securities dealers/brokers may undertake stock transactions, whether arbitrage or investment, without prior Central Bank approval. However, when the purchase/sale of Philippine shares of stock involves a non-resident, whether the transaction is effected in the domestic or the foreign market, it will be the responsibility of the securities dealers/brokers to register the transaction with the Central Bank. The local securities dealer/broker shall file with the Central Bank, within three business days from the transaction date, an application in the prescribed form for registration. After compliance with other required undertakings, the Central Bank shall issue a Certificate of Registration.

Under the Central Bank rules, all registered foreign investments in Philippine securities including profits and dividends, net of taxes and charges, may be repatriated.

Settlement

Payment of the cost of a transaction must be made by the buying client upon receipt of confirmation from the broker, but not later than the settlement date. Regular transactions must be settled on the fourth trading day following the date of the transaction. Certificates sold must be delivered by the selling client before the fourth trading day following the sale.

Brokers tabulate all their transactions in a deliver-and-transfer summary which is submitted to the clearing agent of the Exchange on the fourth day from the date of a transaction. The clearing agent of the Exchange is usually a reputable bank licensed as such by the SEC.

Stock certificates of shares purchased are delivered by the buying broker to the client as soon as they are received from the transfer office and clearing house, if the client has requested that the issuance be in his name.

Payment for shares sold is remitted to the client by the selling broker on the fourth trading day after the sale.

The Rizal Commercial Banking Corporation provides settlement for the Makati Stock Exchange, while the Equitable Banking Corporation provides settlement for the Manila Stock Exchange.

The Twenty Largest Stocks

The 20 largest quoted companies in terms of market value are shown in Table 9.2.

Table 9.2   The 20 Largest Quoted Stocks by Market Capitalisation, as at 31 December 1988

Company	Market Value (Pesos bn)
San Miguel 'A'	18.8
Ayala Corporation 'A'	15.2
Philippine Long Distance Telephone	12.8
San Miguel 'B'	10.0
Ayala Corporation 'B'	6.4
Philex Mining Corporation 'A'	4.3
Bank of the Philippine Islands	4.0
Philex Mining Corporation 'B'	3.0
Atlas Consolidated Mining 'A'	2.9
Atlas Consolidated Mining 'B'	1.8
Benguet Corporation 'A'	1.7
Lepanto Consolidated 'A'	1.6
Philippine Overseas Drilling Corporation 'A'	1.5
Philippine Commercial & International Bank	1.4
Benguet Consolidated 'B'	1.3
Oriental Petroleum Corporation	1.3
Purefoods 'A'	1.2
Anscor 'A'	1.2
Lepanto Consolidated 'B'	1.1
Anscor 'B'	0.8

Source: Manila/Makati Stock Exchange.

Dealing Costs

Brokerage

A broker is compensated for his services in executing orders on the Exchange through commission charges which are paid by both the buyer and the seller. The brokerage commission rate is 1.5% of the transaction value. However, for a transaction amounting to 3,000 pesos or less, the minimum commission charge is 45 pesos.

Transfer Fee

A transfer fee of 20 pesos per stock certificate is charged by the transfer agent for every transfer.

Documentary Stamp Tax

Documentary stamp tax is collected by the transfer agent at the rate of 0.50 pesos for every 200 pesos par value of the stock being transferred or a fraction thereof.

Final Transfer Tax

Sales of stocks listed and traded on the Stock Exchange are subject to a final transfer tax at the rate of 1/4 of 1% of the value of the transaction in lieu of capital gains tax.

Major Securities Houses

Local Securities Houses

A Garcia JR Securities Corporation
4th Floor, Maripola Building
109 Perea Street
Legaspi Village
Makati
Metro Manila
Tel: 8189499 489219

Ansaldo, Godines & Co. Inc.
340 Neuva Street
Manila
Tel: 476161 405706

Anscor Hagedorn Securities Inc.
3rd Floor, Asian Plaza I
Sen. Gil. J. Puyat Avenue
Salcedo Village
Makati
Metro Manila
Tel: 8193151

B L Tan Securities Inc.
3rd Floor, Manila Stock Exchange Building
Prensa Street
Binondo
Manila
Tel: 409836

Barcelon-Roxas Securities Inc.
6th Floor, Padilla de Los Reyes Building
232 Juan Luna Street
Binondo
Manila
Tel: 485003 487421

Citisecurities Inc.
3rd Floor, Manila Stock Exchange Building
Prensa Street
Binondo
Manila
Tel: 409836 409867

Cualoping Securities Corporation
Suite 1804, Tytana Centre Condominium
Plaza Lorenzo Ruiz
Binondo
Manila
Tel: 402929 402466

David Go Securities Corporation
Suite 307, Federation Centre Building
Muelle de Binondo
Binondo
Manila
Tel: 487009 404108

Equitable Securities (Phils) Inc.
3rd Floor, Cacho-Gonzalez Building
Aguirre and Trasierra Streets
Legaspi Village
Makati
Metro Manila
Tel: 891806   494241

I.B. Gimenez Securities Inc.
3rd Floor, Manila Stock Exchange Building
Prensa Street
Binondo
Manila
Tel: 408822   408787

Pryce Securities Inc.
2nd Floor, Basil Petroleum Building
Alvarado Street
Leopagi Village
Makati
Metro Manila
Tel: 8150240

R. Coyiuto Securities Inc.
7th Floor, AIC Centre Building
204 Escolta Street
Metro Manila
Tel: 400817   400995

Squire Securities Inc.
5th Floor, Makati Stock Exchange Building
Ayala Avenue
Makati

Metro Manila
Tel: 8105740   475222

Foreign Securities Houses

First Pacific Securities Philippines
4th Floor, First Holdings Centre
349 Sen. Gil. J. Puyat Avenue
Makati
Metro Manila
Tel: 8163471   484321

James Capel Philippines Inc.
3rd Floor, Cibeles Building
6780 Ayala Avenue
Makati
Metro Manila
Tel: 8105106

Peregrine Philippine Holdings Inc.
Ground Floor, Makati Stock Exchange Building
Ayala Avenue
Makati
Metro Manila
Tel: 8104491/93   8104466/67

Sun Hung Kai Securities (Phils) Inc.
17th Floor, BA-Lepanto Building
Paseo de Roxas
Makati
Metro Manila
Tel: 859876   474682

Listing Criteria

To ensure an equitable and systematic market, the Exchange, under the supervision of the SEC, plays an important role in the stipulation and enforcement of rules for listing and trading.

If a company wishes to raise capital by floating its stocks, it applies for listing at the Exchange subject to its meeting certain requirements prescribed by the SEC and to the submission of certain documents and data, such as:

* The company must have a minimum authorised capital of 50 million pesos, with a positive 12.5 million pesos paid-up capital. 25% of the authorised capital stock must be underwritten and distributed through the member-brokers of the stock exchanges.
* As a rule, the company must have a minimum of 300 stockholders.
* Its securities must be registered/licensed in accordance with the *Revised Securities Act* and be covered by an SEC permit to sell the same to the public.

- Corporate name with a certified true copy of its Articles of Incorporation and By-Laws.
- Amount of its capital stock and number of its shareholders.
- Number and description of shares into which the said capital is divided and the par value.
- Whether the same is fully paid and non-assessable.
- A list of officers and directors of the corporation.
- The location of its offices.
- The name of its proposed transfer agent or its contract with its present transfer agent, if found acceptable by the Exchange.
- Its financial statements for the last three years.
- If there are outstanding bonds and debentures, their amount and character.
- If it is a mining or oil exploration corporation, the status and progress made in the exploration, development, and exploitation work on its properties. In the case of a company engaged in the exploitation and development of mining properties, it must submit certification from the Bureau of Mines that its mining claims/leases are still valid; if the company is engaged in oil exploration, it must submit certification from the Energy Development Board that it has a duly approved subsisting service contract.

Mutual Funds/Unit Trusts

There currently exist three investment trusts which allow investment by foreigners in the Philippines stock markets. They are listed in Table 9.3.

Table 9.3 Mutual Funds/Unit Trusts

Fund	Manager	Inception Date	Listing (if applic.)	Size (US$mn)
JF Philippine Trust	Jardine Fleming	July 1974	Hong Kong	5.2
Thornton Philippines Redevelopment Fund	Thornton	May 1986	Hong Kong	4.0
The Manila Fund*	Indosuez Asia Investment Services	Oct. 1989	London	50.0

Source: Indosuez Asia Investment Services research.
Note: *Closed-end fund.

Rules for Foreign Investors

Foreign Investment Restrictions

Under the Philippine Constitution, foreign nationals may purchase up to 40% of a company's share capital. This is usually by way of issued 'B' shares. Foreign investment over 40% must have the prior approval of the Board of Investments (BOI). Foreign investment below or equal to 40% needs no prior approval. However, the investment must be reported to the BOI and the Central Bank of the Philippines for purposes of capital repatriation and remittance of profits.

Foreign Exchange Control

Exchange control policy is determined by the Monetary Board of the Central Bank, and the regulations are administered by the Central Bank. All ingoing and outgoing capital must have Central Bank authorisation. This authorisation is automatic if transactions are made through an authorised securities dealer. The responsibility for registering securities transactions by a foreign national rests with the securities dealer/broker. While full repatriation of capital is guaranteed, the process is time-consuming.

Taxation

For a non-resident individual, dividends received from a domestic corporation are subject to a withholding tax of 30%.

For a non-resident foreign corporation, dividends from a domestic corporation are subject to a withholding tax of 15%, provided the country in which the foreign corporation is domiciled allows a credit against the tax due from the non-resident foreign corporation. There is an exception in cases where tax treaties are in force.

Capital gains related to the sale, exchange, or disposition of shares of stock in any domestic corporation are taxed, as shown in Table 9.4.

Table 9.4 Taxation on Capital Gains

Net capital gains from shares not traded through a local stock exchange:
    Less than or equal to   100,000 pesos — 10%
    Over   100,000 pesos — 20%
Capital gains from listed shares and traded through a local stock exchange:
    1/4 of 1% of the gross selling price.

Source: Manila Stock Exchange.

Protection of Shareholders

There are several government agencies to protect investors on the subject of fraud, deception, and mergers. The securities industry is regulated by the SEC, a quasi-judicial government agency. Its primary role is to protect the investing public from fraud and deception in securities transactions.

The Securities Investors Protection Fund Inc. (SIPFI) was created to protect investors against losses in case of failure, insolvency, or frauds of member-brokers or dealers. An investor of an insolvent firm may be granted financial assistance up to 10,000 pesos.

The fund is managed by a board of trustees composed of representatives from the SEC, the Makati and Manila Stock Exchanges, the Association of Independent Brokers and Dealers Inc., and the public sector.

Members of the fund pay an initial fee of 10,000 pesos and a monthly due of 1/500 of 1% of their gross monthly volume. The fund now amounts to over 6 million pesos and is made available only to customers of securities firms which are forced to liquidate.

Under the Philippines *Corporation Code*, a merger requires the vote of the majority of the board of directors and two-thirds of the outstanding capital stock holders. Mergers must also be approved by the SEC.

In the case of banks or banking institutions, building and loan associations, trust companies, insurance companies, public utilities, educational institutions, and corporations governed by special laws, the favourable recommendation of the appropriate government agency is also required. A minority stockholder who does not agree to the merger may demand payment for the fair value of his shares.

Available Research

Manila Stock Exchange

Annual Report
Investors' Information Guide, February 1988
Monthly Review
Investments Guide

Makati Stock Exchange

Annual Report
Securities Market Handbook, November 1988
Monthly Digest

10

INDONESIA

Introduction

In the late 1980s, Indonesia has been undergoing a remarkable transformation, particularly with regard to the deregulation and opening up of its small capital market. This development also reflects the fundamental expansion and diversification of its economy away from oil and agriculture (especially timber and plantations) towards manufacturing and service industries, supported by a growing inflow of foreign capital. For the first time since independence in 1948, international businessmen are being welcomed, and have now been assured by the authorities of protection of ownership (up to 49% at least) and repatriation of profits and dividends.

This new confidence has been reflected in the strong performance of the Jakarta stock market in 1988/89. The first international fund for Indonesia securities, the *Malacca Fund* (pioneered by the Indosuez Asia group) was launched and listed on the London Stock Exchange in January 1989; it has since been followed by a number of other closed-end investment funds. It is evident that the impact of this new foreign capital in the local market will be considerable, not only in increased demand for local shares (and, therefore, a growing number of new listings in Jakarta and Surabaya), but also in improving research and reporting standards.

The Republic of Indonesia is situated between the Asian and Australian continents. Extending over 13,667 islands, Indonesia is the world's largest archipelago, with a land area of approximately 1.9 million sq km. Its population, estimated at approximately 175 million in 1988, comprises principally Malays, Melanesians, Arabs, Chinese, and Indians. Islam is the dominant religion (87% of the population), followed by Christianity (9%) and Hinduism (2%).

Indonesia was colonised in the 17th century by the Dutch, who ruled the archipelago until the Japanese invasion in 1942. The country declared its independence in 1945 and an Indonesian nationalist general, General Sukarno, became the Republic's first president. Sukarno also served as the Prime Minister and the leader of the Cabinet. In 1965, an attempted Communist *coup d'etat* was crushed by the military under General Suharto, who was elected president in March 1967.

President Suharto, who was re-elected for his fifth five-year term in March 1988, is the longest-serving president since Indonesia declared its independence from the Netherlands. The president and vice president are elected for five-year terms by the People's Consultative Assembly, composed of 920 elected members. The legislative authority is the House of People's Representatives, which has 360 elected members and 100 members nominated by the president.

Note: US$1.00 = Rp1,773.

Golkar, a coalition of functional groups and armed forces, is the leading political party; in the 1987 polls, it won some 73% of the popular vote. The next elections for parliament will be held in 1992, followed by presidential elections in 1993.

Economy

The Indonesian economy has made a strong recovery since 1986, when it was adversely affected by the fall in world oil prices and the decline in the US dollar. Through a sustained programme of budgetary austerity, currency devaluation, and a relaxation of trade restrictions, the Indonesian government has stemmed the external deficit and maintained domestic fiscal stability.

Figure 10.1   The Jakarta Index, January 1988–September 1989

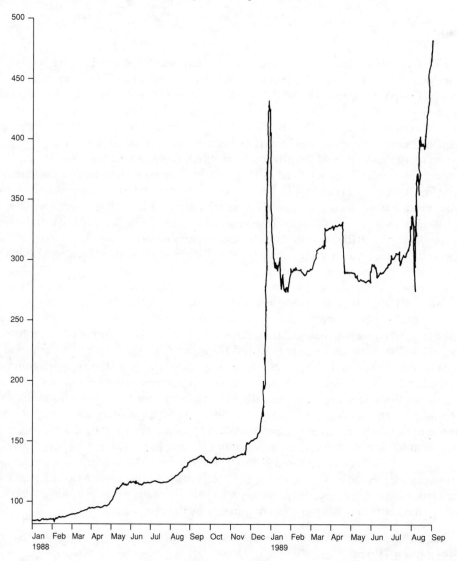

According to the World Bank, strong growth in Indonesia's non-oil and gas exports, especially in the manufacturing sector, helped Gross Domestic Product (GDP) growth to reach 4.2% in 1987. Non-petroleum exports totalled US$9.3 billion during 1987/88, up more than 40% from the previous year. This was the first year in Indonesia's recent history that non-petroleum exports exceeded petroleum exports (see Figure 10.3). The World Bank and the International Monetary Fund (IMF) predict an average growth rate of 5% per annum in GDP until the turn of the century.

Figure 10.2 Indonesian Rupiah vs US Dollar, Weekly, 1982–1989

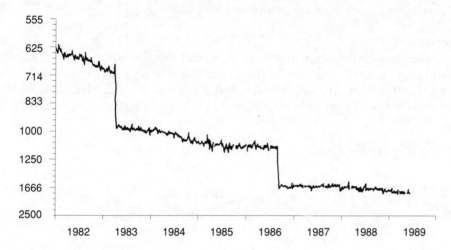

Source: Datastream.

Figure 10.3 Composition of Exports, 1982/83 and 1987/88 (%)

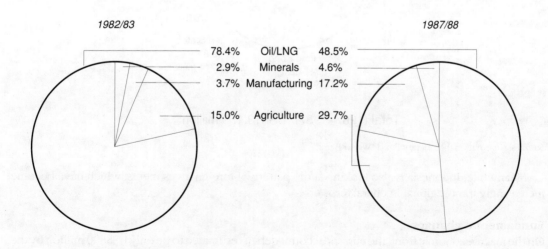

1982/83		1987/88
78.4%	Oil/LNG	48.5%
2.9%	Minerals	4.6%
3.7%	Manufacturing	17.2%
15.0%	Agriculture	29.7%

Sources: International Monetary Fund; World Bank.

Export breakthrough

Non-petroleum exports include such manufactured goods as dry batteries, automotive components, chemical products, paper and pulp, garments, shoes, tennis balls, and handicrafts. This sector increased its share of total exports to 55% in 1988. By 1990, it is expected to account for a 65% share of total exports.

The non-petroleum sector's rapid growth interacts, of course, with the expansion of the banking sector. At the same time, it encourages the government to offer a greater degree of freedom in order to attract foreign investment. In the proposed reform measures, for example, one item will reduce the 'limiting authority' of the Investment Board, which in the past set a scale of priorities that barred new private investments in some sectors, both domestic and foreign.

Foreign investment

In 1987, overseas investment inflows rose 77% compared with the previous year, and accounted for US$1.6 billion in 141 projects. The Japanese led the field in foreign investment, with a total of US$5.65 billion (see Figure 10.4) from 1967 to 1987. The strength and abundance in natural and human resources are expected to continue to attract foreign investments in the Indonesian manufacturing sector.

Figure 10.4   Leading Foreign Investors

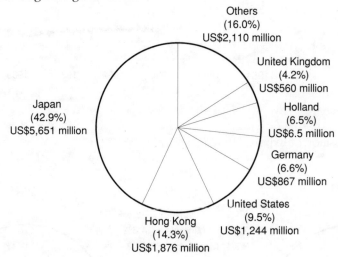

Total (1967–1987) US$13,159 million

Sources: International Monetary Fund; World Bank.

Meanwhile, Indonesia is also looking at the pattern of foreign investments, which have become increasingly intra-regional in character.

Fundamental changes

On the macroeconomic front, the current account deficit (estimated to be only US$800 million by the end of 1988) has declined rapidly, and the debt service ratio has been maintained at the projected level (see Figure 10.5).

Figure 10.5 Oil Prices and Economic Imbalances, 1982/83–1988/89

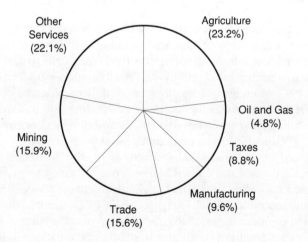

Sources: International Monetary Fund; World Bank.

At a more fundamental level, the agricultural sector has resulted in an average 4% growth over the past decade (see Figure 10.6). And in education, the country's standard is now almost on a par with that of the rest of South-East Asia.

Figure 10.6 GDP by Component, 1988

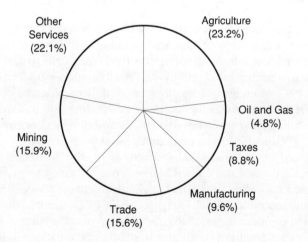

Source: BT Forecast.

Inflation

Inflation, as measured by the composite consumer price index for 17 major Indonesian cities, declined to 7.5% in November 1987, according to recent IMF statistics. The IMF, which has calculated the underlying inflation rate at 5.6%, predicted that it would have settled at 5% by the end of 1988, a considerable achievement in the light of the devaluation of 31.2% of the Rupiah against the US dollar in September 1986 (see Table 10.1).

Table 10.1 Economic Indicators, 1986–1988E

Major Indicator	1986	1987	1988E
Population (mn)	168.0	172.0	178.0
Real GDP (growth %)	4.0	4.2	5.0
Consumer Price Index (growth %)	9.1	8.5	5.0
Central Government Expenditure (% of GDP)	21.4	19.2	17.3
Overall Budget Surplus/Deficit (% of GDP)	-5.0	-2.2	-0.6
Exports (US$bn)	13.8	17.8	19.7
Incl. Oil and LNG	7.0	8.6	8.3
Non-oil	6.9	9.2	11.4
Imports (US$bn)	10.4	11.3	12.5
Overall Balance of Payments (US$bn)	-2.1	1.1	0.4
Net Official Reserves (US$bn)	5.7	7.5	7.9
Total External Debt (US$bn)	44.1	48.6	51.3
Debt Service (US$bn)	5.4	6.4	7.8
Debt Service Ratio (% of exports)	37.1	34.3	37.2

Source: International Monetary Fund/World Bank data, adjusted and attributed to calendar year.

Historical Background

The Indonesian stock market dates back to the early 1900s when the Dutch developed listings for Dutch-owned companies, particularly plantations operating in Indonesia. The market was closed during the 1940s, and an attempt to reopen it in the 1950s, primarily to facilitate the issuance of government bonds and to stimulate the economy, was less than successful. The Exchange effectively remained closed until 1977 when it was formally reopened by presidential decree.

This relaunch of the Exchange was fuelled by both the timing requirement for foreign joint-venture companies to fulfil local ownership regulations and new tax concessions given to public companies. Between 1977 and 1983, nine companies listed their shares.

Following the marked improvement in, and reform of, the securities market in 1977, the government of Indonesia created the Capital Market Policy Council to provide guidance to the Ministry of Finance, and established the Capital Market Executive Agency (BAPEPAM) to institute, regulate, and operate the Indonesian Stock Exchange (ISE). PT Danareksa, the National Investment Trust, was established to promote the equitable distribution of ownership of listed shares through underwriting and issuing mutual fund certificates in small denominations to the public.

In December 1987, the government introduced a series of fundamental deregulation measures (see Table 10.2), the main objective of which was to promote the role of the capital markets as an alternative source of financing. The plan had two principal parts: the creation of a new over-the-counter (OTC) market with simpler listing requirements than those of the Jakarta Stock Exchange (JKSE); and the liberalisation of the existing listing, underwriting, and trading rules. Under new government deregulation packages in December 1987 and 1989, the OTC market — currently called the 'Parallel Market' — began trading in February 1989. The OTC market operates from a room in the same building that houses the small 11-year-old JKSE. The first, and only, issue to date on the OTC market was launched in January 1989 by PT Zebra Taxi, a Surabaya-based taxi company. The issue size was Rp2.5 billion at an issue price of Rp1,500. Under these new regulations, foreign investors are allowed to purchase shares and bonds on both exchanges.

Table 10.2 Capital Market Deregulation Measures

---

1. Imposing a 15% tax on interest in time deposit, certificates of deposit, and saving accounts.
2. Simplifying the process of issuing shares.
3. Allowing foreign investors to participate in the capital market.
4. Introducing bearer shares.
5. Establishing the OTC market.

Source: Jakarta Stock Exchange.

BAPEPAM administers the JKSE and regulates the securities market generally.

As a follow-up to the December 1987 deregulation package, the government introduced a new policy for the capital market on 20 December 1988. The development of the capital market includes the following steps:

1. Establishment of a private stock exchange: in addition to the existing government-operated stock exchange and OTC market, the private sector is also given the opportunity to operate a stock exchange. The establishment of a private stock exchange is subject to the following requirements:
   - the exchange must be a limited liability company;
   - the exchange company must have a minimal paid-up capital of Rp500 million; and
   - all shares of the private-operated stock exchange must be owned by Indonesian citizens or Indonesian national corporations.
2. Opening of stock exchanges in different cities: new stock exchanges to be established where possible in other cities besides Jakarta.
3. Securities trading on the JKSE:
   - Companies which have already listed shares on the JKSE will be allowed to list all remaining shares, previously issued and not listed, on one exchange without the necessity of creating a new underwriting of sale of shares. This action may be taken up to the limit of existing paid-up capital and total shares previously issued.
   - Companies whose shares are registered on other stock exchanges can also register their shares for trading on the JKSE.
   - Insider trading activities are not permitted. Insider trading includes any securities trading activity which involves the utilisation of confidential information, or information not available to the general public, for personal gain.

- Members of the Board of Directors and Board of Commissioners of any publicly traded company can purchase a maximum of 10% of the listed shares of such companies.

Stock Market Performance

At the end of March 1989, there were 24 companies listed on the JKSE (Table 10.3). This figure has been constant for five years until late 1988, whereas the volume of activity grew rapidly in the past two years. The number of listings is now expected to reach 50 within a year.

Table 10.3 Stock Market Performance, 1982–1989

Year	Year-end ISE Index	No. of Companies	Turnover Volume Value (Rp mn/day) (share/day)		At Year End Market Capitalisation[2] (Rp bn)	Dividend P/E Yield Ratio (%)	
1982	95.00	14	20,155	50.7	–	–	13.8
1983	80.37	19	14,030	40.4	–	4.7	17.5
1984	63.53	24	4,914	8.6	–	5.7	14.9
1985	66.53	24	6,602	13.1	89.71	5.7	15.8
1986	69.69	24	5,774	7.3	94.64	5.8	11.9
1987	82.53	24	10,258	21.4	112.08	5.5	13.3
1988	305.12[1]	24	25,781[1]	118.5[1]	434.18	20.0	5.0
1989 (Mar)	335.20	24	29,300[1]	137.5[1]	477.50	20.5	4.8

Source: BAPEPAM.
Notes
1. Estimate by ISA-IS.
2. Market capitalisation for listed shares.

Stock Exchange Details

Address

Capital Market Executive Agency
(Indonesia Stock Exchange)
Jala Medan Merdeka Selatan 13/14

PO Box 439
Jakarta
Tel: 361460 365509
Tlx: 45604/5 BAPEPAM

Trading Days/Hours

The JKSE is open Monday to Friday, with two sessions daily between 10 am and 12 noon, and 1 pm and 3 pm. On Fridays, there is only a morning session. The second session was introduced in December 1989 to cope with the increased volume.

Information on both the Exchange and the new Parallel Exchange OTC market may be obtained from BAPEPAM.

Listings

There are 24 companies listed on the 'Big Board' of the JKSE. (Table 10.4 shows the sector breakdown of the listed companies.) However, it should be noted that the OTC market is becoming increasingly active: current estimates are that at least 50 companies will be listed by the end of 1989, including both Big Board and OTC Listings.

Table 10.4   Breakdown of Listed Companies by Sector, as at 31 December 1988

Stocks	No. of Companies	List Shares Volume ('000)	(%)	Market Capitalisation (Rp mn)	(%)
Financial	3	6,585	10.1	30,776.8	7.09
Consumer	8	22,826	35.0	153,991.4	35.47
Industrial	6	14,041	21.5	93,724.0	21.59
Pharmaceutical	5	6,833	10.5	45,520.2	10.48
Services	2	14,918	22.9	110,165.1	25.37
Total	24	65,203	100.0	434,177.5	100.00

Source: BAPEPAM ISA-IS.

By world standards, turnover is small, averaging less than US$70,000 per day in 1988, although this has picked up substantially in 1989.

In 1976, the government established a State Investment Trust, PT Danareksa, in an attempt to stimulate share ownership amongst the private sector and to assist in the development of the Exchange. PT Danareksa issues certificates similar to unit trusts, which are sold to the public. It is estimated that PT Danareksa currently hold 35–40% of the Exchange's issued shares, although they have recently started to release some of their holdings in an effort to satisfy the current demand.

Disclosure

Listed companies on the JKSE and the OTC market are subject to various disclosure and reporting requirements. Companies must submit financial statements to BAPEPAM no later than 120 days after the close of the company's financial year. Furthermore, companies are obliged to notify BAPEPAM within 30 days of any event which may materially affect their operations. Companies must also provide any additional reports that BAPEPAM may request.

Listed companies must publish a balance sheet and profit and loss statement, audited by a public or government accountant, within 120 days of the close of the financial year. Publication is to be in at least two Indonesian-language newspapers, one with national circulation and the other at the company's place of domicile.

The Twenty Largest Stocks

Table 10.5 shows the 20 largest quoted companies in terms of market value.

Table 10.5   The 20 Largest Quoted Stocks by Market Capitalisation, as at 31 December 1988

Company	Industry	Market Capitalisation (US$mn)
Unilever	Consumer	257.0
Jak Int Hotel	Hotels	95.4
Goodyear	Rubber	83.9
Sucaco	Cables	72.3
Semen Cibinong	Cement	71.6
Multi Bintang	Beverages	70.7
Tificorp	Textiles	69.6
BAT Indonesia	Tobacco	55.3
Sepatu Bata	Shoes	44.2
Panin Bank	Finance	37.1
Hotel Prapatan	Hotels	32.9
Sari Husada	Foods	27.3
R.V.I.	Chemicals	26.3
Centex	Textiles	23.9
Delta Jakarta	Beverages	20.4
Bayer Indonesia	Pharmaceutical	16.8
Merck Indonesia	Pharmaceutical	15.6
Unitex	Textile	15.4
Panin Putra	Insurance	8.4
Squibb	Pharmaceutical	8.4

Source: Jakarta Stock Exchange.

Major Securities Houses

PT Aksara Kencana
Jl. Prapatan Raya 20
Jakarta
Tel: 348198

PT Aperdi
Gedung Bursa
3rd Floor
Jl.M. Merdeka
Selatan 14
Jakarta
Tel: 353054 365509 Ext. 184/187

PT Danatama Makmur
Gedung Danareksa Annex
Jl.M. Merdeka
Selatan 13
Jakarta
Tel: 3801928 3801929

PT Dhanamas Buana Wirasata
Gedung Bursa
3rd Floor
Jl.M. Merdeka
Selatan 14
Jakarta
Tel: 365509 Ext. 181

PT Dharmala
Wisma Dharmala Sakti
Jl. Jenderal Sudirman No. 32
Jakarta 10220

PT Eferindo Agung
Gedung Bank Niaga
4th Floor
Jl.M.H. Thamrin 55
Jakarta
Tel: 330507 360408 Ext. 509

PT Intan Artha Exchange & Co.
Gedung Bursa
3rd Floor
Jl.M. Merdeka
Selatan 14
Jakarta
Tel: 347958 349002

PT Interkomarta Jasa
Gedung Bursa
3rd Floor
Jl.M. Merdeka
Selatan 14
Jakarta
Tel: 365509 Ext. 179

PT Makindo
Gedung Bursa
3rd Floor
Jl.M. Merdeka
Selatan 14
Jakarta
Tel: 359707 359927

PT Murni Segara Lestari
Gedung Bursa
3rd Floor
Jl.M. Merdeka
Selatan 14
Jakarta
Tel: 377149 365509 Ext. 174

PT Pratama Penaganarta
Jl. Kemang Raya No. 98
Kebayoran Baru
Jakarta
Tel: 7999844 7980151

PT Ramayana Artha Perkasa
Kompleks Ketapang Indah
Block B 3/19
Jl. KH Zainul Arifin
Jakarta
Tel: 6399535 6283258 6283257 6596551

PT Tri Pratama
Gedung Bursa
3rd Floor
Jl.M. Merdeka
Selatan 14
Jakarta
Tel: 365509 Ext. 180

Listing Criteria

The requirements for a company seeking a listing on the JKSE include the following:
1. limited liability;
2. domicile in Indonesia;
3. a minimum fully paid-up capital of Rp200 million;
4. profitability for the two financial years immediately preceding the company's application for registration; net profits for the latest year must be at least 10% of the equity; and
5. its financial statements for the previous two years must have been audited by a registered public accountant.

Several companies are anticipated to be listed by the end of 1989 (see Table 10.6). In addition, up to ten new private/state-owned companies are in the pipeline for new listings.

Table 10.6   New Listings in 1989

Company	Type	Market	Size of Issue (Rp bn)
Ficorinvest	Non-bank fin. inst.	JKSE	5.0
Jaya Pari Steel	Steel	JKSE	4.0
Darmo Grande	Real estate	JKSE	—
Bandung Plaza	Shopping/hotel complex	OTC	12.0
ASM	Container manufacturing	OTC	3.0
Sofyan Hotel	Hotel	OTC	2.5

Source: Jakarta Stock Exchange.

Mutual Funds/Unit Trusts

There has been a rapid growth of interest on the part of international fund managers in the Indonesian stock market following deregulation at the end of 1988. Table 10.7 lists the existing funds.

Table 10.7   International Funds for Indonesia, 1989

Name	Manager	Inception Date	Size (US$mn)	
Malacca Fund	Indosuez Asia Investment	1/89	35.0	Closed End
Indonesia Fund Inc.	Jardine Fleming	3/89	20.0	Private
Indonesia Growth Trust	Royal Trust Asia Limited	3/89	6.0	Open End
Jakarta Fund	Thornton	8/89	20.0	Closed End

Rules for Foreign Investors

Restrictions on Foreign Ownership

For all companies, there are both legal and company limitations on foreign shareholdings. Foreigners can invest directly in securities issued by certain Indonesian corporations (including certain listed corporations). Foreign ownership of equity of the corporations concerned should not exceed specified percentages ranging from 95% to 25%, and is in certain cases subject to mandatory reduction within specific time-limits as prescribed by the Indonesian government. For most securities, foreign ownership of equity is limited to a maximum of 49%. Of the 24 listed companies, 16 are restricted to new investors, as they are foreign joint-venture companies where the foreign partner already holds more than 49%. The eight companies that are open to foreign investors are shown in Table 10.8.

Table 10.8   Companies Open to Direct Foreign Investment

PT Sucaco	PH Hotel Prapatan
PT A.J. Panin Putra	PT Jakarta International Hotel
PT Sari Husada	PT Semen Cibinong
PT Pan Union Insurance	PT Delta Jakarta

Source: Jakarta Stock Exchange.

Foreign Exchange Control

Indonesia imposes no controls on the flow of capital or income into or out of the country, other than that loans from non-Indonesian lenders with a maturity of more than one year are required to be reported on a regular basis and, if made to specified categories of Indonesian borrowers, require approval from the Indonesian Central Bank and the Ministry of Finance.

There are no restrictions on the repatriation of sale proceeds or dividends to a foreign investor.

Exchange Rate

The Indonesian government has maintained its freely convertible currency despite substantial declines in petroleum revenues, pressures on the balance of payments, and speculation against the Rupiah in 1986 and 1987.

The Rupiah is linked to a basket of currencies of Indonesia's principal trading partners. However, the government has allowed the Rupiah to depreciate against the US dollar in an effort to preserve the competitive gains achieved as a result of the 1986 devaluation (see Figure 10.2).

Taxation

Under current Indonesian law, there is no capital gains tax or income tax liability arising from the sale of Indonesian securities by funds or foreign individuals, provided they are not carrying on the business of dealing in securities in Indonesia through a permanent establishment there.

However, foreign investors are subject to a 20% withholding tax on dividends deducted by the Indonesia company. Domestic investors are subject to a withholding tax of 15%, and any capital gains are treated as income and taxed at the progressive personal tax rate.

Protection of Shareholders

The principal regulatory organisation for shareholders of publicly listed companies is BAPEPAM. The agency has the power to suspend trading in stocks of companies quoted on the Exchange, and/or to delist companies, in order to protect the interests of public investors.

Shareholder protection has generally been provided for by the Articles of Association of the company which, under Indonesian law, must be approved by the Minister of Justice before the company is deemed to exist.

Insider trading and other forms of market manipulation are addressed in provisions of the December 1987 Ministerial Decrees concerning the supervisory and control powers of BAPEPAM. These powers are of a preventative nature or in the form of sanctions.

The protection of the interests of public shareholders against fraud or default by members of the Exchange is monitored by BAPEPAM through the implementation of various measures.

There are currently no specific laws or government regulations regarding takeovers and corporate mergers in Indonesia.

11

INDIA

Introduction

Few spectacles in the world are more expressive of human vitality than the Bombay Stock Exchange. Raucous sound, vivid gestures, colourful costumes, and a dense mob of brokers in the dilapidated surroundings of the exchange building (complete with antiquated telephones placed on the edges of balconies and scaffolding) portray the vibrant share market of India, a nation in the process of turning away from a planned economy towards the free market.

India is the most surprising and the least known of all the Asian markets. Its capitalisation, whilst only medium sized (US$35 billion, or about the same as Singapore), is markedly small in relation to its large economy (US$275 billion), its vast population (over 800 million), its wealth, and its territorial extent. It is, therefore, a startling fact that there are nearly 6,000 shares listed and more than 10 million shareholders in the country. Bombay, as the oldest exchange in Asia (1887), has no less than 509 individual stockbroking members, and another 50 seats for professional or institutional members.

Approximately one-third of the market capitalisation is in the hands of this large number of small Indian investors; one-third belongs to 'Project Sponsors', meaning multinationals or large Indian corporations, such as Tata, Birla, Reliance, and Bajaj; while the final third of the market is held and actively traded by a few state-controlled institutions.

Historical Background

The earliest recorded capital market dealings in India were transactions in the loan stocks of the East India Company towards the end of the 18th century. The enactment of the *Companies Act 1850*, which introduced the concept of limited liability in India, together with increased European demand for Indian cotton on the outbreak of the American Civil War in 1861, served to stimulate activity in the securities markets. In fact, as Anthony Rowley notes in his book, *Asian Stock Markets — The Inside Story* (Far Eastern Economic Review, 1987):

'When Indians mention the "great share mania" it might be assumed they are referring to the 1985/86 bull market when many share prices doubled and stock indices reached all-time highs. In fact, the term is used to describe the remarkable market boom of 1860–65 at the time of the American civil war when a cotton famine brought unprecedented demand for Indian stocks and unprece-

Note: US$1.00 = Rs16.75.

Figure 11.1   Financial Express Equity Index, Daily, 1982–1988

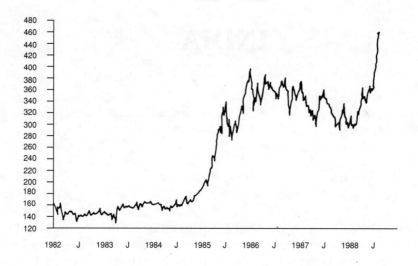

Figure 11.2   US Dollar vs Indian Rupee, Weekly, 1982–1989

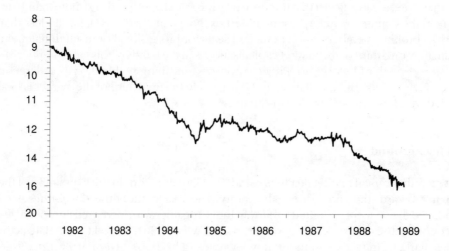

Source: Datastream.

dented inflows of gold and silver into Bombay to pay for it. The Bombay stock market went wild — until it crashed in 1865.'

In 1887, the first stockbrokers' organisation, the Native Share and Stock Brokers Association, was formally established, later becoming the Bombay Stock Exchange. As further stock exchanges were established, they were placed under the exclusive regulation of the central government. Under the *Securities Contracts (Regulation) Act 1956*, only those stock exchanges recognised by the central government were permitted to function, and the central government was vested with wide powers of supervision and control over all stock exchanges. Soon after the implementation of this Act, the exchanges at Bombay, Calcutta, Ahmedabad, Delhi, Madras, Hyderabad, and Indore were officially recognised.

From 1956 to 1976, the Indian stock market recorded moderate growth. In the 1969–70 Union Budget, preferential tax rates were introduced for listed companies in an effort to promote listing and public ownership. The most significant event affecting the securities markets during this period was the enactment of the *Foreign Exchange Regulation Act 1973* (FERA). Under the FERA, Indian corporations with more than 40% foreign shareholdings were generally required to reduce their foreign ownership. As a result, many such corporations offered equity to the Indian public. These offerings were heavily oversubscribed and served to increase the liquidity and broaden the investor base of the Indian securities markets.

Growth in the capital markets in India has gained significant momentum in the 1980s. The market has witnessed unprecedented buoyancy over the last three years and has become more broadly based, with an increase in the diversity of financial instruments being floated. Larger amounts of capital are being raised from a growing number of investors. The important fundamental factors contributing to these trends are an increasing rate of gross domestic savings (currently standing at 22% of disposable income), and a growing preference in the household sector for financial assets to deploy its savings.

The importance of the capital market as a prime mobiliser of funds for the corporate sector was recognised long ago. However, active steps to create the right environment for channelling resources into it have been taken only in recent years. Consequently, the corporate sector has increasingly been raising resources from the capital market rather than banks and financial institutions. Railways, power, and telecommunication undertakings of the government are also raising funds directly from the household sector in order to reduce their dependence on government funds. This is facilitated by the fact that the trend towards investment in marketable instruments has spread from the major metropolitan areas to semi-urban areas. The investor population has multiplied in the last decade and is now estimated to be around ten million.

The Indian capital market has added another dimension to its growth with the successful launching of the *India Fund* in 1986 (listed on the London Stock Exchange), and the *India Growth Fund* in 1988 (listed on the New York Stock Exchange). This can be seen as a manifestation of the confidence that the international community places in the Indian economy, as well as a reflection of the emerging maturity of the Indian capital market, which has now made its mark on the map of international capital markets.

There are now 16 stock exchanges in India (see Figure 11.3), but Bombay, which accounts for over 80% of stock market capitalisation, is by far the most important, followed by Calcutta, Delhi, Madras, and Ahmedabad. Trading in these five exchanges accounts for over 90% of total turnover, and they are the only ones to be connected in by the PTI electronic Stockscan service. Within this subset, Bombay and Calcutta are the only ones which provide adequate liquidity to the trader.

Figure 11.3 Stock Exchanges in India

Source: The Stock Exchange Foundation.

The improvement in the quality and quantity of information available has considerably reduced inter-exchange arbitrage opportunities.

Calcutta may not be the main exchange, but the number of its listed companies exceeds even that of the London Stock Exchange.

The market for new issues has played a significant role in view of the rapid growth of industries witnessed in recent years. There has been a quantum jump in the number of new issues floated and the capital raised from the primary market. The consents for capital issues by the Controller of Capital Issues (CCI) increased more than tenfold, to around Rs55.7 billion in 1987–1988, over the 1980–1981 figure of Rs4.7 billion (see Figure 11.4).

Figure 11.4 Consents for Capital Issues, 1980/81–1987/88

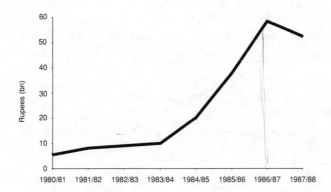

The new issues market witnessed an unprecedented response during 1985, reflecting the increasing confidence and interest of investors in industrial securities. Most of the new issues were oversubscribed several times during the year. From 1986 onwards, investors have become more discerning. While the number of issues and capital raised showed a significant increase in 1986, only issues made by companies with a proven record, or new projects in high-growth areas incorporating modern technology, were oversubscribed. By its performance, the primary market has indicated that it has sufficient depth and potential to absorb even large volumes of capital issues during the years ahead (see Figure 11.5). The development of the primary market during the last three years has also been characterised by innovative instruments such as tax-free bonds floated by public sector undertakings, convertible debentures by private corporations, and the issue of Mastershares by Unit Trust of India (UTI) through the formation of a closed-ended mutual fund in 1986. All of these have received encouraging support. In 1987, SBI Capital Markets successfully issued Magnum, an income-oriented mutual fund of Rs1,000 million which assures a minimum dividend of 12% pa, and bought deals were introduced for the first time to assist new companies with their initial public offers. The subsequent unloading of shares will serve to widen the secondary market.

Figure 11.5 Capital Raised from Market, 1983/84–1987/88

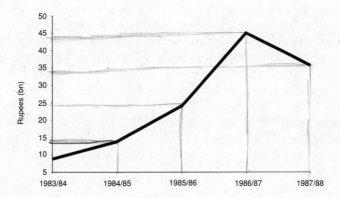

The new issues also attracted investments from Non-Resident Indian (NRI) investors (see Figure 11.6). Direct NRI investment in 1986 was 319% higher than in 1984. The *India Fund*, which was floated on the London market in 1986 for GBP 60 million, was oversubscribed more than twice and the actual subscription accepted was for GBP 75 million. All foreigners were eligible to subscribe to the issue. The *India Growth Fund*, another offshore fund launched in the United States in July 1988, attracted US$60 million.

Figure 11.6   Investment by Non-Resident Indians

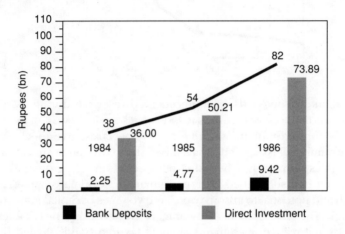

In response to the process of liberalisation of the industrial economy initiated in the early 1980s, corporate investment surged. The new economic policy relaxed a number of controls on industrial investment, production, distribution, and prices. The gross domestic capital formation (GDCF) at current prices rose from 1% of GDP in 1980–1981 to 24% in 1987–1988, and GDP itself rose by an average of 5% from the 1980s as against the trend rate of 3.5% in the preceding three decades. Large investments in new capacity, and expansion and modernisation of existing plants, have taken place in several industries such as fertilisers, cement, aluminium, power, telecommunications, electronics, manmade fibres, automobiles, and other consumer durables, opening up wider possibilities for investor participation. Aggressive promotion of public issues by companies and issue managers has been another supporting factor as investors have become more aware of the benefits of investment in securities. Fiscal and tax concessions given from time to time have encouraged investments in new security issues. The unprecedented buoyancy in the secondary market during 1985–1986 provided a great spur to the primary market. With the stock market recovery, which began in April 1988, investor support to the new issues has been gathering momentum. Among new issues, Reliance Petrochemicals Ltd's (RPL) jumbo issue of Rs5.4 billion fully convertible debentures received an overwhelming investor response and attracted oversubscriptions up to Rs13 billion, giving a new impulse to the primary market.

Stock Market Performance

The four indices that are commonly used to indicate trends in the equity market are the Reserve Bank of India (RBI) Index, the Economic Times (ET) Index, the Financial Express (FE) Index, and the Bombay Stock Exchange (BSE) Sensitive Index of Equity Shares. The RBI Index provides the most comprehensive historical data but is compiled on a weekly basis only. The other indices are calculated on a daily basis using more actively traded shares and are most commonly used to measure day-to-day changes in the market.

Stock exchange operations in India are largely uniform, so that the operations of the BSE can be taken as representative of all the stock exchanges. Securities are traded on the stock exchanges through brokers. Seventy-six actively traded shares are classified as 'specified' shares. Delivery of and payment for the 'specified' shares may be carried forward to subsequent periods by payment or receipt of the difference between the contract price and the making-up price fixed by the BSE at the end of each settlement period.

There are generally no restrictions on price movements on any security on any given day, but the BSE has the right to impose such restrictions at any time. This right has occasionally been exercised when wide fluctuations have occurred. Margin requirements are imposed by the BSE in respect of 'specified' shares and are required to be paid at the end of each settlement period at such rates as may be fixed by the BSE. In addition, a daily margin is imposed in respect of all shares. Adequate margins are collected from members having large outstanding positions in relation to their financial capacity.

The yearly turnover for equity shares on the BSE grew steeply during 1986 to Rs136 billion, ie about three times the 1982 level. The turnover then fell to Rs87 billion in 1987, but with the buoyant conditions prevailing in more recent years, the turnover has again improved substantially.

There is an active secondary market in government securities. The major participants in the market are banks, insurance companies, and other financial institutions which are required to hold a certain percentage of their assets in government securities. Buying and selling government securities by these institutions constitutes the secondary market. The bulk of the trading takes place in the over-the-counter market through a limited number of approved brokers.

Table 11.1 Stock Market Performance, 1961–1986

Market Indicators	1961	1975	1984	1985	1986
No. of listed companies	1,203	1,852	3,882	4,344	4,744
No. of stock issues of listed companies	2,111	3,230	5,485	6,714	7,258
Paid-up capital of listed companies (Rs bn)	6.75	21.42	50.82	60.76	73.64
Market value of paid-up capital of listed companies (Rs bn)	12.16	28.05	99.84	210.77	223.43

The secondary market in India has been greatly reactivated during the 1980s. The increasing number of scrips listed on the stock exchanges, now over 500 as against 180 in 1975, and the dramatic rise in prices on some of the active counters, have substantially enlarged market capitalisation from Rs28.05 billion in 1975 to over Rs319 billion in September 1988.

Although India's market capitalisation is third among the emerging market countries, it is modest compared with the capital markets in developed countries. In India, market capitalisation is only around 9% of GNP, compared with between 35% and 90% for other emerging countries like South Korea and Hong Kong. This reflects the considerable potential for growth in capital raised from the market and the potential for a rise in stock prices in the years ahead.

The price/earnings ratio (PER) on the Indian Stock Exchange has been in the range of 9 to 12 since 1987. The market leaders, and the shares of many of the multinationals, have much higher ratios (15–35). The average PER in the Indian capital market is low by international standards.

Stock Exchange Details

Addresses

The Bombay Stock Exchange
Phiroze Jeejeebhoy Towers
Dalal Street
Bombay 400023
Tlx: 011 5925 STEX IN

Ahmedabad Stock Exchange Association Ltd
Manek Chowk
Ahmedabad 380001

Calcutta Stock Exchange Association Ltd
7 Lyons Range
Calcutta 700001
Tlx: 021 7414 CALSTOCK

Cochin Stock Exchange Ltd
Exchange House
37/1003 T.D. Road
P.B. No. 3529
Ernakulam, Cochin 682011
Tlx: 885 6298 COST IN STOCK

Delhi Stock Exchange Association
3 & 4/1B, Asaf Ali Road
New Delhi 110002
Tlx: 65317 DESA IN UPKARI

Gauhati Stock Exchange Ltd
Saraf Buildings Annexe
A.T. Road,
Gauhati 781001

Hyderabad Stock Exchange Ltd
5-1-711/712 Bank Street
Hyderabad 500195
Tlx: 425 6053 HSE IN

Jaipur Stock Exchange
Rajistan Chambers Bhaban
MI Road
Jaipur 302003
Tel: 141 74904

Kanara Stock Exchange Ltd
11th Floor, Syndicate Bank
Mission Street Branch
Mangalore 575001
Tlx: 311 STOCK IN STOCKANARA

Ludhiana Stock Exchange Ltd
Lajpat Rai Market
Clock Tower
Ludhiana 141008
Tlx: 0386 429

Madras Stock Exchange Ltd
11 Second Line Beach
Madras 600001
Tlx: 041 8059 MSEX IN MASTEX

Madhya Pradesh Stock Exchange Ltd
67 Bada Sarafa
Indore 452002
Tlx: 735 244 MPSE IN INDSTEX

Magadh Stock Exchange Ltd
Bihar Industries Assn Premises
Sinha Library Road
Patna 800001
Tlx: 22 407 MSEA IN MAGEXCHANG

Pune Stock Exchange Ltd
2nd Floor, Maharashtra Bank Building
Baji Rao Road
Pune 411002
Tlx: 145462 PSEX IN PSEX

Uttar Pradesh Exchange Association Ltd
14/76 Civil Lines
Kanpur 208001

Trading Days/Hours

Normal trading hours are from 12 noon to 3 pm, Monday to Friday, but some kerb trading occurs unofficially outside these set times.

Settlement

Transactions have to be carried out by a registered broker, who will issue a standard contract note after the order has been executed. Brokers deal with jobbers on the exchange much in the same manner as in London before the 'big bang'.

Following the establishment of a stockholding corporation, trading in the major stocks was simplified, and settlement for many of the most-traded issues is now computer based. At present, the normal account period is 14 days.

Stocks are divided into two lists (A and B), with different settlement regulations, as follows:

A Stocks ('the forward list'). This group is made up of about 70 scrips with the most-traded names and is the most important market segment both in terms of capitalisation and turnover. Settlement in these shares, also referred to as 'specified shares', may be carried forward for a time not exceeding six settlement periods.

B Stocks ('the cash list'). Settlement of these shares, also known as 'nonspecified shares', must be concluded at the end of the account period. There is little scope for active trading in these shares as settlement may well be delayed two or three months and transaction problems are frequent.

The Twenty Largest Stocks

Table 11.2 shows the 20 largest companies by market value. It should be noted that for all 915 companies in the BSE, capitalisation currently stands at Rs34,343.32 million.

Table 11.2   The 20 Largest Quoted Stocks by Market Capitalisation, as at 23 December 1988

Company	Market Capitalisation (Rupees mn)
Reliance	2,335.35
Tisco	1,668.93
Bajaj Auto	778.26
Larsen & Toubro	768.49
Telco	754.57
Hindustan Lever	690.57

Company	Market Capitalisation (Rupees mn)
GNFC	500.46
Tata Chemicals	481.03
Colgate Palmolive	475.53
GSFC	400.88
Indo Gulf Fert	391.63
Century Enka	353.79
Century Textiles	346.06
Food Special	324.00
J K Synthetics	319.63
Grasim Inds	296.57
Nocil	289.80
Oswal Agro	288.05
Hind Aluminium	282.03
Asian Paints	264.35

Major Market Players

Estimates of the total number of private investors in the equity market are very significant: the most conservative would place the figure at 12 million, while other estimates are as high as 18, according to definition and means of survey. However, it is generally acknowledged that, as a group, individuals hold the largest amount of equities — over 35% of the market. The other major groups are financial institutions (25%), joint stock companies (22%), and government bodies (20%).

The major players in the market are a handful of institutions which are under direct or indirect state control. They usually trade large blocks and, for tax reasons, they tend to be medium-term holders. The most important of these are:

- Unit Trust of India
- Life Insurance Corporation
- General Insurance Corporation
- Industrial Development Bank of India
- Industrial Reconstruction Corporation of India
- Industrial Credit and Investment Corporation of India
- Industrial Financial Corporation of India.

Pension funds are absent as they are not allowed to hold equities in their portfolios, and banks are mainly confirmed primary market underwritings.

The domestic scene is dominated by Unit Trusts of India (UTI) — which was established in 1964 — and by other state-controlled institutions. UTI presently numbers 1.8 million shareholders, and its portfolios include stock from 850 companies with total available funds of Rs 94 billion (US$6 billion). UTI funds are now available to NRIs.

Dealing Costs

Stamp Duty

For ordinary and preference shares, 0.5% of the value of the contracts, or part thereof calculated on the amount of consideration, is payable.

For debentures, stamp duty is affixed at the prescribed rates in force in the state where the company's registered offices are situated. These charges can vary considerably.

Commissions

The general brokerage commission for all stock transactions is set at 1.5%, with a minimum amount for small transactions.

Brokerage

These will vary, but they are usually between 0.25% and 1% and, in the case of public offerings, 1.5%.

Listing Criteria

Capital issues are governed by the *Capital Issues (Control) Act 1947*. The powers of the central government under the Act are exercised by the CCI, whose office is a division of the Ministry of Finance. Issues of equity and preference shares, debentures, and rights issues above Rs10 million come within the scope of the regulatory provisions of the Act and require the consent of the CCI. Well-defined guidelines are prescribed, and for issues falling within these, consent is readily granted. Admission of securities to listing is regulated by the *Securities Contracts (Regulation) Rules 1957*.

Mutual Funds/Unit Trusts

The first two funds for international sale were authorised in late 1986. The first, a closed-end tax-exempt fund, was launched by Unit Trust of India and Merrill Lynch. The second fund was launched by S.G. Warburg merchant bank and a management company controlled by the Birla family. At least 60% of the shares in this fund must be held by NRIs.

In July 1988, the *India Growth Fund* was launched. A subsidiary of UTI acted as adviser, while Merrill Lynch and Nomura Securities Market had the task of marketing the fund internationally.

The Indian government has recently permitted more commercial banks and financial institutions to launch mutual funds. Recently, Canara Bank and the State Bank of India, as well as the Bank of Baroda together with the Life Insurance Corporation and the General Insurance Corporation, have defined their own plans to establish funds.

Such was the success of the *Children's Fund*, that the UTI followed it up with the launch of a *Parents Gift Growth Fund*, a five-year closed-end fund, by which Indians wishing to take care of their aged parents could invest a fixed amount to provide them with a steady monthly income. This combination of family feeling, charity, and sound investment principles has perhaps only been rivalled by the Quakers in England, whose Friends Provident Funds attempt to combine ethical and moral principles with profitable stock selection.

The Unit Trust of India is, of course, well known internationally for being the manager of the first fund investing in the Indian stock market. The *India Fund* was launched in August 1986 with GBP 50 million and listed on the London Stock Exchange. Over its first two years, it rose over 50% in Sterling terms, despite the rupee's steady 8% annual depreciation and a large discount to asset value in the London market price. This was followed in 1988 by the US$60 million *India Growth Fund*, which was listed in New York.

A more enterprising product was the privately placed *India Investment Fund*, a venture capital fund aiming to buy into small Indian companies before listing, managed by Grindlay's Bank, a long-established British bank with old roots in the subcontinent.

Rules for Foreign Investors

There are significant barriers to a foreign investor's direct entry into the market. Such investors must be licensed by the Reserve Bank of India and then only 'non-resident Indians' are allowed to acquire a stake in an Indian company. The classification includes only those who are of Indian descent, as specified by the Reserve Bank of India. Foreign companies which are at least 60% owned by NRIs may be authorised to purchase equity. There are limits even for NRIs, either *de facto* or *de jure*, as companies have sometimes refused to register the transfer of shares to a legitimate buyer.

Foreign investors have been able to access the markets via the funds as described above under Mutual Funds/Unit Trusts. However, even some of these funds are destined largely for NRI investors.

The definition of an NRI is broad enough to include citizens of Indian origin who hold other passports.

Foreign Exchange Control

The *Foreign Exchange Regulation Act 1973* provides the basic regulatory framework for foreign exchange transactions. The Act regulates ownership of equity as well as the exchange of currency. However, the Ministry of Finance issues detailed guidelines regarding the control of companies. The Reserve Bank of India has total control over the remittance of foreign funds. There are no restrictions on the repatriation of profits, royalties, dividends, or capital, provided the original investment was approved by all the appropriate authorities.

Taxation

Dividends are subject to a withholding tax of 25% for non-resident companies, while a foreign individual will pay the higher rate of 30%, or a percentage on income exceeding Rs18,000, where marginal rates will vary from 25% to 50%.

Capital gains stand at 65% for a foreign company's profits for shares which have been held for less than one year. For individuals, the gain is treated as ordinary income. There are significant reductions for gains on longer-term holdings: 20% on gains in excess of Rs10,000 for non-resident individuals, and 40% in the case of companies.

Wealth tax is applicable to non-residents whose holdings are valued at Rs75,000 or more.

Protection of Shareholders

Regulation of the securities market has usually been considered fairly ineffectual, and several undesirable practices and structural inadequacies have led to severe erosion of investor confidence. The Securities and Exchange Board of India (SEBI) was established in April 1988 as part of a plan to evolve comprehensive legislation and to rationalise the complex set of regulations now in effect.

A compensation fund was established in 1986 to protect the victims of fraud, but on the whole the individual has to resort to criminal proceedings to gain compensation.

Listed companies are now required to publish half-yearly unaudited accounts in the newspapers, and requirements for publication of financial data are being tightened. However, disputes concerning the larger transactions, such as takeovers, are often subject to informal governmental scrutiny.

Insider dealing legislation is limited to officers of a company and their use of information known exclusively to themselves for their own advantage.

Available Research

On line
Prices listed on pages IISA to IISC of Reuters provide open, closed, and previous closed levels for each of the 32 selected stocks, as well as the BSE Index at close.

International press
Brief daily reports are published in the *Asian Wall Street Journal* as well as on a weekly basis in the *Far Eastern Economic Review*. Both of these publications carry features on the Indian economy as well as on the more general political scene.

Prices, turnover, and other quantitative information
Each stock exchange compiles a daily list of quotations which is available on subscription. A more practical format can be found in the monthly *Stock Exchange Review*, published by the Bombay Stock Exchange. This booklet is also a useful source of official announcements.

Credit ratings
The Credit Rating Information Services of India Limited (CRISIL) was established by the Industrial Credit and Investment Corporation of India, Unit Trust of India, ADB, and an international consortium of banks. The range of securities rated includes debentures, fixed-deposit programmes, short-term instruments, and preference shares. There will be a significant discrepancy between their ratings and those of other international rating agencies. Domestic sovereign debt is rated AAA by CRISIL but Indian sovereign debt is rated A2 by Moody's (below investment grade); the two are therefore not easily compared.

Indices
The most widely used index is the Economic Times of India Index. The paper also provides subsector indices. The Financial Express and Bombay Stock Exchange, as well as the weekly Reserve Bank of India Index, are available as well, but are rarely referred to in the international press.

Research reports

Most of the larger financial institutions have research departments who will publish reports and provide copies on request. Those which are most widely known are the Reserve Bank of India bulletins and Annual Reports, the UTI Investment Research Department Report, and, on a subscription basis, the Corporate Investment Research and Consultancy Report, which is a weekly review of the capital markets.

Other Addresses

Unit Trust of India
13 Sir Vithaldas Thackersey Marp
New Marine Lines
Post Bag No 11410
Bombay 400 020

Securities and Exchange Board of India
Nariman Bharan, 14th Floor
Nariman Point
Bombay 400 021
Tlx: 011 2193

The Credit Rating Information Services of India Limited
Nirlon House, 2nd Floor
254 B Dr Annie Besant Rd
Worli
Bombay 400 025

12

PAKISTAN

Introduction

The Islamic Republic of Pakistan, covering an area of 803,943 sq km, is bounded by Iran and Afghanistan to the west, northwest and north, by India to the east and southeast, and by the Arabian Sea to the south.

Pakistan is divided into four autonomous provinces, each with its own capital: the Northwest Frontier Province (Peshawar), Punjab (Lahore), Sind (Karachi), and Baluchistan (Quetta). The national capital is Islamabad.

Like the Republic of India, Pakistan became independent on 15 August 1947, primarily as a result of the efforts of the 100 million Muslims of the Indian subcontinent under the leadership of Muhammad Ali Jinnah. The country inherited those contiguous districts of the former Indian empire which had a Muslim majority.

The state of Pakistan was set up under the 3 June 1947 *Partition Plan*, often referred to as the Mountbatten Plan, which was accepted by the three main Indian parties — the Indian National Congress, the Muslim League, and the Akali Dal, representing the Sikhs. The *Indian Independence Act* of July 1947, which was based on the Partition Plan, endowed the new state with its constitutional and legal sanction.

Pakistan's former eastern wing became the independent People's Republic of Bangladesh after the Indo-Pakistan war of December 1971.

Economy

In 1988, the economy of Pakistan performed reasonably well despite the fact that the main economic indicators showed a mixed picture. Growth in real GDP at 5.8% was moderately high by recent standards. Net exports increased by 24% and the current account deficit in balance of payments remained approximately 2.25% of GDP. The inflation rate, according to State Bank of Pakistan estimates, was 6–7%. This figure was substantially higher than in 1987, but was still in line with the projection considered acceptable for the Sixth Economic Plan.

The agricultural sector responded well to the incentive of adequate and guaranteed support pricing for major crops and is currently absorbing technological changes with modern financing practices.

Note: US$1.00 = Rs20.9.

Figure 12.1 Pakistan Rupee vs US Dollar, 1982–1989

The contribution of the manufacturing sector to overall GDP increased to 20% in 1988. However, the growth in manufacturing, at 7.6%, was lower than in 1987 as a result of disturbances in some parts of the country.

Gross domestic investment, estimated at 15.7% of GNP in 1988, showed a marginal decline from 16.1% in 1987. The national savings of 13.3% of GNP in 1988 showed some improvement compared to the annual average rate of 12.5% in the period 1981–1987. The domestic savings rate improved to more than 9% in 1988 against only 5.1% during the period 1981–1987.

The rate of inflation, which was in the range of 3.6–5.4% in 1987, increased in 1988 to 6% when measured by the Consumer Price Index and 7% when measured by the GDP deflator. The increase in the rate of inflation during 1988 was a direct result of the drought which reduced the supply of certain perishable agricultural commodities in Pakistan.

The growth of the economy continues to be strong, and future potential remains promising.

Historical Background

The Karachi Stock Exchange was set up in the Chartered Bank Building on 18 September 1947. It was registered on 10 March 1949 under the *Companies Act* of 1913 as a company limited by guarantee. Although the initial membership was 100 firms, scarcely ten of those were active as brokers. The membership list comprised entrepreneurs of trade and industry who envisaged the development of a healthy corporate sector in Pakistan.

Initially, only five companies were listed on the Karachi Stock Exchange, with a paid-up capital of PRs37 million (US$1.8 million). The first quotation was printed in the daily newspapers of 17 April 1948. Pakistan's second stock exchange, located in Lahore, has never garnered more than a small share of total trading activity.

Membership of the Karachi Stock Exchange is of two types — active and non-active. The membership currently stands at 200, with about 50% active as brokers. Only active members are permitted to trade on the floor of the Exchange and to appoint authorised agents to act on their behalf.

The management of the Karachi Stock Exchange is vested in the President, along with the 14 directors of the governing board directly elected by the general body of members.

Most shares quoted on the Karachi Stock Exchange are of major industrial and financial institutions. In many instances, the shares are held by controlling families or government institutions, including the Investment Corporation of Pakistan, leaving only a limited number for actual trading on the market by individual investors.

Stock Market Performance

The performance of the Karachi stock market during the period 1984–1988 is shown in Table 12.1.

Table 12.1   Stock Market Performance, 1984–1988

Year	Stock Market Index	Market Cap. (US$bn)	No. of Listed Companies	Rupees/US$
1984	168.3	1.34	347	15.36
1985	166.5	1.49	362	15.98
1986	199.9	1.82	360	17.25
1987	228.4	2.16	378	17.49
1988	262.7	2.51	422	18.65

Source: Karachi Stock Exchange.
Note: The Karachi Stock Market Index has a base of 100 set in 1980–1981.

Stock Exchange Details

Addresses

Karachi Stock Exchange (Guarantee) Ltd
Stock Exchange Building
Stock Exchange Road
Karachi
Tel: (9221) 233581
Tlx: 2746

Lahore Stock Exchange (Guarantee) Ltd
17 Bank Square
PO Box 1315
Lahore
Tel: (9242) 57265
Tlx: 44821

Trading Days/Hours

Both the Karachi Stock Exchange and the Lahore Stock Exchange are open from Saturday through Wednesday. Trading is from 10.15 am to 2 pm in the Karachi Exchange (however, some kerb trading occurs unofficially outside these set times), and from 10 am to 11 am on the Lahore Exchange.

Transactions on the Stock Exchange

The main type of security dealt in on the Karachi Stock Exchange is the ordinary share. Institutional and private activity account for 25% and 75% of trading respectively.

The Karachi Stock Exchange has two trading sections — the Ready (spot) List and the Cleared (forward) List. The Ready (spot) List transactions are done through the open outcry method whereby member firms trade in a given scrip once the company in question is called out by a representative of the Exchange's Quotation Department. These transactions are settled within 24 hours of the contract being executed between the members.

The Cleared (forward) List transactions are only allowed in five companies. Cleared List trading is regulated by the rules and regulations governing forward delivery contracts. The five companies on the Cleared List all have a relatively large capital base with sufficient floating stock to prevent one investor from accumulating a large stake.

Trading is permitted in marketable lots, while trading in odd lots is settled directly by the members themselves.

Settlement

Settlement is carried out through the clearing house of the Exchange in accordance with the clearing schedule notified by the Exchange on a monthly basis. Settlement instructions on the Ready List are made on a weekly basis, while the instructions to deliver and settle accounts on the Cleared List are made on a monthly basis.

The Twenty Largest Stocks

The 20 largest quoted companies, as determined by market capitalisation, are shown in Table 12.2.

Table 12.2 The 20 Largest Quoted Stocks by Market Capitalisation, as at 31 December 1988

Company	Market Capitalisation (Rupees bn)
Pakistan International Airlines	2.32
Bankers Equity	1.18
Karachi Electric Supply Corporation	0.79
National Refinery	0.77
Pakistan National Shipping Corporation	0.58
Sui Gas Transmission	0.52
Sui Northern Gas Pipelines	0.44
ICI Pakistan	0.36
State Enterprise Mutual Fund	0.29
Pakistan Oilfields	0.27
Pakistan Tobacco	0.25

Company	Market Capitalisation (Rupees bn)
Cherat Cement	0.21
Pakistan State Oil Company	0.20
Southern Gas	0.17
Pakistan Packages	0.17
Exxon Chemicals	0.16
PICIC	0.15
Glaxo Laboratories	0.14
Dawood Hercules	0.14
Milk Pak	0.14

Source: Karachi Stock Exchange.

Dealing Costs

Brokerage

Brokerage commissions to institutional and individual investors are charged at different rates, as shown in Table 12.3.

Table 12.3 Standard Brokerage Charges

Market Value	Rates for Institutions (Rupees/share)	Rates for Individuals (Rupees/share)
Up to PRs19.99	7	8
PR s20.00 to PRs29.99	11	13
PRs30.00 PRs49.99	13	20
PRs50.00 PRs74.99	20	30
PRs75.00 PRs99.99	33	65
Over PRs100.00	53	125

Stamp Duty

The rate of stamp duty for the transfer of shares is 1.5%, subject to a minimum of PRs1.0.

Listing Criteria

The procedure for companies wishing to initiate a new listing is regulated by the Listing Rules of the Exchange. A formal application for admission to dealings must be made on the standard form in writing to the Stock Exchange by the company or member concerned. The Exchange places the application on the notice board for the information of members one week prior to its consideration by the board.

If the company applying for the listing is in compliance with the Exchange's listing regulations, then listing takes place approximately 35 days from the publication of the prospectus in the local newspapers. It is a common practice, however, that once a prospectus is published in the newspapers, trading immediately begins between individuals as private share deals. The exchange is attempting to discourage this type of trading even though trading in unlisted securities is prohibited under s. 8(2) of the *Securities and Exchange Ordinance 1969*.

Mutual Funds/Unit Trusts

There are currently no Pakistan funds available to international investors. However, non-resident Pakistanis may buy into funds managed by the following local managers:
- Investment Corporation of Pakistan Mutual Fund Series 'A' (18 funds);
- State Enterprise Mutual Fund (represents shares of public listed enterprises) (one fund); and
- Modarabas (Islamic term for mutual fund or leasing company), which has three funds, namely *Habib Modarabas*, *First Grindlays Modarabas*, and *Modarabas Al Mali*.

Rules for Foreign Investors

Foreign Investment Restrictions

At present, foreigners are not permitted to invest directly in Pakistan's listed securities. However, investment is allowed provided formal permission has been granted by the State Bank of Pakistan and the Ministry of Finance. Repatriation of such proceeds, including capital gains and dividends, is governed by cl. 6 of the *Foreign Private Investment Act* of 1976.

There also exist special rules for non-resident Pakistanis investing in the Karachi Stock Exchange, both on a non-repatriable and repatriable basis.

Non-repatriable basis
Pakistani nationals residing abroad are permitted to invest in the shares of public limited companies, National Investment Trust Units, and government securities provided the securities are purchased by authorised banks on behalf of the investors on the basis of non-repatriation of capital and dividends. Such securities must be registered at the Pakistani address of the investors and retained by the authorised banks.

Repatriable basis
General permission has been given to Pakistani nationals living abroad to invest in shares on a repatriable basis, subject to the following conditions:

1. the full value of the shares is received from abroad through normal banking channels or paid from a foreign currency account maintained in Pakistan;
2. shares are held for at least one year; and
3. disinvestment proceeds and dividends will accrue in Pakistani rupees and its repatriation will be in foreign currency based on the prevailing exchange rates on the day in question.

Protection of Shareholders

Shareholder protection is covered by the *Companies Ordinance 1984* and the *Securities and Exchange Ordinance 1969.* Although these ordinances exist, market manipulation via insider trading continues to proliferate. In 1989, the Stock Exchange is attempting to draft a new section of the *Securities and Exchange Ordinance* in order to deal more effectively with this practice and to ensure full disclosure of corporate developments to all necessary parties.

Available Research

The Karachi Stock Exchange (Guarantee) Limited Annual Report
State Bank of Pakistan Annual Report
State Bank of Pakistan — Equity Yields on Ordinary Shares
State Bank of Pakistan — Index Numbers of Stock Exchange Securities
State Bank of Pakistan — Monthly Bulletin

13
NEPAL

Introduction

The modern history of Nepal began in the latter half of the 16th century when the followers of a northern Indian Rajput family settled in the town of Gurkha, in central Nepal. The Gurkha king, Prithvinarayan, conquered the whole of Nepal in 1768, founding the Shah dynasty which reigns to the present day. From 1826 to 1951, Nepal was ruled by a family of hereditary prime ministers, the Ranas, who pursued a policy of close co-operation with the British powers in India. However, the movement against British rule by the Indian National Congress had its repercussions among Nepalese intellectuals and politicians, who pursued a similar policy through the Nepali Congress Party for a more democratic government. This led to a revolution by which the royal family line, represented by King Tribhuvan — the ninth descendent of the dynasty — returned to power.

A general election in 1959 resulted in an overwhelming victory for the Congress Party. However, at the end of 1960, King Mahendra, who had succeeded King Tribhuvan, imprisoned the prime minister and dismissed the ministry, replacing it with a system of Panchayat 'democracy for a village' government under which political parties are not allowed.

Economy

In 1988, Nepal's population was estimated at approximately 18.3 million, with a relatively small GDP of US$3.4 billion. The per capita income is only US$164, making Nepal one of the poorest Asian countries.

Nepal's economy has always been handicapped by the fact that the country is land-locked, with largely undeveloped internal communications. The mountainous Himalayan region covers approximately 80% of Nepal's land mass, while the remaining 20% comprises the Terai. The Terai is generally considered to be a lifeline for the country, although only 17% of the region is suitable for cultivation.

Prior to the 1950s, there were virtually no roads in Nepal. Since then, largely with Chinese, Indian, and US aid, Nepal has developed a network of roads which by 1985 covered in excess of 6,000 km, more than nine times the total in the 1950s. However, inflation, due to the increase in oil prices, has had a serious impact on these development projects.

Note: US$1.00 = Rs27.70.

Figure 13.1   Nepal Rupee vs US Dollar, 1982–1989

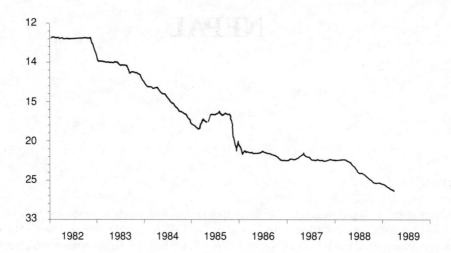

According to the World Bank, Nepal's economic growth since 1960 has barely kept pace with the increase in the country's population, averaging only 0.5% per annum to 1985. As a result, Nepal is considered by the World Bank to be one of the 25 least developed nations in the world.

Nepal is an overwhelmingly agricultural country, with a mainly subsistence economy. Agriculture is the largest productive sector, producing almost 60% of GDP and contributing more than 61% of total export earnings. Manufacturing and other industry contributes only about 10% to GDP.

Tourism is a major source of foreign exchange, as Nepal attracts more than 200,000 visitors annually. The Nepalese currency is the rupee. Figure 13.1 reflects the depreciation of the rupee against the US dollar by 16.7% during the 12 months to 31 December 1988.

Historical Background

The Stock Exchange of Nepal, considered tiny on a global scale, is located in the capital city of Kathmandu. It opened for trading in 1976, while equity shares first traded in 1984 when the government attempted to raise capital for manufacturing-based industry and to develop private investment opportunities.

As of 1986, the Kathmandu Securities Exchange Centre comprised only 13 companies. This number had increased to 26 by 1988 and currently stands at 31. Transactions on the Exchange are very sporadic. In fact, turnover can remain listless for weeks at a time. The total market capitalisation at the end of 1988 was estimated by a local source to be Rs800 million (US$32 million).

Stock Market Performance

The total volume transacted through the Kathmandu Securities Exchange in 1988 was Rs648 million (US$26 million). The trading breakdown of listed shares, government bonds, and Treasury bills is shown in Table 13.1.

Table 13.1 Market Turnover, 1988

	Amount (US$mn)
Shares	0.3
Government Bonds	16.3
Treasury Bills	9.4

The 1988 average price/earnings ratio was approximately 25, while the dividend yield was almost 2%.

It should be noted that foreign parties are not permitted to invest in the Kathmandu Stock Exchange at the present time.

The Kathmandu Stock Exchange is still at an early stage of development. Changes by the regulatory authorities regarding expansion of the Exchange and foreign investment could very well occur in the 1990s, although the pace of such reforms may be slow.

14

SRI LANKA

Introduction

At the time of publication of this book, Sri Lanka remains in a volatile political situation that is not very encouraging to international investors. However, taking a longer-term view, this island nation has many important assets, including its fertile soil, favourable climate, and well-educated population, together with a basically sound infrastructure. The long tradition of tea, rubber, coffee, and clove plantations was the foundation of the Singhalese stock market, and suggests that when peace returns to this troubled island, there will be good investment opportunities in Sri Lanka.

Historical Background

The origins of the Colombo share market date back to the 19th century. During this period, economic activity in the country was dominated by the British mercantile community. The principal commodity until the mid-1870s was coffee, but when the coffee plantations were destroyed by a leaf fungus, the British mercantile community decided to switch to tea. However, excessive remittance of money abroad during the heyday of the coffee plantations resulted in a lack of funds to finance the transition from coffee to tea. In order to mobilise the necessary resources, it was decided to float public limited liability companies in both London and Colombo to raise funds by way of share issues to the public. This move culminated in the birth of the Colombo share market in 1896.

The governing body of the Colombo share market was initially known as the Colombo Share Brokers' Association. In 1904, the name was changed to the Colombo Brokers' Association which formulated a set of rules based on the London Stock Exchange, with modifications to suit local conditions. These rules were further revised in 1955.

At the turn of the century, the rubber industry also made rapid progress as a result of relatively high prices and an increase in acreage planted. The initial capital required by the new rubber companies was also collected through share issues to the general public.

The development of the tea and the rubber plantations paved the way for a number of other commercial companies which provided back-up services to the estate sector. As a result, the Colombo share market in the late 1920s comprised mainly plantation companies, with a handful of commercial establishments which had also raised their initial capital through the market by way of public share issues.

Note: US$1.00 = Rs34.5.

Figure 14.1 Colombo All Share Index, 1985–1988

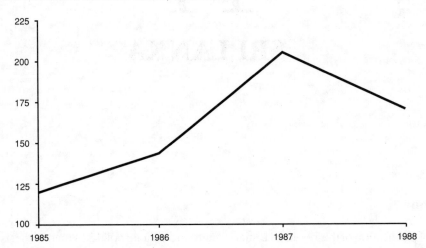

Activity in the Colombo market prior to 1948 was not confined totally to locally registered companies. Shares of companies registered in London (sterling companies), Bombay, and Singapore were also freely transacted until the introduction of the *Exchange Control Regulations* in June 1948, which transformed the Colombo market into a fully domestic market.

Since Independence

The Colombo share market failed to make any satisfactory headway between Independence in 1948 and 1977 as a result of changing economic policies from one government to the next.

The limited progress achieved in the development of the stock market over a period spanning a little more than seven decades suffered a further setback with the introduction of the *Business Acquisition Act* in 1970. The introduction of land reforms in 1972 and the subsequent nationalisation of plantations dealt a fatal blow to the stock market, bringing it to a virtual standstill.

Figure 14.2 Sri Lanka Rupee vs US Dollar, Weekly, 1982–1989

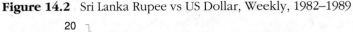
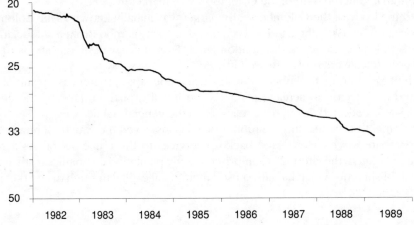

The adverse effects of nationalisation were compounded by delays in the payment of compensation to the shareholders for assets taken over by the government. However, the decision by the government elected to office in 1977 to pay compensation to shareholders for assets taken over, with a minimum interest rate of 10%, and the introduction of liberal economic policies which resulted in the emergence of the private sector as a dominant force in the economy, rekindled hopes that the share market might survive.

On 2 July 1984, a trading floor open to the public replaced the 'call over' system of trading which had existed since 1896. This historic development was due mainly to the pioneering efforts of the chairman of the Colombo Brokers' Association, Mr Mallory Wijesinghe.

The ensuing period led to confusion among the investing public when another group of individuals, calling themselves the Stock Brokers' Association, operated a trading floor in competition with the Colombo Brokers' Association. However, a survey of the Sri Lankan capital market conducted by the Asian Development Bank at the request of the government of Sri Lanka led to the merger of the two rival trading floors to form a unified stock exchange under the Colombo Securities Exchange.

The Colombo Securities Exchange is organised in the form of a company limited by guarantee and is a non-profit-making organisation formed for the development of the stock market.

The membership of the Exchange is confined to stockbrokers; at present, there are eight full-member firms. The Executive Committee, the main policy-making body of the Exchange, consists of the seven founding members of the Securities Exchange.

Stock Market Performance

The impact of the national crisis in Sri Lanka is apparent in both the Index and the number of listed companies. However, turnover has shown appreciable growth over the same period (Table 14.1).

Table 14.1 Stock Market Performance, 1984–1988

Market Indicator	1984	1985	1986	1987	1988
Colombo All Share Index	Not Available	122.22	141.38	217.97	172.44
Annual turnover (Rs mn)	32.9	79.0	140.4	355.5	380.0
Daily turnover: Average (Rs mn)	Not Available	0.33	0.60	1.46	1.61
Volume of Shares Traded (mn)	3.1	4.8	6.1	17.3	13.2
Volume of Transactions (No.)	2,776	4,148	8,525	14,964	13,027
Mkt Capitalisation (Rs bn)	Not Available	10.02	12.03	18.73	15.57

Source: Colombo Stock Exchange.

Stock Exchange Details

Address

Colombo Securities Exchange (Gte) Ltd
2nd Floor, Mackinnon Building
York Street
Colombo
Tlx: 21124 Mackinnon Ce

Trading Days/Hours

The Colombo Securities Exchange trading floor is open from Monday to Friday (except on public and mercantile holidays). Trading is conducted from 9.30 am to 11.30 am. The Exchange is centrally controlled by a trading floor manager and proceedings are conducted on an open outcry system.

Policy-making decisions for the Exchange are made by an Executive Committee comprising seven members elected from the eight broking firm members.

Types of Market

The activities of the stock market can be categorised into two sectors: the primary market and the secondary market. The primary market is involved in raising new capital, either by way of public issues or rights issues for existing share holders.

A company intending to go public and contemplating a listing on the Stock Exchange must meet the listing requirements of the Exchange. A member firm of the Securities Exchange is required to sponsor applications in respect of any new issue, whether public or subsequent. The main function of the sponsoring broker is to advise the company about the various requirements of the Exchange and to file the application with the Exchange. Once approval is granted for the company to proceed with the public issue, the sponsoring broker as well as the other brokers will commence marketing the shares on behalf of the company.

Settlement

Payments in respect of purchases and sales shall be made to the broker firms and clients respectively on or before the settlement day. The Colombo Securities Exchange operates on a two-week settlement basis, with the sellers' prompt falling on the second and fourth Fridays of each month and the buyers' prompt falling two days prior to the sellers' prompt.

Disclosure

Listed companies are required to report to their shareholders and the Exchange on a half-yearly basis.

The Twenty Largest Stocks

The 20 largest quoted companies, as determined by market capitalisation, are shown in Table 14.2.

Table 14.2 The 20 Largest Quoted Stocks by Market Capitalisation, as at 31 December 1988

Company	Market Capitalisation (Rs mn)	Turnover (Rs mn)	Profit/Loss after Tax (Rs mn)	Dividends per share	Earnings per share (Rs)	Price Range 1988	
						High	Low
Ceylon Tobacco	2,639.6	5,386.5	196.2	2.85	4.33	78.00	48.00
Property Dev.	808.5	194.9	117.9	1.50	1.79	17.00	11.50
Nestlés	584.5	593.9	28.2	0.50	0.63	22.00	10.25
Hayleys	570.0	977.3	110.9	3.30	22.41	168.00	62.00
Haycarb	453.5	170.8	48.5	3.30	10.38	105.00	38.00
Pelwatte Sugar	443.9	387.0	(254.8)	Nil	—	8.00*	
Colombo Drydocks	391.5	N/A	(82.5)	Nil	—	4.00*	
Bata	353.4	480.1	33.8	2.25	3.47	48.00	33.00
Commercial Bank	323.8	N/A	51.3	3.00	17.12	120.00	64.25
Pure Beverages	315.1	434.4	15.5	1.50	2.53	89.00	35.00
Lanka Milk Foods	293.7	601.2	76.8	1.50	2.56	16.25	9.00
Sampath Bank	278.9	N/A	N/A	—	—	116.00	8.50
Cargo Boat Dev	255.0	14.9	10.7	4.00	3.14	82.00	41.25
Dipped Products	250.0	133.5	45.4	3.00	9.09	120.00	35.50
Hotel Developers	248.9	N/A	(245.7)	Nil	—	7.00	3.00
Hatton Nat'l Bank	209.0	N/A	33.1	2.50	15.56	103.00	74.25
Ceylon Grain Elevators	202.5	460.6	35.9	Nil	2.39	10.00	9.00
Shaw Wallace & Hedges Ltd	201.4	205.2	26.1	4.00	6.91	85.75	41.25
Colombo Land & Dev. Ltd	188.8	N/A	32.8	2.00	2.82	24.00	18.25
Singer Sri Lanka Ltd	179.7	632.6	39.1	2.50	8.43	37.00	32.00

Source: Colombo Stock Exchange.

Note: * No movement.

Dealing Costs

Brokerage

Once a transaction is concluded, the broker firms will despatch a contract note to their respective buyers and sellers within 24 hours. In addition to the value of the shares, the buyers will have to pay a brokerage fee amounting to 1.5% of the total consideration (as shown in Table 14.3). Brokerage accrued is paid to the broker firm for services rendered. On the selling side, in addition to the value of shares, the client will pay 1.5% of the total consideration as brokerage.

Table 14.3 Dealing Costs

(a)	*Standard Brokerage Charges* on Listed Company Shares	:	1.5% of the total consideration from both the buyer and the seller over Rs10,000 of par value – 0.2%
(b)	*Stamp Duty*	:	1% of total consideration

Membership

Membership of the Exchange is restricted to stockbrokers who in turn are permitted to act as intermediaries or agents of buyers and sellers.

At present, there are eight member firms of the Exchange, all of whom operate on the floor and enjoy full member status.

Major Securities Houses

The major securities houses are as follows:

Bartleet & Co. Ltd

Bartleet House
65 Braybrook Place
Colombo 2

Serendib Trust Services Ltd
34 W.A.D. Ramanayake Mawatha
Colombo 2

Forbes & Walker Ltd
46/38 Navam Mawatha
Colombo 2

Somerville & Co. Ltd
137 Vauxhall Street
Colombo 2

John Keells Ltd
130 Glennie Street
Colombo 2

J.B. Stock Brokers & Financial Services (Pvt) Ltd
150 St Joseph Street
Colombo 14

Mercantile Stock Brokers Ltd
55 Janadhipathi Mawatha
Colombo 1

City Investment Services (Pvt) Ltd
York Arcade Building
27-4/1 York Arcade Road
Colombo 1

Mutual Funds/Unit Trusts

There are no mutual funds or unit trusts presently available for investment in Sri Lanka.

Rules for Foreign Investors

Foreign Investment Restrictions/Exchange Control

According to the prevailing *Exchange Control Regulations*, participation by foreigners in the Colombo market is restricted. Foreigners should first apply for exchange control approval, and their transactions are subject to a 100% capital gains tax under the *Finance Act*.

Taxation

Taxation on dividends and capital gains received by shareholders is as shown in Table 14.4.

Table 14.4   Taxation on Dividends and Capital Gains

Dividends	:	A 20% withholding tax is applicable
Capital Gains	:	Less than 20 years/over 15 years – 12.5%
		Less than 15 years/over 5 years – 17.5%
		Less than 2 years – normal rates applicable to other income

Note: The first Rs12,000 earned per annum as dividend income is not liable to income tax.

Available Research

Colombo Share Market Report
Colombo Securities Exchange Facts and Figures
Central Bank of Sri Lanka Annual Report, 1988
Colombo Securities Exchange — *Securities Council Act*
Colombo Securities Exchange — Stock Market Daily

15

BANGLADESH

Introduction

Bangladesh, situated on the vast delta of the Ganges, is probably the poorest and most overcrowded nation in the world. The national per capita income is estimated at only US$125 per annum, yet the resourcefulness and intelligence of its people are equal to the adverse natural circumstances. Although the stock market is not yet open to international investors, it would be wrong to dismiss the country's prospects or its capital market, as the growth in the number of companies listed in the past 12 years (from 9 to 111) amply indicates.

The objective in re-establishing the Dhaka Stock Exchange in 1976 was to establish a securities market governed by just and equitable principles of trade, as well as to conduct business in securities with due regard for the public interest and for the protection of investors. The Exchange provides a channel for companies to seek capital funds from the public, and also a place for investors to buy and sell shares of the quoted companies. The Exchange is a non-profit-making public company and, as such, its income and property are applied solely towards the objectives of the Exchange; no portion is paid or distributed to its members in the form of dividends or bonuses.

At present, the Dhaka Stock Exchange is one of the world's most highly regulated stock exchanges, being governed by the *Securities and Exchange Ordinance 1969* and the *Securities and Exchange Control Rules 1971*. The 111 listed companies currently trading on the Exchange (including mutual funds and debentures) are classified into 12 sections, as shown in Table 15.1.

The Dhaka Stock Exchange is registered as a public limited company with limited liabilities under the *Companies Act 1913* and *Securities and Exchange Ordinance 1969*. The Exchange is a self-regulatory body in the conduct of its own affairs.

Historical Background

The Dhaka Stock Exchange Limited was originally incorporated on 28 April 1954 under the name of the East Pakistan Stock Exchange Association Limited. Subsequently, on 23 June 1962, it was renamed the East Pakistan Stock Exchange Limited, and on 14 May 1964 the name was again amended to the Dhaka Stock Exchange Limited. Though incorporated in 1954, formal trading did not begin until 1956 at Narayanganj. In 1958, it was shifted to Dhaka and became fully functioning at the Narayanganj Chamber Building, Motijheel C.A.

Note: US$1.00 = Taka 32.7.

Table 15.1 Classification of Listings, 1988

Sector	No. of Listings
Banks	9
Investments	7
Engineering	16
Food and Allied Products	16
Fuel and Power	3
Jute	11
Pharmaceuticals and Chemicals	13
Paper and Printing	5
Service	2
Textile	14
Miscellaneous	11
Debentures	4
Total Listed Securities	111

Figure 15.1 Growth Pattern of Dhaka Stock Exchange, 1976–1988 (Taka billion)

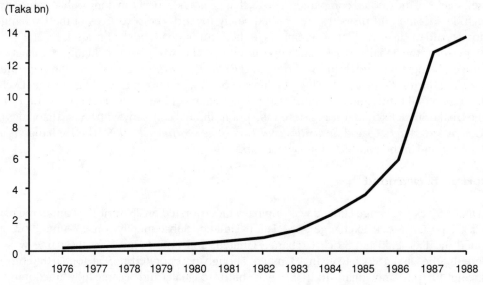

Source: Dhaka Stock Exchange.

Figure 15.2 Bangladesh Taka vs US Dollar, 1982–1989

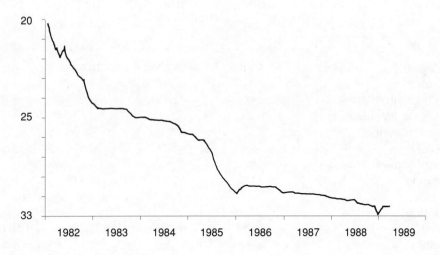

Source: Datastream.

The trading activities of the Exchange were suspended when Bangladesh became independent in 1971 as a result of the economic policy of the new government. With the change of economic policy implemented by the government in 1976, trading activities were finally resumed, with a total of nine listed companies. The total paid-up capital on the board was Taka 137.52 million. By the end of December 1988, 111 companies were listed on the Dhaka Stock Exchange, with a total market capitalisation of Taka 13.6 billion.

Stock Market Performance

Tables 15.2 and 15.3 show the highlights of the stock market during the period 1984–1988.

Table 15.2 Stock Market Performance, 1984–1988

Market Indicator	1984	1985	1986	1987	1988
Taka/US$	26.00	31.00	30.80	31.20	32.27
Total No. of Listed Securities	58	72	82	92	111
Total No. of Listed Shares Debentures and M.F. Certificates (mn)	62.35	85.50	99.60	105.28	123.06
Total Issued Capital of All Listed Securities (Taka bn)	1.54	2.06	2.66	3.15	3.66

Market Indicator	1984	1985	1986	1987	1988
% Increase of Issued Capital	54.42	33.18	28.81	18.72	16.32
Average Issued Capital (Taka mn)	26.66	28.61	32.35	34.24	33.01
Total Market Capitalisation of All Listed Securities (Taka bn)	2.26	3.49	5.73	12.67	13.56
% Increase of Market Capitalisation	86.29	54.78	64.08	121.11	6.99
Average Market Capitalisation (Taka mn)	38.90	18.51	69.89	137.73	122.14
Price/Earnings Ratio	6.12	5.50	6.80	20.58	7.83

Table 15.3 Turnover of Shares and Debentures, 1984–1988

	1984	1985	1986	1987	1988
Total Turnover Volume in Shares					
Debentures ('000)	215.50	591.80	849.1	1,876.30	1,023.90
Value (Taka mn)	10.10	32.27	47.86	177.67	130.03
% Increase of					
Volume	5,375.93	43.48	120.97	-45.43	
Value (Taka)	2,229.14	48.29	271.27	-26.81	
Daily Average Transaction					
Value (Taka '000)	50.20	116.10	170.30	662.90	490.70
Annual Transaction					
Value (Taka mn)	10.10	32.27	47.86	177.67	130.03

Source: Dhaka Stock Exchange.

Stock Exchange Details

Address

Dhaka Stock Exchange Limited
Stock Exchange Building
9th Floor, Motijheel C.A
Dhaka – 1000
Bangladesh

Trading Days/Hours

The trading hours of the Dhaka Stock Exchange are from 11.30 am to 1.30 pm, except Thursday, when trading starts at 11 am and closes at 1 pm; the Exchange remains closed on Fridays and other bank and public holidays.

Settlement

Unless otherwise stipulated at the time of the bargain, contracts entered into shall be for either 'ready' or 'immediate' delivery. In the case of 'immediate' delivery contracts, the seller must deliver the documents to the buyer on the next working day after the date of the contract. In the case of 'ready' delivery contracts, the seller must deliver the documents to the buyer between the third and seventh working day after the date of the contract. In the event of non-delivery, the buyer should forthwith report the matter to the Complaint Subcommittee.

If the buyer fails to so report, the Subcommittee, when called upon to adjudicate, will do so on the presumption that the period for the performance of the contract was extended by mutual consent of both the buyer and the seller. This presumption will also apply in the case of claims for patents and differences relating thereto. The Subcommittee shall not adjudicate any of the non-delivery cases referred to in this rule unless the report is made to the Subcommittee within a period of 90 days from the date of the contract. If the 90th day falls on a holiday, the case can be filed on the next working day. This rule shall not apply in cases of delivery of shares listed in the Clearing Schedule or of government securities or debentures.

If the buyer fails to take delivery of the shares tendered on the third working day, the seller will have an option to charge interest at 2% above the bank rate for one day's grace before reporting to the Complaint Subcommittee.

Disclosure

All companies listed and quoted on the Exchange shall forward to the Exchange copies of:
- statutory and annual reports and audited accounts, as soon as issued; and
- all notices before they are published or sent to the shareholders, and file with the Exchange certified copies of resolutions of the company as soon as they have become effective.

The Twenty Largest Stocks

The 20 largest quoted companies, as determined by market capitalisation, are shown in Table 15.4.

Table 15.4 The 20 Largest Quoted Stocks by Market Capitalisation, as at 31 December 1988

Company	Market Capitalisation (Taka mn)
Bangladesh Tobacco	2,900
Glaxo Bangladesh	2,060
Bangladesh Oxygen	1,209
Bata Shoe Company	879
Rupali Bank	466
Reckitt & Colman	392
Sonali Paper & Board Mills	349
City Bank	300
Eastern Cables	270
United Commercial Bank	264
Arab Bangladesh Bank	250
Burma Eastern	252
IFIC	244
Uttara Bank	205
Dhaka Vegetable Oil	200
National Bank	192
Pubali Bank	181
National Tea Company	168
Ashraf Textile Mills	148
Bangladesh Shipping Corp.	144

Source: Dhaka Stock Exchange.

Major Types of Investors

The Investment Corporation of Bangladesh (ICB), a state-owned and controlled agency, has the role of market maker on the Dhaka Stock Exchange. The ICB also co-ordinates institutional investors wishing to invest in the stock market. Additionally, the ICB is also the manager of six ICB mutual funds, which allow Bangladesh nationals to invest in the stock market.

Investment Corporation of Bangladesh
Shilpa Bank Bhaban
11th Floor
8 D.I.T. Avenue
Dhaka – 1000
Bangladesh

Dealing Costs

The standard brokerage charges include stamp duty, commission, tax levies, clearing fees, and other relevant costs.

Brokerage Commission

Members are entitled to charge brokerage at the following rates on the purchase or sale of shares, government securities, and debentures:

1. *Brokerage on interest-bearing securities:*
   On all government securities — 1% of the face value.
   On municipal or port trust debentures — 1% of the face value.
   On joint stock company's debentures — 1% of the face value.
2. *Brokerage on all shares:*
   Preference, ordinary, preferred, deferred, or any other kind of shares — 1% of the market value of the shares, subject to a minimum charge of Taka 10 for each transaction.

Major Brokers

There are currently 195 members of the Dhaka Stock Exchange, including the Investment Corporation of Bangladesh. According to the Dhaka *Securities and Exchange Ordinance 1969,* no person other than a full member of the Dhaka Stock Exchange shall transact any business in any security as a broker or a jobber on the Exchange.

Some of the major brokers are listed below:

Selah Uddin Ahmed
Room 415, Stock Exchange Building
9th Floor, Motijheel C.A.
Dhaka—1000

Delwar Hossain
Room 407, Stock Exchange Building
9th Floor, Motijheel C.A.
Dhaka—1000

Kazi Firuz Rashid
Room 408, Stock Exchange Building
9th Floor, Motijheel C.A.
Dhaka—1000

A.S. Shahudul Huque Bulbul
Room 503, Stock Exchange Building
9th Floor, Motijheel C.A.
Dhaka—1000
Tel: 231935 239882

Khwaja Ghulam Rasul
Room 613, Stock Exchange Building
9th Floor, Motijheel C.A.
Dhaka—1000

A.R. Chowdhury & Co.
Room 316, Stock Exchange Building
9th Floor, Motijheel C.A.

Dhaka—1000
Tel: 256444

MD Abdullah Bokhari B.A.
Room 505, Stock Exchange Building
9th Floor, Motijheel C.A.
Dhaka—1000
Tel: 250841 259374

Shafi Ahmed
Room 401, Stock Exchange Building
9th Floor, Motijheel C.A.
Dhaka—1000
Tel: 231935

Kamal Edbar
Room 417, Stock Exchange Building
9th Floor, Motijheel C.A.
Dhaka—1000
Tel: 230803

MD Abdul Mannan
Room 308, Stock Exchange Building
9th Floor, Motijheel C.A.
Dhaka—1000
Tel: 255505 254635

MD Shahjahan Thakur
Room 408, Stock Exchange Building
9th Floor, Motijheel C.A.
Dhaka—1000
Tel: 502337 328890

Mustafizur Rahman
President
Bangladesh Commerce & Investment Limited
19 D.I.T. Avenue
Dhaka—1000
Tel: 411154 259991

Listing Criteria

Listing Requirements of Securities

Trading on the Dhaka Stock Exchange is made in listed securities only. A company or issuer who intends to list any of his securities on the Exchange shall submit an application on the prescribed forms of the Stock Exchange according to the Listing Rules, as modified on 13 December 1979. Upon receipt of an application, the Exchange may, if it is satisfied after making such inquiry as it may consider necessary that the applicant fulfils the conditions prescribed in this behalf, list the security for dealings on the Stock Exchange. There exist various prerequisites for admission to the official list of the Exchange. At present, public companies having paid-up capital in excess of Taka 10 million are required to be listed on the Stock Exchange.

In addition, companies which list their shares on the Exchange are entitled to a 5% tax reduction on an annual basis.

Minimum Issued and Paid-up Capital of Listed Companies

No company with an issued and paid-up capital of less than Taka 1 million can be listed on the Stock Exchange.

Rules for Foreign Investors

Foreign Investment Restrictions

The *Security and Exchange Control Rules 1971,* among other things, effectively prohibit foreign investment in securities listed on the Dhaka Stock Exchange. Citizens of Bangladesh living overseas may, however, invest in the local stock market.

Foreign Exchange Control

At present, repatriation of dividend income and capital of joint ventures, or multinational companies' investment in stocks, is not permitted by foreign nationals.

Taxation

Taxation regarding dividend income

Any dividend income of an assessee, other than a company received from a public limited company, is exempt from taxation. Shareholders of a private limited company will also be entitled to the exemption if the company is converted into a public limited company within two years from the first day of July 1987.

For the purpose of exemption under this paragraph, a public limited company shall include a company in which not less than 50% of the shares are held by the government.

Exemption of capital gains from tax

Capital gains arising from the transfer of government securities and stocks and shares of public limited companies which fulfil the conditions laid down in para. 8, part B of the Sixth Schedule of the *Income Tax Ordinance 1984* shall be exempt from income tax if the sale proceeds are reinvested within two years in similar securities, stocks, or shares.

Available Research

Stock Exchange Publications

Daily quotation of all listed stocks
Monthly Stock Exchange Review
Annual Fact Book
Listing Rules of the Dhaka Stock Exchange Ltd
General Rules, Regulations and By-Laws for Ready Delivery of Contracts of the Dhaka Stock Exchange Ltd
Memorandum and Articles of Association

Additional Research Publications

S. Hug and A. Hug, *Investors' Guide to the Dhaka Stock Exchange*
The Bangladesh *Gazette*
Dhaka Stock Exchange Report
Dhaka Stock Exchange Securities and Exchange Ordinance 1969
International Monetary Fund — International Financial Statistics

16

CHINA

Introduction

At first sight, it seems impossible that a Communist country can allow the existence of stock markets. After all, the central principle of Marxism (and even more so of Maoism) was to abolish private capital wealth and privately owned property, and to place the means of production under state ownership. In China after 1949, as in the Soviet Union after 1917, measures were swiftly taken to enforce this idea and to nationalise all companies, especially large companies in the important fields of industry, shipping, and banking.

However, since 1978, China has tacitly admitted that the centrally planned economy and the system of state ownership have failed to deliver the goods. In that year, Deng Xiaoping introduced the 'responsibility system', starting with the farmers, which abolished central quotas for agricultural production and replaced them with the free-market system under which farmers could sell their own produce in the market. In the ten years since then, many farmers have become wealthy; they now own cars, and in many cases have bought their own houses as well as long-term leases on their land. China has always had a large middle class, and substantial private savings are often hidden away. Together with the new wealth of the peasant farmers, a significant amount of savings could be channelled into share markets. China's savings rate is already one of the highest in the world. In 1987, it was officially estimated to be 38% of GDP (see Figure 16.3).

Chinese leaders are now pushing for a faster implementation of the programme to privatise housing, both as an end in itself, and as a means to absorb the surplus demand for agricultural products and consumer goods (ie to ease inflation). They are also studying proposals for developing capital markets in the country in order to tap its vast reserves of personal savings and to provide funds for the development of state-owned enterprises.

One such proposal has recently been put forward by a group of young economists who are eager to import to China ideas associated with Western intellectual movements, such as Reaganomics and Thatcherism. The economists in question argue that public ownership is no longer the premise of socialism, and that a shareholding system would provide a more solid foundation for the country's modernisation efforts.

Financially, a huge amount is at stake (state-owned enterprises have fixed assets valued at US$190 billion and account for two-thirds of China's industrial production), so critics could argue that potential investors would not be able to acquire a stake in companies which are presently in the

Note: US$1.00 = RMB3.50 (official rate).

public domain. The economists apparently anticipated this criticism, for they advised the government to issue 'asset certificates' (ie vouchers) that could be used in place of money to purchase shares in state-owned enterprises. The certificates would be issued to institutions (replacing the subsidies which they receive from the government) and individuals (in exchange for giving up their right to lifetime employment). Cash, as well as certificates, could be used to buy stocks. The authors of the proposal are strongly in favour of allowing foreigners to become shareholders.

Figure 16.1   Stock Markets in China, 1989

Figure 16.2 RMB vs US Dollar, 1978–1988

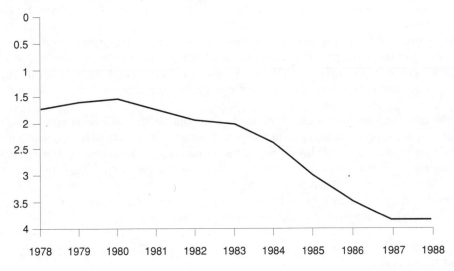

Figure 16.3 Gross Domestic Investment and Savings as % of GDP, 1987

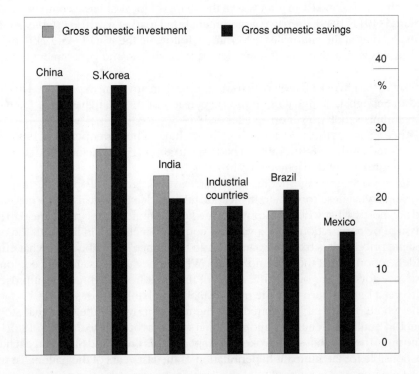

Source: World Bank.
Note: * These are official rates. Recently, the RMB was traded in an exchange centre at RMB7.0 = US$1.

A recent comment in *The Economist* (2 September 1989) pointed to competition for sales, rather than ownership, as the overriding spur to efficiency, provided managers in state-owned companies are free to manage.

'[P]rofit-sharing can be and is used as an incentive for workers and managers in state-owned enterprises in many countries (including China) without either share ownership or a stock-market. If incentives need to be strengthened by giving employees a stake in the business, shares can be issued even if there is no stockmarket to trade them on. They will pay a dividend related to profits.'

While the case for stock markets in China seems unassailable, this proposal constitutes a radical blueprint for restoring property rights in the country. The fact that the official response to it has been favourable suggests that economic liberalisation still looms large on the policy agenda in Beijing and that, although there is disagreement about tactics, the long-term commitment of Chinese leaders to reform should not be doubted. This commitment ought to manifest itself in the near future in concrete steps to broaden the scope and improve the functioning of capital markets in the People's Republic of China — a development that would be welcome in Hong Kong.

Historical Background

The first stock market in China was established in Shanghai in the 1890s, towards the end of the Ching Dynasty. At that time there were two markets: the most active market was in foreign, typically US and British, shares; and the secondary market was in the shares of local Chinese companies. During the republican period (1911–1949), an active government bond market was also established in Beijing. During the final period of the nationalist government following the war (1945–1949), the Shanghai Stock Exchange was very active, and foreign shares, local shares, and government bonds were all traded.

However, by 1948, a hyperinflation which was worse than anything experienced in Germany in 1923 resulted in Shanghai, culminating in the suspension of the Shanghai Stock Exchange even before the Communists took power on 1 October 1949.

Shanghai once again has the most active bourse in China. When it reopened in 1986, there were only two shares listed, but by 1988 the number had risen to about 25 and included the shares of banks, department stores, textile, and machinery companies.

In the Shanghai Stock Exchange, trading takes place in the large hall of one of the major Shanghai banks and is a somewhat desultory affair. In fact, the title 'stock exchange' is a little misleading. The 'stocks' listed are mostly what would be known elsewhere as bonds; that is, they are loan stock with debentures issued by corporations with a variable coupon which rises in line with the company's profits. The share price itself is fixed. Also to call it an 'exchange' might be somewhat euphemistic since it is widely reported that there are no sellers. When a new issue is announced, long lines of Shanghainese investors appear outside the doors of the bank from daybreak, as it presents a rare opportunity to get a better return than the rates available on bank deposits.

During the whole of 1987, it is reported that the total turnover of the Shanghai stock market reached about US$2 million. General opinion in China seems favourable to the idea of stock markets; yet at the same time, the idea that stockbrokers and speculators on the old Shanghai exchange were somehow responsible for the rampant hyperinflation of the last years of the nationalist regime still resides in local memory and is referred to as the 'irrational practices of the past'.

Reliable statistics are very hard to come by, but it is reported that more than 6,000 companies have issued shares in China over the past five years. During 1988 alone, it is reported that 2,483 companies offered shares to the public, with an unverifiable total value of about US$5 billion (according to newspaper reports). The first reported joint stock company was the Tian Qiao Department Store, which was established in Beijing in 1984.

In 1986, in addition to Shanghai, stock markets were established in Wuhan, in the central part of China; and in Shenyang, in Liaoning Province in the northeast. Smaller markets were also established in Jilin, Henan, and Hubei (see Figure 16.1). In April 1989, a senior official in Guangzhou reported that a stock exchange was planned there.

According to Zhang Yanning, Deputy Director of the state Structural Reform Committee, the state is in favour of carrying on a shareholding system. The central government is allowing the experiment and is tolerating the system's existence, but it hopes that in the course of rectifying the 'irrational practices of the past', new equally irrational practices will not emerge.

China has four types of stock: capital stocks, fixed assets stocks, increased stocks for raising funds, and increased stocks for setting up new shareholding companies. The types of shareholding companies include group stock, joint stock, in-house stock, public stock, financial stock, and compound stock. Stock ownership is generally divided into state stocks, enterprise stocks, and private stocks. As a whole, Chinese 'listed' companies lack a unified pattern as many of them were established in a rush to follow the example of others.

The main problems for the state posed by the companies are as follows:

- Most stocks have no guarantees against risk.
- In some in-house stock companies, private stocks often gain high interest and bonuses, while the state stock's interest is depressed to a very low level. In order to raise funds, the interest of the private stocks is one or two times higher than that of enterprise stocks in some cases.
- Some share-issuing companies are set up without making realistic valuations of assets. Some simply make asset valuations according to the net asset value in the account books, and some even deliberately underestimate the asset value at the expense of the state and enterprises.

The view of the Structural Reform Committee is that in some places, the area of experimentation is too large and liable to run out of control. China's economists, however, are said to be almost universally in favour of the shareholding system, the most prominent advocate being Professor Li Yining of Beijing University. Since the beginning of China's 'open door' economic policy turnabout in the early 1980s, Professor Li put forward the idea of China 'going along the company shares road' and has been promoting it ever since. Professor Li and other economists such as Lin Tongwei, think shareholding could be a route to improving the contract responsibility system and thus solve two problems at once.

The main drawback of the 'contract responsibility system' is its inability to increase state revenue even though it may increase the economic returns of an enterprise. In effect, the state has to subsidise the losses caused by the price hikes of raw materials. In 1988, the local budget showed that the profits of enterprises practising the contract responsibility system rose by 20.3% compared with the previous year, but the income tax and regulatory tax handed over to the state went down by 9.5%.

Lin Tongwei, amongst other economists, believes that the state should turn from indirectly managing enterprises — actually unhook itself from enterprise administration — and control enterprises only through shareholding. In implementing the shareholding system, the enterprise's fixed assets would be appraised and turned into shares, and if necessary, could be lent to the enterprise. As shareholder and creditor, the state's part in the enterprise would be only to receive dividends and interest. This would be a transformation of the ownership system which would enhance the sense of responsibility in managing state property and increase efficiency and therefore return. And, at the same time, it could raise funds from the public and solve enterprises' chronic capital shortages.

There are other ways in which China might convert contract responsibility to shareholding.

One would be for the establishment of a contract responsibility enterprise with foundation funds (for mortgage against risks) contributed by the staff, to turn into shares which the staff would hold. Fixed assets would also be evaluated and turned into shares. Another method would be to organise a joint stock company by combining enterprises. Two or more enterprises, combined and with their assets appraised and turned into shares, could form a joint stock company satisfactorily.

A third way would be to raise funds and set up a shareholding company which would buy shares from the enterprise and control the shares, thus turning the operation into a stock enterprise. And a fourth route would be to use foreign capital from Hong Kong, Taiwan, and Macau to transform an enterprise into a shareholding operation.

Shenzhen Special Economic Zone

It has been reported by the Hong Kong press that Chinese shares have been sold for the first time to foreigners. The shares were issued in January 1989 by a conglomerate 'Vanke', formerly state-owned. The company has a five-year track record and has interests in real estate development, trading, video-cassette recorder production, and jewellery manufacture.

This new share market is evolving in the Special Economic Zone of Shenzhen (see Figure 16.1), bordering Hong Kong. There is no stock exchange as yet, nor even a trading hall, and only two companies — the Shenzhen Development Bank and Vanke — have so far issued shares to the public. Both companies became 'listed' by obtaining the permission of the central bank, the People's Bank of China, to sell shares. The shares were then sold direct to the public by the companies and their sales agents. Investors filled in a form, handed over cash or cheques, and were given either scrips or receipts.

When Vanke went public with a RMB28 million (US$7.5 million) equity issue, there were no underwriters in the conventional sense. Two sales agents each agreed to sell RMB6 million (US$1.6 million) for Vanke. The state-backed Shenzhen Securities Company received a fee for guaranteeing the sale of its portion of the shares, while the Bank of China's International Trust and Consultation Company agreed to sell the shares on a best efforts basis, with no fees involved. Vanke itself undertook the sale of the rest of the shares. As broking commissions were paid by the company, it did not matter to the investors whether they bought the shares directly from the company or from an agent.

The RMB8 million (US$2.1 million) flotation of the Shenzhen Development Bank in May 1987, and another RMB5 million (US$1.3 million) issue in March 1988, followed smiliar procedures. The bank's shares were sold to the public by an agent — the Shenzhen Securities Company, which has since acted as broker and occasional market-maker for the issues. It also provides a physical marketplace where trading can be conducted. Turnover since March 1988, when trading began, reached RMB1 million (US$268,067). The shares, which have a face value of RMB20, fetched RMB35 at the height of the market trading.

Some of the bank's shares, denominated in Hong Kong dollars, are available to foreigners. Central bank officials say that they are stricter when it comes to foreign ownership of a Chinese financial institution. However, Vanke has been allowed to earmark RMB10 million (US$2.7 million) of its shares for foreign purchase. The big question for the non-Chinese investor is how he can convert his dividends and, when he sells, his investment into hard currency.

The country's central bank has agreed to let investors exchange their Renminbi at the local swap centres, where foreign and domestic currencies are exchanged at rates determined by market demand, though within a band set by the central bank. Sources at the Shenzhen branch of the central bank say they expect Vanke, which has hard currency income through its trading activities, to provide the foreign exchange for investors. However, if the company is temporarily short, there is a tacit understanding that the central bank, through the swap centres, will provide funds. Investors will not be left holding nonconvertible Renminbi.

Vanke, in line with international practice, published financial details about itself before the flotation. It valued itself at RMB12 million (US$3.2 million) and recorded earnings of RMB3.61 million, thus giving the company a price/earnings ratio of 3.32. Shenzhen Development Bank has not disclosed its financial details.

In June 1988, Gold Cup Automobile, a company in the northeastern provincial capital of Shenyang, announced its intention of issuing dollar-denominated shares which would be available to overseas investors. However, at the time of going to press, the company had not received permission from the central bank to go ahead with the issue.

This year, the central bank is expected to announce regulations for the Shenzhen share market, and it is currently working on a regulatory framework for the share market of all China.

The Securities Exchange of China in the 1990s

China has shown a willingness to experiment and to use the idea of a 'share market' to promote its national economic development. One of the keys to the successful management of these stock exchanges will be, of course, having trained people, as well as finding domestic capital and savings. In Shanghai, an advantage has been the input of a number of 60–70 year-old stockbrokers who remember the way in which business was conducted in the 1940s. Their know-how went some way towards facilitating the reopening of the exchange in 1986. But this begs the obvious question: 'Why should China not use the well-established Hong Kong stock market, with its international image and a market capitalisation of nearly US$85 billion?' We may well imagine that in the years before and after 1997, the tendency will be for Chinese corporations to turn more and more to the Hong Kong market to raise capital from international investors. In fact, there are already a number of smaller companies listed in Hong Kong (such as Tian An) that have virtually all their operations inside China.

After June 1989

China's progress towards modernisation appears to have received a severe jolt, at the very least, following the events of 4 June 1989. However, despite the disappointment of the hopes of the political 'Liberals', it appears that the economic liberals, willing to experiment with new systems and to encourage further foreign investment, are still in the ascendancy. China's watchword in the months immediately following the tragic events in Tiananmen Square was: 'Business as Usual', and for this reason the author has thought best to leave the preceding paragraphs about China unchanged, although they were written in the happier and more optimistic times preceding June 1989.

Other Markets in the Communist Bloc

Other communist countries, notably Vietnam, may also attempt to follow such free market concepts, including the establishment of domestic capital markets. (Of Laos, Cambodia, and Burma, little can be said here: the economies of the first two remain impoverished, and their populations small, whilst Burma is still undergoing political turmoil, the outcome of which it is too early to predict.)

At the time of writing, a communist country, Hungary, has formally announced the reestablishment of its stock market, and an international fund has been incorporated to invest therein. The 'Hungary Fund' Inc., launched in New York, undoubtedly depends to a large extent on the support of wealthy Hungarian emigrés (in fact, the minimum subscription was set at US$500,000) or bold institutional investors. But this is also true of the socialist Asian nations such as China and Vietnam, where more than 80% of direct foreign investment emanates from the deep pockets of the overseas Chinese communities. China itself has benefited from this trend since 1978, to the tune of over US$10 billion (see Figure 16.4).

Figure 16.4   Direct Foreign Investment in China — Cumulative, 1982–1988

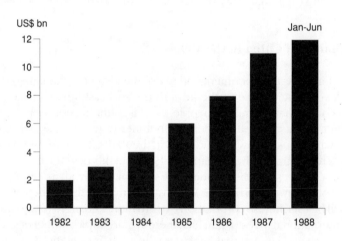

The case of Vietnam is instructive. It is less than 15 years since Saigon was a thriving free marketplace, with an active foreign exchange and real estate market. The time that has elapsed in most communist cities since a free market last existed exceeds 40 years (eg, Budapest and Shanghai), and thus more than a generation. It appears to an outside observer that Saigon, or Ho Chi Minh City, may be in a favoured position to benefit from the more recent experiences of its managerial staff in the practice and mentality of the marketplace.

Y